The Life of an Ordinary Woman

ANNE ELLIS — 1929

The Life of an
ORDINARY
WOMAN

Anne Ellis

Foreword by Carol Bly

Introduction by
Lucy Fitch Perkins

HOUGHTON MIFFLIN COMPANY

Boston

For information about permission to reproduce selections from
this book, write to Permissions, Houghton Mifflin Company,
2 Park Street, Boston, Massachusetts 02108.

Library of Congress Cataloging in Publication Data

Ellis, Anne, 1875–1938.
    The life of an ordinary woman / Anne Ellis : with an introduction by
Carol Bly.
        p.   cm.
    ISBN 0–395–54412–2 (pbk.)
        1. Ellis, Anne, 1875–1938.   2. Women pioneers — Rocky Mountains Re-
gion — Biography.   3. Women — Rocky Mountains Region — Biography.
4. Mines and mineral resources — Rocky Mountains Region — History.
5. Rocky Mountains Region — Social life and customs.   I. Title.
CT275.E38515A3   1990
978′.02′092 — dc20   90–34334
[B]   CIP

Printed in the United States of America

HAD 10 9 8 7 6 5

Houghton Mifflin Company paperback 1990

To INA and GERALD CASSIDY, ore-sorters, who among much waste discovered some native silver; to JULIA and ROYCE ARMSTRONG, the 'two travelers,' who grubstaked and encouraged a weary prospector; and to my sister, JOSEPHINE COLE, another old-timer, who helped me to remember.

ILLUSTRATIONS

ANNE ELLIS — 1929 *Frontispiece*

A FAMILY GROUP 86

I HAD MY PICTURE TAKEN WITH A BUNCH OF MINERS IN FRONT OF THE HOUSE OF LORDS SALOON 108

THERE HAS ALWAYS BEEN SOME ONE TO STAKE HIS MONEY ON A MINE IN BONANZA 152

JUST BELOW MY BOARDING-HOUSE AT INDEPENDENCE WAS THE DEPOT (NO. 1) WHICH HARRY ORCHARD BLEW UP 208

HERBERT WAS GETTING THREE DOLLARS A DAY IN THE EMPRESS JOSEPHINE MINE 232

WE LIVED ON HIGH-GRADER'S HILL IN GOLDFIELD 250

JOY'S GRAVE 282

FOREWORD

Anne Ellis was the perfect taker for Plato's wonderful maxim that "the unexamined life is not worth living." When we imagine him saying it, though, we don't imagine a nearly destitute girl and, later, woman of the early Colorado mining towns who snapped up every book and every cultural experience she could — and who, with verve and curiosity and humor, followed Plato's dictum exactly. She watched and evaluated life as it came along.

It is her inherent literary instinct that makes Ellis's memoir a thousand times more lively than most personal histories of rough life in the American West. Ellis liked Dickens and Zola as well as the easier novelists; from girlhood on she read a lot and wanted to write. She has none of the narcissism common to the memoirist: Ellis's idea was deliberately to find out everything going on, not just in her own purview but in others' lives as well — the frightening work conditions in the copper and gold tunnels, the dangerous cage that sometimes ground off men's arms and legs as it dropped a thousand feet to the mine bottom, the lives and ideas of the fancy women, the fates of the old and indigent who slept in mine tunnels until they were discovered and removed.

Anyone who is a watcher and evaluator leads two lives: the ordinary one, with its mix of emotions and practical necessities, and a second one of retiring inward for several seconds each day or each week to ask, Is this actually *good*? Is this all right? Is this grossly unfair, or absurd?

Ellis was no drab moralist. She had nice balance. A believer in industrious motherhood, she also had an amiable toleration of whores; though bored or exasperated by her husband, she admired his valor in bearing pain. She energetically inquired into everything: even as a child she broke the rules by going into the fancy house. She took in the practical technology of life — how you lick quartz to make the gold specks show, how you coordinate signals so the engineer doesn't haul the cage full of men right up into the shive wheel.

Narratives by pioneers who lived first and wrote afterward tend to be strung through with beads of nostalgia and some romanticizing. Their authors sometimes wind up defending the hardships as if they were a moral force in themselves. Gratitude for one's past life is a handsome emotion, but it often furs over the old, gross injustices that many present-day readers want to know about — especially those readers who think of social history as useful kit for making changes. Since Ellis, spirited, even willful, did her thinking as she went along, the finished book lays no scrim across any of its here-beautiful, there-horrible truths. She early learned, probably from her enthusiastic reading of Dickens, to hunt up and not forget the rough-and-tumble particulars: if a neighbor ran a yellow-cat farm as a cottage industry, raising the cats for their skins, Ellis didn't pass up mentioning it. But it is the outcroppings of judgments that mark *The Life of an Ordinary Woman* as literature. *These* annals of the poor are not short and simple: this book is well outside the stereotype.

FOREWORD

Ellis was not a stereotype of anything — especially not of the effects of poverty. Nor was she the stereotyped victim of male negligence and brutality, although the men of her life — father, stepfather, and one of her husbands — were runaways and bullies. Although far too tired much of the time, midst all her brave contrivances to keep the children warm, fed, and clothed, she wasn't the stereotype of a driven, unthinking person. She always looked around, standing on her "moral sense," which, she tells us, her one and only true love gave her.

Ellis had a funny mix of goals for herself, one or two of them straight Louisa May Alcott. She made a constant effort to use less slang. She burned her old love letters because her ridiculous husband (number one) asked her to. At the other end of the virtues continuum, she served meat and homemade breads to her miner boarders three times a day, with two vegetables, two pieces of pie, and a choice of other desserts at supper, even though she was very short of money. She often reported that she was "frantic" to have money and things — a moral weakness she didn't get over until after the death of one of her children. It seems incredible that she chastised herself for being materialistic when she was stepping about the kitchen dodging the two by six stringers because a previous owner had torn up the floorboards for fuel. At other times Ellis was absolutely pragmatic. She grazed her animals in a neighbor's field. She ran up and down a mountainside with water buckets all one day to help extinguish a mine fire — and to bring about an abortion.

It is curious what memoir writers feel proud of and

what they regret. Ellis criticized herself for being an inconsiderate daughter, a negligent wife on occasion, and a negligent mother, according to the conventional standards of the time. She cheerfully boasted of her physical daring: she put herself between her little sister and a rattler that had given its warning "like seeds in a blue-flag pod." She took satisfaction in her ebullient behavior — talking too much and too loudly in public and on the train: on the other hand, she loved the Joshua trees, the high-desert spring flowers, the shuddering cottonwoods. One of her more wretched homes leaned right up against a stable: it was classy of Ellis to take pleasure in hearing the horses stamping and snorting at night.

Some of her irritations were very modern. She despised the way men gave themselves permission to be surly, drunk, or both when times were hard, and the way their women commiserated as if they didn't have to bear the same hardships — sober, what's more. She disdained the way women credited silent men with wisdom when they were just too lazy to think and therefore had nothing to say. Present-day feminists might wonder that Ellis, though nettled by men's arrogance and women's accommodation of their arrogance, didn't confront or interfere. Her stance was literary rather than sociological; the way men and women related to one another was a matter of eternal verities, not acculturated behavior one could militate against. She nonetheless saw their behavior for the psychological enormity it was.

Being a mining wife was worse than being a farm wife because mining is an addictive lifestyle. Colorado miners

FOREWORD

would conn this rumor or that rumor about the Empress Josephine or the Bonanza or the Exchequer, then shift from stake to stake or camp to camp. That life set home-making women's teeth on edge. The historian Patricia Nelson Limerick credits the extractive-industry mental-ity of "get in, get rich, get out" with "shaking up" the West generally.[1] Some women got the feel of mining and successfully invested in or ran mining operations.[2] But Anne Ellis's life was at the bottom of all that, and her friends were friends-in-desperation. They related in a way that could be called female bonding, like the male bonding front-line soldiers comfort themselves with.

I think we waste Ellis's work if we read it only as a story of economic conditions that were not benignant to women. If we want a better life for everyone (and such a desire is always floating about in the minds of people who read books), it is more useful to see Ellis as a cultur-ally effective person than as an economically failed per-son who happened to keep a record and have ideas. Here is why: her life was partly conducive to writing and think-ing and partly not. Her mother and stepfather read aloud in the family — but Anne Ellis grew up in such poverty she hadn't energy or time to write regularly. Despite all, she took on an activity that we now know makes people conscious thinkers: she examined her life and kept rec-

1. Patricia Nelson Limerick, *The Legacy of Conquest* (New York: W. W. Norton, 1987), p. 100.
2. Sandra L. Myres discusses these women in *Westering Women and the Frontier Experience, 1800–1915* (Albuquerque: University of New Mexico Press, 1982), p. 264.

[xi]

FOREWORD

ords. She is more a colleague of Rebecca Harding Davis than a sociological resource.[3]

Of course this book will be read as a handbook to life in an early Colorado mining town, but its real heft is in Ellis's grasp of what it means to take part in culture — to see and keep records and have your own ethical ideas. In any event, it is extraordinary to read about such a bright person leading such a harsh life.

CAROL BLY

---

3. Davis wrote "Life in the Iron-Mills," which can be found in *Norton Anthology of Literature by Women*, ed. Sandra Gilbert and Susan Gubar (New York: W. W. Norton, 1985).

INTRODUCTION

Two friends of mine, who were taking a horseback trip through the Colorado mountains, found themselves at nightfall of a September day, some years ago, in a wild region, far from the destination which they had hoped to reach.

Bringing the horses to a standstill on the summit of a ridge, they searched the landscape spread before their eyes, hoping to find a suitable camping spot for the night.

To their surprise and relief, they saw a group of tents not far away, clustered among the pines of the mountain slope. Urging their tired horses forward, they soon reached the encampment, which proved to be that of a telephone construction gang, and following a most appetizing smell of fresh-baked bread and cinnamon rolls, they were led by their trusty noses directly to the cook tent. Determined if possible to secure food and a night's shelter in this unexpected refuge, they entered the tent.

There was no one in sight to greet them, but soup was simmering on the stove, the tent was orderly and clean, and lying face down on the white oilcloth of the table was a copy of 'Hamlet.' The two looked at each other inquiringly. What sort of person could it be who cooked for a construction gang and read Shakespeare in odd moments?

Their mute question was soon answered. A tall,

slender woman in early middle life, with alert blue eyes and a wealth of light brown hair, entered the tent. She was dressed in a lavender gingham dress with a fresh white apron over it, and pinned to one shoulder was a little bouquet of wild flowers.

This super-cook was Anne Ellis, a woman reared in the poverty, ignorance, and hardships of Western mining camps, who knew the pioneer life of the West as few people now living have ever known it, and who had brought to her experience of life an extraordinary wealth of courage, perception, humor, and philosophy.

It took little penetration to perceive that she was the good angel of this camp of laborers and that she made an art of ministering to their needs. Her skill and kindness in catering to their personal tastes won from them such appreciation and loyalty that they vied with one another in bringing home 'cook's bouquet,' and the flowers and ferns with which she always decorated the table. Later, when she entered politics and ran for office, the support of these men was an active factor in her triumphant election.

The two travelers and Anne Ellis became friends, and later she summed up in a single remark to them her whole philosophy of cookery. 'Give me,' said she, 'a well-cooked, well-served meal, a bouquet, and a sunset, and I can do more for a man's soul than all the cant ever preached. I can even do it without a sunset!' And she could. Some time after this first meeting with her new friends, Mrs. Ellis was stricken with a severe illness, and for a time it seemed that the vivid flame of her life might flicker out in the sanitarium where she found refuge, but the indomitable spirit which had carried her through unnumbered hardships in her career as maid, wife, and widow, and which had sustained her in earning a living for herself and her two children by sewing, cooking, or any other task which came to hand, flamed again in this campaign against the last enemy.

At the suggestion of one old-time friend and with the encouragement of her two new ones, she decided to employ her enforced leisure in writing her recollections of a phase of our national life which has now passed from the earth. Having made this decision, she characteristically did not wait until morning to begin to carry it out.

Writing to her friends in the wee small hours, she says:

'Not yet daylight and I am starting the Book! I am going to follow your suggestion and make a record of the early mining days, a record of times and customs already past and gone. I will try to write truthfully — why not? Not trying to dress it up or make it any better or in any way to change it. You know Herbert Quick said, "The life of the most ordinary man is interesting and priceless. The trouble is no one can write such a life." But I'm going to try it! It will be the life of a very ordinary woman, hundreds just like it all around you, only mine happened to be lived for the most part in the excitements and hardships of mining camps.

'The record will be in pieces like a crazy quilt, as it comes back to me that way — all in bits. It is so

INTRODUCTION

hard to bring out of the garret of my memory things laid by thirty — yes, forty-five years ago. And my thoughts are hard to control, like the heart of one who never knew he had a heart "until it began to break." I always thought I had a mind until I tried to think.

'I have known in my life only the most ordinary people, and always like to read of them, so I can and will write of just such folks as myself. There are so many millions of this kind who never write memories, but believe me, they have thoughts, hopes and aspirations which they cannot express and are never given credit for.

'I will try so far as I can to remember the terms and slang used in those days. Just think how hard I have tried to use good English and to express myself without slang, never thinking the time would come when I would want to recall it.

'I will use a form of punctuation of my own, which will be something like this — when one is beginning he takes a long breath, for this use a capital. When he stops for breath, a comma, and when it is all gone, a period. Don't know the use of a semi-colon, but expect it is when one thinks he is out of breath and isn't.

'You read of people who write that they always had the urge to do so, but I did not. Many times funny, sad and strange things have happened and I have wished some one knew of it who could really write, but I knew it was beyond me. Although if a good fairy offered me a gift, this is the one I would take, because of the fact that it reaches the very poor, while singing and painting may not come their way.

INTRODUCTION

'Up to six weeks ago I never saw a painting and never yet have heard a great singer, but ever since I could read I have had wonderful companions in books. It seems strange, my writing a book myself, and if it is ever said "she does it well" or "poorly" it will remind me of Ouida's dancing dogs. When some one exclaimed, "How wonderfully they dance," another replied, "No, the wonderful thing is that they dance at all."'

So Anne Ellis began this extraordinary narrative, finding in the labor of writing it distraction from pain, and unconsciously revealing in the process a character of such force and endurance that it interprets not only her own history but the history of her period as well.

She is the world of Bret Harte become articulate in the first person singular. Her manuscript at length found its way into my hands and received instant recognition from a group of discriminating listeners to whom portions of it were read. The narrative was too long for publication in its original form and required careful editing and rearrangement.

This difficult task was intrusted to Kathleen Carman Dodge, who brought to it literary experience and skill as well as an enthusiasm for the manuscript itself.

The book which resulted lies open before you.

LUCY FITCH PERKINS

The Life of an Ordinary Woman

THE LIFE OF
AN ORDINARY WOMAN

.·.

CHAPTER I

Not because of, but in spite of ancestors
we should try to be and do something.
A. E.

OF course one starts with ancestors. For years I did
not know this. I thought one had only a mother, and
I yet think of our mother as the ancestor. And in-
deed she is the root, stem, and branches of my family
tree, and now that I think of it, she was like a tree —
so generous and just as close to nature. Her name
was Rachel Swearengen. She was a tall, small-boned
woman, with lots of black hair braided in two long
smooth braids crossed over and wound around the
back of her head. She had small, well-shaped hands
which she bequeathed to each of her children.

I think she was born in Tennessee, and it is a sort
of a tradition that her people had slaves at one time.
They moved to Missouri when she was small, and
before the Civil War had cattle, horses, and hogs, and
a home. Her mother was crippled with rheumatism,
and had to be carried out of the house when they
heard 'bushwhackers' were coming. Her father did
not take sides in the war — but she said he 'leaned
toward the North.' I am afraid not far enough, how-

ever, as some bushwhackers, finding a gun hid in a bed left by a Confederate cousin, did kill him, calling him into the yard and shooting him. She said he tried to scratch some message on the ground before he died, but they couldn't make it out. The bushwhackers burned the house and drove off all the cattle and horses, killed the hogs and left them lying there. After stripping one uncle, they drove him away in front of them and the family never saw him again. At one time Mama, while peeking through the cracks in a corncrib, saw an uncle killed. I never could see why they picked on her people and wonder if they could have been carrying water on both shoulders. I do know that after her father was killed, her oldest brother, John, joined one of these bands of bushwhackers and stayed with them until after the war was over. This same brother belonged to the Jesse James gang, and I have heard that at one time there were seven Swearengen men chained together on their way to jail in Ozark, each one near seven feet tall, and weighing near two hundred pounds, and after they were in the jail they just pulled it down around them and walked away.

Her girlhood was hard, doing men's work — barefoot — in the fields. John, her oldest brother, was her guardian. He whipped her with the plough lines whenever anything went amiss; she was strong and could stand it, but Dogie (the name given to any weak motherless undergrown calf) was not strong and could not; so she did this young brother's work also and tried to shield him from John. On her arm was a huge scar that came about in this way: she and her brother were cutting corn, and since it was done more easily one way than another, they quarreled about it and fought with corn-knives. I don't know how he came out, but her arm must have been in a dreadful state to leave this big scar. Mama's times of rest were spent digging poke root, jimson weed, and ginseng, which could be sold to buy a much-prized and longed-for sprigged calico dress.

She has told me of going to camp meeting as though it was an event; of going or wanting to go to a dance; of dancing on a puncheon floor (logs with the top smoothed off by hand), the cracks so wide that the dancers jumped them.

Mama never went to school a day in her life, and it was always a great sorrow to her that she could neither read nor write. I feel sure she would have been a brilliant woman if given a chance. She has told me of a loft where tobacco was hanging — she would be sent to bring down some and would stop and nibble it, and in this way learned to use it. As a child I was ashamed of this. I did not know she was just forty years ahead of the times! She had no sense of fear, but a great love and understanding of all animals — could and did doctor any of them. She was as strong as a man. Once, when I was a little girl, a man with a load of lumber was stuck in a mud hole near our house; while whipping, swearing, and urging his team, he felt the wagon give a heave and found Mama had lifted the back end out.

She often used the Southern expression that, when

one is doing well, 'he is eating his white bread now.' She never had a white-bread time.

I suppose my father seemed wonderful to her. He had a good education for those times, and was, or tried to be, a 'gentleman' always, and to get along with as little work as possible. Mama was married when she was sixteen, and her brother John gave her eight hundred dollars as her share of their property. My father started a store with this, but soon grew tired of it, as he did of all things.

On her wedding day, an Easter Sunday, she had new brogans. She had gone barefoot before, and after the ceremony slipped away and was found at a small creek with her shoes off, wading to cool her swollen feet. My father's people felt it a disgrace; in fact it was a brother of my father who told me this in a low voice, breaking it easy so I could stand it. It was he, too, who told me of breaking down the jail, this in almost a whisper, and that we had Indian blood (on my mother's side, of course), and that he had heard that one of my female ancestors (still on my mother's side) had been burned for a witch. He thought that I might live it all down and I could depend on him not to spread it. Now, this is what I call some start.

I have heard that Mama's brother John's death came in this manner: he had grown tired of his meek, brow-beaten wife Sukie, and had used cave-man methods on a nephew's wife, stealing her and taking her to his home. All the family were in fear of him, but the nephew thought this was going too far even for John, so he went and killed him. I should have liked to meet John. He must have had all the qualities that make a man if they had only been thrown in the right direction. He was strong, very brave, and certainly had the courage of his convictions.

And now we come to my father's side of the family.

My father's father walked from Missouri to Colorado at the time of the 'Pike's Peak or bust' boom, and, in spite of plains and mountain Indians, died with his scalp on and his boots off. I am not quite sure whether he deserved credit for this pilgrimage or not. I know he enjoyed the adventure, and no doubt it was easier to fight Indians than poverty; but it seems to me that the brave one was my grandmother, left in Missouri with a large family on a rocky hillside farm. Back of my father there were only vague reports, never favorable, but this may have been because Mama told me. She also told me, when I was extra lazy, of an aunt who tried to be a lady and would walk mincingly across the floor holding her hands in front of her like a penguin; of an uncle who was so spoiled and such a glutton that his mother would get up in the night and make coffee and hot biscuits for him. Lots of times she said I took after him. She told me, too, of an uncle, who, a tiny boy, when the men were 'baching,' would climb upon a chair to turn the bacon in the skillet. This boy she liked and said she wished I was more like him, but she summed up the whole tribe as 'po' white trash.'

And now my father! Charming, good-looking, cheerful, honest, and artistic — no bad habits, but hating work, and just simply not there when it came to providing for his family. A good promoter, but he would never stick to anything. He really did have good ideas, if he had only held on. Each new plan sounded so plausible, and even when you knew him you couldn't help feeling it would be a sure-enough success this time. If Fate had given him a rich man for a father, he would have made a charming gentleman. I think he might have been called a 'faddist,' because he changed his religion as often as he did his job. First, I think he called himself an atheist; then in Bob Ingersoll's time a Freethinker; in Brand's time, an Iconoclast. He was also a writer for, and a reader of 'The Iron-Clad Age'; and then it was Science, Theosophy, and New Thought. He had a way of making one think he just happened to be down on his luck at that particular time, but was going to make the best of it. His head was 'bloody but unbowed,' and, like Micawber, he was always sure something would 'turn up.' I do not know how long the store flourished, but I do know my father got white pants to work in, and an expensive pair of scales. I think the pants were expensive, too. I believe his talents lay in getting ready to do a thing, and if they had been better directed I might have been the daughter of a statesman, an efficiency expert, or perhaps a real-estate king.

My father can still put up such a good talk, and is so honest and sure of himself, and has such faith in whatever it is that he happens to be interested in at the moment, and has such a secret of holding friends, that he can find some one to back each new venture. And who knows? He may make it yet.

CHAPTER II

Pioneers: 'The cowards never started and the weak ones died by the way.'
CARL SANDBURG

I DO not know how far it is from Christian County, Missouri, to Custer County, Colorado, but it must have seemed far, traveling with oxen. I can almost hear my father say, 'These old mossbacked backwoods Missourians are dead in the shell and don't know it. We will go West where there are chances for a man, and there we will found our fortunes.'

And such chances as there were, too! Think of the farming land they passed, and of the fine ranches they drove over! Only they were not looking for ranches — they wanted mines, where, as they thought, riches came overnight and without work.

Did my young mother dread this journey, or look forward to it? I think that, in spite of the fear of the Indians (and this was a dreadful fear), she did look forward with her heart full of hope. I know a woman who made this journey just before her baby was born. That baby is now an old man, and he always goes peeking around corners, sidling, slipping, and watching, in constant fear of the Indians. Whenever I see a covered wagon going along, in imagination I see my mother sitting up there, framed in the bow, a baby in her lap, only now these wagons have horses, and our teams were always oxen. I fancy she would walk a good deal — it seems oxen are more easily

[8]

goaded on if one walks beside them. The tragedy of a broken neck-yoke still remains with me, broken where there were no tools or material to mend it.

Then the dread of fording the rivers; of being swallowed up in quicksand; of never having enough provisions! My father was the kind who traveled, trusting to Fate to provide, and it did — but Mama was Fate! She would be dressed in a slat sunbonnet (pushed back most of the time — she had to be free), a tight basque, and a full skirt made of calico or linsey woolsey, and if not barefoot, she probably wore a pair of brogans. She had an old blue army overcoat, and in after years I thought she meant this when she sang, 'Faded coat of blue.'

She would look forward and be happy, thinking of the home she was going to have 'out there,' and then look back and cry, thinking of the friends she had left. She was like this. I would have only looked forward. With all the work and hardships, she was 'eating her white bread' then, although she did not know it. At night my father would bring out his banjo — all day he would have a headache and would have to lie in the wagon. It was cured when the sun went down and the day's work was over. Then they would all sit around the camp-fire, and sing, and some would dance while others patted 'Juba.' All troubles were forgotten while they planned the things they would have, and do, when they 'struck it rich.'

My father's father and his family were along. A young uncle, who had not been weaned yet, would slip up to his mother's side, and lean on her, then the men would laugh and make fun of him, and would make him perform. After he danced and sang, 'I am a nigger, and don't give a damn; I rather be a nigger than a poor white man,' they would let him nurse.

At one time — it seems I remember it, but I fancy it was told me — the men go after buffalo, shoot one, and stampede the rest, which head for the wagons, and we are saved only by a miracle. Another time — and I am quite sure I remember this — I sat down in a cactus. I think now Mama must have been expecting another baby; anyway, I was weaned on the road on brown sugar and cornbread — no milk — and yet I survived! Some of the pioneers did have cows. Many of the cows would get sore feet and would have shoes made of old pieces of leather laced on them.

Mama would hunt and gather the dried buffalo chips for fuel when they camped. She would, when they were near the muddy Platte, dip this water, leaving it to settle; I wonder what in! What did people use before the time of the five-gallon tin oil can? I cannot imagine any new country without them. I have seen them used for almost every purpose — houses built and covered with them, stoves made of them. I have used them always for bread cans and wash boilers. To make the water settle more quickly, my mother would gather, very carefully, pear cactus and split it more carefully, throwing it into the water. The slime in this cactus gathers up every bit of dust and gravel, leaving the water beautifully clear.

THE FEAR OF INDIANS

A dreadful fear of the Indians was born and grown into me. As a child I had three gripping fears — starvation, Indians, and ghosts. Long after I had outgrown the fear of not having enough to eat, and the fear of a ghostly hand being laid upon my shoulder from behind, I still had horrible dreams of trying to hide from Indians; of running from them till my feet rose from the ground and I ran in the air — hundreds of times have I had this dream. This, no doubt, came from my mother's fear of them. Before I was born there was a treaty with the Utes, by the terms of which the Utes were to get twenty-five thousand dollars per year for their land. The year I was born, the attention of Congress was called to this, and in justice to the Utes they were urged to pay; then gold mines were discovered on Indian land, and the 'Utes must go.' Chief Ouray (the Arrow) got one thousand dollars per year from the Government for keeping peace.

At this time Meeker had been trying to teach the Indians to farm. They, like the rest of us, didn't want to be uplifted — so in 1879 occurred the Meeker massacre. We were crossing the plains at the time; we heard of this and were dreadfully frightened — being told how the Indians took Meeker's stiff body and ran it along the ground as one would a plough — this in derision of the lessons in farming.

For years Chief Colorow was used to frighten me — he was an Indian outlaw and a very bad *hombre*. I thought he had special designs on me because of my long yellow hair, and many times in my dreams have

I felt him lift it from my head and seen it dangling from his belt.

Driving over northeastern Colorado my people feared the Cheyenne and Arapahoe Indians. Every one kept watch every moment, many times being frightened by a mirage, or they would see a line of objects running all in a row toward them as Indians would, or they might be going from them like frightened, lumbering animals — these usually turned out to be the ever-shifting tumble weeds driven by every passing wind.

Always, when I think of pioneers, I see my mother, a baby on her arm, working, working, ever hopeful, seeing something to laugh at, cooking for the men, feeding the cattle at night, doctoring both the men and cattle. She was a born doctor. In after years she would go any time of the day or night to bring some one's baby into the world, doing everything and then finishing up with the washing. They might say, 'You know you are not a regular doctor so cannot charge anything, but we will give you five or ten dollars.' Sometimes they did and sometimes they did not. But it was all the same to her if they needed help.

We did not stay very long in any place, and were always poverty-stricken. We came into Pueblo and camped at the edge of the town, with nothing to eat. And this brave country woman leaving her baby in camp with oh! such a fear pulling at her heart that the baby might toddle out under the feet of the oxen or fall into the fire, or into the evil-looking Arkansas river, took one of her most prized possessions, a pieced quilt, and went into the city to sell it for food. While she would not be afraid when the mad buffalo charged down on them, the noise, the unfriendliness of the rushing crowds in this strange city, did raise such a lump in her throat, such a weakness in her stomach, but she went bravely on. In after years, she felt it a disgrace that she had once begged in Pueblo. Thus it is, some of the noblest things we do we are ashamed of, and sometimes are proud of such little, piffly things.

There followed years of hardship for Mama, cooking and washing in mining camps. Then the gipsy grandfather (he wasn't really; just Dutch. Are there Dutch gipsies?) thought it might be better back in old Missouri. 'No chance here for a man who was really up and coming.' So back we and the oxen went. After being there for a time, the West again was 'the place for opportunity.' I have crossed the plains three times in an ox team, but do not remember much — the cactus, of course, and one time a little white house with hollyhocks in the yard. How I longed to be in that house! I must have been about three years old then. Another time I remember seeing sunflowers beside the road and being told they followed and turned with the sun, and thought, 'How wonderful!' Our last move left us in Silver Cliff, Colorado, now called West Cliff. Here a baby brother died. I remember feeling quite grand riding in a carriage, and wondered why Mama cried when she looked at the little white box in front.

I think it was here, or near here, that my father taught a term of school; at any rate, I bragged that my father was a school teacher, and must have had some reason. I do know that at about this time he sold, or was the means of selling, a mine, and made a few hundred dollars. He then went to Buffalo and never returned to us.

Later on there was a divorce, but whether my mother or my father got it I do not know, nor whose fault it was. Probably, as in most such cases, each one was partly to blame.

CHAPTER III

If it were not for poor people writers would lack a lot of material.
A. E.

So we are left, my young mother and two babies. I cannot think that at the time my father left he did not expect to return, but I fancy it was his first taste of the life he so longed for. He was young and a man, and they often do not have the tie toward a child which a mother finds so hard to break. I seem to remember the watching and waiting for a letter; I am sent for the mail very often and am always disappointed; so one day I pull myself up to the shelf at the post-office window, just so my eyes can see over it, and ask the postmaster, 'Well, when will there be a letter?' And did one ever come, and who read it for her, and what did it say? I don't know. There must be a special heaven for eager wives, anxious mothers, and longing sweethearts, who have turned away from post-office windows disappointed, but hopeful for another day. When there are two babies to take care of each day, and one has to take in washing in order to feed them, there is not much time for sorrow.

After a time we go to Querida, where Mama is married again. I have no memory of this time, but pray that she was happy. I do not think she works so hard now; not for a time at least.

This new husband, Henry, was a miner. I suppose she had washed for him. He had a fair education, a charming manner, and no bad habits; all the good qualities one would look for in a husband; but he was utterly without feeling. In fact, I don't see how she came to choose two such absolutely selfish men, unless it was because of the fact that she was so good-hearted herself, and never happy unless doing for others.

More passing pictures — my first doll, a china one, a boy breaks her head off; I cry — and try to fasten it on again with sand and spit; a pan of moss roses mama had brought from home; they freeze and she sheds tears over them.

Henry, my stepfather, had a brother who was married to a very young girl. I am staying with her nights, while her husband is on night shift at one of the mines. A circus comes to town, and we have no money to go. When the parade goes past her house, she opens the door and stands on her head in the open doorway — I don't know whether to show derision, or merely to let them know she can stage a circus herself if she cares to. She tries to have me get on my head beside her, but I make a poor job of it and double and flop over, and the people in the parade look and laugh. I know this is something I must never tell my mother.

Another time we are getting ready for the day. Mama, with the baby on her hip, is trying to get breakfast, put up Henry's lunch, and dress me all at the same time; she has got as far as my red flannel petticoat (I sleep in my underwear made of flour sacks) when she discovers we have no eggs, and asks Henry to go and get some. But he is peevish, and says it is all her fault, anyway, she should have remembered; so she, desperate, tells me to go to 'Shorty's' and get some. We had a bachelor neighbor called Shorty, also the butcher downtown went by this name; and I, so little, and not understanding, went the long way to town. I knew I didn't look right without a dress on and arms all bare, so I stopped outside the door and pulled out a string of beads I had on next to my skin. I thought, 'Shorty will see these, and then it will not be so bad.' I asked for eggs; he had none, so I took liver instead, and as I returned home this started to ooze through the paper and over my arm. A dog came up to smell it: this frightened me and I began to run; and the dog came on faster. I stumbled and fell, running a big stick into my leg, and the scar is there today. Some one picked me up and carried me home, and the worst of all was I had broken the string and lost my beads!

My father, after he left us, had married a woman in Buffalo, New York, a widow with one daughter. She was supposed to have money, but it did not last long. They come to Silver Cliff to live, and I am invited to go over and visit. This is my first social event. I remember Mama shirred up a big blue handkerchief for a hat for me, and that I was all excited hearing of the wonders of a circus I might go to.

Maude, the daughter on the other side, had very pretty clothes, and the evening before the circus, I decided in my small mind I wanted to wear some of them. According to my ethics it would never do to ask for them, so I took off my blue-and-white striped apron, pulled a mattress open, and pushed it far in.

The result was I wore a red plaid silk dress of Maude's, made long-waisted, with two rows of pearl buttons on either side, running the full length of it. The end of this dress was tragic. I took a little dead goat to some baby mountain lions just caught and in a cage waiting to be shipped; when I reached the goat in to them they reached for me, caught their paws in my dress and tore it off. Another dream vanished!

We go to the circus! I am the owner of a balloon, quite the finest thing which has happened to me so far. When I returned to the house, I put it behind me for safe keeping. I hear a noise, look for my balloon — nothing there! This seems unbelievable, so wonderful just a moment ago, and now just a string! I cried.

I am six this May; my brother is two years younger, and there is another baby coming. The mines are shut down, and Henry must go to another camp. Several men without work have gone to Bonanza, a booming town in the upper end of the San Luis Valley, and there he goes and we are alone again, with the same waiting for mail. I wonder if there was ever a fear in Mama's heart that he too might never return.

When one cannot read, one thinks a lot, and if one is carrying a baby and there is no money in sight, the thoughts are troubled. When the mail does come, the young sister-in-law must read it to her, and what if she does not get it all? Or to tease her, what if something is held back? You wives, who get so much between the lines, she was denied even this. But one day a letter does come with money, and we are to go,

ANOTHER MIGRATION

so the packing begins. Mama sings now. We load into a wagon and are off through the Wet Mountain Valley.

When Chief Ignacio had objected to signing the treaty giving this tract to the Government, Chief Ouray told him it was no use to fight; 'The white men are as numberless as the leaves on the trees and every man has a gun.' A German army officer, realizing the worth of this land, bought most of the valley and started a colony of German farmers there. Here Mama sees the ranches and longs to live on one of them. She was a woman of the soil. Then on through the Sangre de Cristo Range. The fathers who named this must have seen it for the first time with the red sun pouring over the snowy top and down the purple sides. This range runs the full length of the valley and on into New Mexico. I wish every one might see it; to me, it is wonderfully beautiful.

It is now the latter part of September, the loveliest time in Colorado. The quaking aspen and scrub oak are all colors of red, yellow, green, and orange. Mama rides along, all her worldly possessions in the wagon with her, the team never going faster than a walk. She loves the trees with their never-ending motion. She would not know the story I hear later, why these trees always trembled. It is because Christ, on the way to Calvary, passed under an aspen, and it commenced to tremble and quake in sympathy, and never through all the years since then has it stopped.

All this beauty Mama will soak in, and will give

[19]

to the child soon to be born. We pass more ranches and herds of cattle, she always wishing she had them. On and on up Kerber Creek and into the mountains, where we come at last to a very narrow place in the road and are stopped by a big bar — a toll gate, where every team or pack train has to pay to get through. Bonanza is one mile farther on. She is tired and anxious to arrive — she feels that her time is near, and she must get a big washing done, so as to have everything in order when the baby comes. At the edge of the town is another toll gate, and now we are passed, and in the place where we are to live so many years.

Our little family drove into Bonanza in the fall of 1882. The camp was discovered in 1880, following the Leadville boom. Men were wild with the silver fever and the mountains were full of prospectors. The first discovery in the Kerber Creek district is said to have been made in Copper Gulch by a man hunting horses, who stumbled over the rich float and located it, calling it the White Iron. Kerber Creek was named after Captain Charles Kerber, who in 1865 was mustered out from Fort Garland, and in looking for a pass through the mountains went up this stream. Following the locating of the White Iron was the discovery of the Cornucopia, the Bonanza, the Rawley, and the Revenue. The Bonanza had the best showing — pay dirt right from the grass roots — and to-day it is still a paying mine.

This is the story of its location as told by C. M. Buck, a mining authority and an old schoolmate of mine:

'The discovery and location of the Bonanza Mine

was one of the most daring and exciting events of the early history of the camp — according to Eli Weddington, one of the pioneers of the district, he being an actual witness to most of the following events.

'Pete McCardle and John Stansbury, two pioneer prospectors of that day, had just located the Exchequer group of four claims, about a mile and a half north of the town of Bonanza. This was early in the summer of 1880. Their claims apparently also covered the group known as the Bonanza group.

'Pat Cuddington and Jennings, two other prospectors, followed them a few days later with their burros and prospecting outfit. Not knowing the ground was covered by McCardle's and Stansbury's claims, they began to dig on what proved later to be the very top of the Bonanza vein. They had dug but a few feet, when the rival claimants, McCardle and Stansbury, who were working on their claims in the Exchequer group, higher up the hill, discovered them. They immediately procured their six-shooters and came over to where Cuddington and Jennings were working. Flourishing these small cannon in a menacing fashion, and with language more forcible than elegant, they ordered the trespassers to move. They did not, however, leave the vicinity, but simply went back to their camp to bide their time for a more favorable opportunity. Watching their chance, they went back the first time they saw their rivals had left the ground, and made exact copies of their location notices. A careful study of these revealed the fact that the way their rivals had claimed the ground, their hole — Cuddington's and Jennings's — was not within McCardle's and John Stansbury's boundaries. Fearing that McCardle and Stansbury might discover this discrepancy and change the course of their locations, they lay low until the day before the time to have the claims surveyed and recorded. Early in the morning of the last day they set forth with picks and shovels and armed to the teeth. McCardle and Stansbury were greatly surprised, about nine o'clock that morning, to see dirt flying from the hole they had ordered their rivals to vacate. Grabbing their guns, they proceeded to investigate. As they drew near the hole, the shoveling ceased and no one could be seen. When within about twenty feet of the hole, two huge six-shooters appeared above the collar, simultaneously with the command 'Hands up.' McCardle and Stansbury were taken by surprise and promptly raised their hands. Cuddington and Jennings then rose up and proceeded to explain.

'"The time limit on your location notices to have your claims surveyed and recorded expires to-day. If we get this claim surveyed and recorded before you do yours, our claim will hold, and we propose to beat you to it." McCardle and Stansbury lost no time in leaving for Salida by horseback for a surveyor, but they were too slow; Cuddington and Jennings already had a man on the road to Saguache for the same purpose, their man arriving several hours before their rivals. As a consequence of this little dispute, Cuddington and Jennings became the owners of the Bonanza.'

GENERAL GRANT AT BONANZA

The Rawley has worked off and on all these years and to-day is a big concern. Harry Payne Whitney, of New York, owned a large interest in it. In 1880, when ex-President Grant was returning from his trip around the world, he stopped off in Denver to visit his friend John Routt, Territorial Governor of Colorado. They heard of the Bonanza boom, and Grant, who was particularly short of money at this time, decided to look Bonanza over, hoping to recoup his fortunes here. They drove in a livery rig, since the railroad was not built into Salida till 1881. Salida is sixty miles from Bonanza. They camped at Sedgwick for a week or two. Grant had a Japanese servant with him, but most of their provisions were sent from Salida already cooked. Grant offered forty thousand dollars for the Bonanza Mine, which was promptly refused — for by now the owners were charging one dollar per head just to look at this hole down only a few feet. Grant also offered one hundred and sixty thousand for the Exchequer — he was lucky the owners did not take him up. He left without investing. After leaving, he went to Central City, another mining camp, where in his honor, they had a walk made of silver bricks from his carriage to the door of the Teller House.

Bonanza is ten thousand feet above sea level, lying in a narrow gulch, the mountains rising high on either side. A street and creek run down the middle. In one place the creek runs under and across the road. This is covered with a wooden culvert which has been the worry of three generations of mothers; whenever a child is lost, they run first to look under the culvert. Most of the houses have the back end or kitchen built in the hillside. A good many are of logs; some of frame; the lumber for these frame buildings being packed in on mules or burros. In these days there were many tents large and small.

There were then three towns on Kerber Creek. The farthest up was Exchequer; a mile below this is Bonanza; a mile below this is Sedgwick, which I think an Englishman must have named. I do not know how many people there were here in the height of the boom. In speaking of the population, you didn't count people, anyway, you counted saloons and dance-halls. There were thirty-six saloons and seven dance-halls.

Bonanza was not as rough and tough as most new camps, because in the very beginning it was incorporated as a city, and always had all the town officials. Sometimes it took almost the entire population to fill the offices. Judge Slaughter held court every day, and woe betide any evil doer, as the judge's lowest fine was forty dollars and costs, and he fined at the drop of the hat. Non-payment of fines meant the calaboose and bread and water. Bill Tripp, a bad man from Silver Cliff, was jumping streets (claiming land used for streets) both he and his woman, Mollie May, paying little attention to law and order. Judge Slaughter put the Indian sign [1] on them by declaring,

[1] The Indians were supposed to put a distinguishing mark of some sort on any prisoners who were reserved for special torture. Hence, to put 'the Indian sign' on any one meant, to inspire him with terror. *Ed.*

'I've seen and settled more hell than you could ever raise.'

For many years now, Sedgwick and Exchequer are gone; the house torn down and moved away, and Nature quickly covers these gashes cut in the mountain-sides where cellars and foundations once were. We lived in Exchequer long after every one else had gone, and came to think of it as our town. Only Bonanza to-day is left of all these towns, and some of the old-time buildings are standing and being used; but they are so stooped and gray with age that they lean on each other for support; the windows are all broken, like blind eyes; and the sidewalks so torn and warped that they look like twisted hands.

It is seventeen miles from the narrow-gauge railroad which runs over through the San Luis Valley. In my time everything was brought in on pack trains and ore wagons, and to-day, while they use many trucks, still these freight teams make the trip.

From town, going over and through the mountains to Shirley, there was, and still is, a toll road built by Otto Mears, the Pathfinder, and he was a sure-enough road-builder! Some of this road is very good yet, and, where it is graded on the high mountain-sides, it still winds in and out among the trees. Nature seems to know it for a good job and does not try to cover it. I have heard that Mears built this road before an election — not that a road was needed especially, but he did need votes. He was a man of wonderful judgment; for instance, a few years before this he had a store in Saguache, and a pioneer woman told me 'he swapped tobacco and whiskey to the Indians who would come in from the agency — no roads — galloping their horses over the chico till they looked like waves.' She also told me this story: 'Once all our husbands was out burying a man who had been killed in a drunken shooting scrape — some of them had been drinking a lot too — so us wives went up to Mears's Store — Nancy Tuttle, the blacksmith's wife was sick and couldn't go — and we went in and smashed in the heads of the barrels and poured the whiskey into the road. Mears never said a word, just looked on, but, lo and behold, when our husbands got their bills they were charged with all that whiskey, between four and five hundred dollars' worth. Money so scarce, too. Nancy was sure glad she had that sick spell.'

More memory pictures: we are moved in, but not settled, in a one-room house; there is a door in front with a window on either side; three steep steps lead up to the door, which opens right on the road; along this road dash men and women on horseback; the women are on side saddles and are dressed in long wide skirts, tight basques, and stiff hats with veils floating behind them. The dress I remember best was double-breasted with gilt ball buttons running up and down either side of it. When they galloped, the little tails on the basques went flippy-flop in a very graceful manner, or at least I thought so.

The 'fancy girls' all had their favorite horses and rode each day. There were other horses ridden to the mines, the bridle thrown over the horn, when they would all return on the run, to their stables.

A NEW BABY SISTER

Going by our house are strings of burros with the panniers on either side packed full; on top of this a roll of bedding, then drills, picks, and shovels on top of all. There are the freight teams coming down with ore or going up with supplies, and the stage dashing by with its passengers. All of this is very strange to us. My brother and I keep Mama in hot water all the time, for fear of the creek on one side and the busy road on the other.

The second day after we are here — Mama is not unpacked yet, but does get her washing done — comes a fall of snow, the first of the year. Nothing would do but Henry must go hunting; 'a shame to miss out on such a good tracking snow.' At daylight he leaves. After he is gone Mama's time has come. My brother and I are out playing, and there alone, with no fire, no wood to build one, nothing to do with, her heart wrung with worry over these two small children out on the busy road (they do climb in a tub left in the creek, tip it over, but scramble out), she has her child, does everything needful for it and herself, as best she can without warm water, then gets up, comes to the door, and asks a passing miner to get her children for her (all wet and muddy from their spill). She never mentions this little new girl on the bed; instead she tells us what to find to eat — the foremost thought of all mothers. In the evening the good man returns, and I believe cooks us all a meal, then goes to town, treats all the boys and is treated in return, because he has a new baby in his house. He comes home feeling as though he had really done it all himself. He even names his new daughter after his sisters, Josephine May.

In the mean time this mother lies there content, listening to the soft breathing of her older children sleeping on the foot of her bed, her hand on the little round head of this last one, curled up at her side. She is very drowsy, but before throwing her long black braids over the pillow, she thinks a prayer, and smiles; all is well.

CHAPTER IV

Women dream many dreams and see many
visions while bending over the washtub.
A. E.

Now comes a heavy snow, and we are all penned up
in one small room, each time the door is opened the
wind driving the snow in and across the floor. Around
the tiny stove, German socks and overshoes are drying; across one corner is stretched a rope; this also
holds clothes left to dry. Mama complains because
this snow had not come a few weeks before, when she
had seen it from a distance, lying on the high mountain peaks, and had longed for some of it to eat, fearing if she did not get it she would mark this new baby.
She believed very strongly in marking babies.

Most of the winter we live in this one-room house,
then move to another, with a front room and a lean-
to kitchen. This is necessary, because Henry's father
from New Hampshire is coming visiting. When he
does arrive, he brings a huge cake of maple sugar,
which is put on the saw-buck and sawed in two, we
children, meanwhile, grabbing for the sweet sawdust.
He was very good to us and from him I heard my first
Mother Goose rhymes, but I did not enjoy them as
most children do. I was too old, and I could make no
sense of a 'cow jumping over the moon,' and knew
that a dish never did 'run away with a spoon.'

Grandfather and we children slept in the kitchen;
Mama, Henry, and the baby in the front room.

THE LIFE OF AN ORDINARY WOMAN

Never did we have a 'parlor,' for by the time we were grown and could have one, they were 'living-rooms.' In front of our bed a piece of canvas hung; around this, in the early morning, would come the smell of pancakes and the sound of coffee being ground.

By now the boom is commencing to wane, and most of the miners are out of a job. Henry got a job cutting a survey trail or line. Have you ever noticed a clean cut through the pines or an aspen grove, otherwise covering a mountain-side? These are survey trails cut when making a survey on a claim.

Mama is a fine manager, but each day our meals are slimmer until things get desperate. One night a butcher shop is broken into and all the meat stolen. A great to-do follows, and Mama wonders who 'had the gall to do it'; and Henry would like to know 'who in blazes did do it.' There is talk of searching each cabin, and Mama points out to us the dreadful punishment which comes to thieves, while all the time, rolled in a piece of canvas, and pushed far back under the bed, is a quarter of black frozen meat. This I wasn't supposed to know, and, as I was a canny youngster, I kept it to myself. I do know, however, that Henry didn't have a hand in it; he hadn't the nerve.

Two of the men who were in on this deal were Si Dore and Picnic Jim. Dore had been a sailor, now he was a timber-man, and a very good one. He drank a good deal, and, although I never saw him drunk, he always smelled of it, as most of these men did. They always kept a jug, and would have an eye-opener on getting up in the morning, an appetizer before breakfast, a snifter before dinner, one to settle the stomach after eating, a friendly glass with any one who might show up in the course of the day, and a hot sling before going to bed. Dore was supposed to be a devil after women, and had a fast woman living at his cabin most of the time. There were strong objections to my visiting him so much, but I did it anyway — he was generous with his nickels and dimes, and always asked me to eat — good codfish and mackerel, and biscuit over which he folded a very dark white cloth on taking them from the oven.

One winter he made me a sled, with real irons on the runners. (I made sleds, my only tools a hatchet and saw, but never went so far as to have irons on runners.) He was a wonderful hunter and I would stand by the hour, listening to his stories (if one exclaimed in wonder, and praised him he was more generous) and watching him clean his gun. When any one broke the sight on his gun, Dore made fine new ones of pearl buttons. He had a dog which slept with him, and was very dear to him; in some way it was killed, and Dore had quite a funeral, followed by a big drunk. Always when you mentioned this dog tears came into Dore's eyes.

Once Mama made him a buckskin shirt, shedding many tears over it, it was so hard to sew. She also did his washing, and it was then, when I delivered his laundry, that I did my visiting. His cabin was not clean like Eli's, but Eli was an exception; Dore's was just the usual miner's cabin — a bunk built in one corner, a mattress of straw or pine boughs and over this blankets, with a top cover of canvas, and a pillow with a dark calico slip (quite shiny in the middle). At the head of the bed is a shelf, either nailed, or on pegs set in the logs; on this shelf are matches, a candle, pipes and tobacco, shaving mug and razor, and a small box holding thread, needles, and buttons. Against the wall is a home-made table, on which are cans containing sugar and salt; also a can of condensed milk, a few tin plates and cups, these being turned upside down when not in use, to keep mice and dirt out. Over the dishes, knives and forks, the dish-pan was turned; on top and covering all this was spread the not very white dish-towel, made from an old flour sack. The chairs were of blocks of wood, or two pieces of board nailed on a slant, with a seat fastened on; the stove was a tiny sheet-iron affair, with a coffee-pot on the back. Under a curtain in the corner hung their 'other clothes'; near the door, on a box turned on end, would be a water-bucket and wash-pan.

I don't know when Picnic Jim first came to our house; I think Henry discovered him and brought him one evening to play the mouth harp; Picnic was an expert on this. He could play all the music he had ever heard, imitate animals, and usually ended by using an empty (or maybe there was water in it) tin can. This was his masterpiece. He was a drunkard, but a harmless and good-natured one. This first night he won Mama's heart by telling her of his mother

who lived in Denver and worried about him. He had
a few pack jacks and I never knew him to work in
the mines. I think he gambled and hung around the
saloons a great deal.

Mama was often brought to task by her neighbors
for letting us children be with Picnic so much. We
would go camping and be gone for days at a time, but
in spite of the fact that he was as bad as painted, and
put in lots of his time at the sporting houses, all we
ever learned from him was worth while; stories of
cities; how to pack a jack, and all the tricks of camping. I fancy he put up with us only because our house
was such a good place to go for a meal, a warm wel-
come, plenty of buttermilk to sober off on. The worst
I ever knew him to do was to sing, 'Chippie, get your
hair cut.' He sang this always, hummed the words to
himself, and came out strong on the end —

> 'Chippie, get your hair cut, hair cut, hair cut,
> Chippie, get your hair cut, short like mine.'

However, by coaxing, he did promise to teach me the
can-can (supposed to be the worst ever), in which
there was high kicking as near as I could find out. So,
I went around, trying out on limbs of trees, or anything as high, or higher than my head, against the
time when Picnic would teach me — but he never
did.

On one of our trips, Picnic made what he called an
Irish stew. A boy from town, somewhat tough, said,
'I don't want any of your hishy-hashy-hell-fired
stew'; and Picnic, who did not intend to have any

rough stuff in his camp, grabbed him up and sat him down on the red-hot sheet-iron stove, saying, 'Bet that will hold you for a while'; but it didn't, and when the smoke and boy were cleared away, everything was peaceful.

According to Picnic, his wants were few, 'A woman and a bottle of whiskey.' Sort of a 'Jug and Thou' person. After all, his was a pretty good plan. No matter if he had just made a winning, or if hungry, down and out, or getting over a bad case of snakes, his answer was always the same to the inquiry —

'How are you?'

'Oh, having a Picnic.'

This winter was the first time I had ever heard of Santa Claus, and again it was to hear of something wonderful coming my way, only to lose it. I, with neighbor children, plan on all the things we are to have. It seems Santa brings toys and candy, so I decided on a doll for myself, and a wagon for Ed, leaving it to his judgment what to bring the baby. Christmas night our stockings are hung up, and we go to bed with high hopes; but morning finds these stockings as lank and raggy-looking as the night before. We were so disappointed, and after this I pretended there was a Santa Claus for the other children, and through all the years managed to fix something for each one of them, using old cigar boxes, pieces of tin foil, scraps of silk, and tissue paper, cutting the pictures from fruit cans, using them to decorate the work box, pencil box, cornucopia, or whatever I happened to be fixing. The hurt I felt when I saw these empty stockings has been with me always, and after my own children came, never did they find an empty stocking, although the stuffing was ofttimes pitiful. Mama saw how hurt we were and said, 'Never mind, he will come to our house New Year's.' It seems we did not have a payday till the first, and then Santa Claus did come, and leave shoes and stockings, but the thrill was gone; also my belief in Santa Claus.

While we lived in this house there was a presidential election, with stirring times, speeches, parades, and bonfires; also much talk. In those times an election was looked upon as a vital and personal matter, and was the subject of all talk at home and school. School children had many fights.

Each side held meetings and dug up all the latest talent to speak or sing. No, I will not say talent, because once I recited. My piece came just after a young lawyer had pounded the table, clawed the air, calling all Democrats all sorts of names, saying that his 'honorable opponent' (such a sneer after 'honorable') 'must be driven out of town, carrying his law books under his arm.' He wasn't driven out, but did leave with his books in a box, and was afterward a prominent Denver lawyer. When my turn came, the chairman announced, 'Now a staunch little, golden-haired Republican will speak for us.' (Applause.)

I climb up on the platform, feeling as though I had swallowed a flatiron (or some people call them sad-irons, and this felt just so), my knees wobbling, like those of a newborn calf. The evening before my hair had been braided in tight braids, and was now let fly

loose, and frizzed all around my shoulders; I had on
my linen duster apron (one had to be very careful not
to wrinkle it); my shoes were newly blacked, and
smelled of it. I swallowed a few times and started in
a weak, small voice.

'Bing' (I suppose this was *being*, but I came out
strong on the *bing*)

> 'Bing one morning in May,
> Gathering flowers neat and gay,
> The prettiest little boy I ever did see
> Came walking along by the side of me.
> Shall I go bound, shall I go free?
> Shall I love a pretty boy that don't love me?
> Oh, no, no, love shall never conquer me.'

This, of course, was not an election piece, but was
the only one Mama knew to teach me.

Once Slippery Joe told me: 'In the spring of 1876
I was workin' in Lake City; one day I saw all the boys
gatherin' in front of a cabin. I figgered somebody had
locked horns, so sauntered over, an' by gol! it was
a woman talkin' politics, "Wimmin's Rights," she
called it. She said she was a school teacher somewhere back East an' she only got nine dollars a month
an' men got twenty-four an' it riled her an' she hit the
trail a-talkin' — an', kid, it don't look like a square
deal, does it?'

'How was she dressed, Slippery?'

'Nuthin' fancy, but good black silk, I guess, white
collar and cuffs, a right purty breastpin on. She was
a good talker an' we all took in what she said, but I
bet it'll be a cold day before I ever vote for a woman.'

'Was she married?'

'She didn't look it. Her name was Susan B. Anthony. Another woman with her was called Elizabeth Cady Stanton. They was ridin' horseback from one camp to another.'

At one election Otto Mears gave prospective voters hams, bacon, and sacks of flour, much better, it seems to me, than cigars or whiskey. Another time I remember a spring wagon being filled with men much the worse for wear, and many cases of very, very bad eggs. The wagon was driven up and down the streets and each Republican's house was rotten-egged. Today, if one of those frame houses still stands, there are stains on it where the eggs oozed down.

All this election talk, of what dread times we would have if Cleveland was elected, how we would 'go to the dogs,' how all the mines would close, and we would starve, filled my small mind until I started to worry over it. I knew if we grew any harder up than we now were, we couldn't stand it. I did not know how to pray, but brought my mind to dwell on the subject, and wished hard that the Republicans would get in. But they didn't, and I could see no change in our way of living, either for better or worse; and from that day to this, political talk has passed over my head. When they speak of a certain party getting in and bringing prosperous or dull times, in the background I see a thin, white-faced child very much worried over nothing.

Once, when things had gone worse than usual, I decided to commit suicide, my plan being to crawl into a big snowdrift, and die there. I thought how sorry they would feel in the spring when the snow went off, and I was found. I hoped I would not look like a cat we had found early one April! — but — Mama had just made two custard pies, the frosting sweating huge drops of gold, and had put them on the cupboard shelf to cool. So I put off the dreadful act till they were eaten, and always since then, there has been something, if not a pie to save me.

Crowded as we were, there was always room for guests. Once a preacher came, Mama being one of those good souls who entertained preachers. This one rode a horse seventeen miles over a high mountain pass, coming to town once a month, thinking he was doing his duty toward these miners. One time he came just after Christmas, and Mama in her hurry between stove, children, and setting the table, rushed to the clothes pack, grabbed up something, thinking it was our one tablecloth (made of four floursacks sewn together), and spread it on, only to find it was a huge white shirt which had been left for her to mend. When supper is over, the preacher tells us of Christmas in Saguache, and the presents given him, among them a huge wax doll, which he said he would bring to Jose the next trip. (I suspect he liked his meal and was looking forward one month.)

Well, right there I decided to have that doll, and started in to coax it from Jose. Each day she would give it to me (Oh, but I was good to her!), and each day it would be taken back. At the times when it was mine I would sit in the window and watch for him.

THE FATE OF A WAX DOLL

As the end of the month drew near, I had it cinched, had taken her fat hands and crossed her heart for her, and wished for her, that she would die if she took it back another time. Now I strain my eyes for him; he must come before she gets over her good spell! One day he comes in sight — but with no bundle showing! On he comes, now he is in the house, but with nothing in his hands! This is terrible.

Finally, I ask, 'Where is the wax doll at?'

He answers (how can he talk so low when it is so tragic?), 'Really, my little dear, it is unfortunate. At the time they gave me the doll, they also gave me nuts, candies, and other goodies, and when I made my former trip, to keep them safe from mice, I placed everything, including the doll, in the oven. When I returned it was quite chilly, and I built a fire, forgetting the contents of the oven, and there you are.'

Yes, there I was, with a most dreadful lump in the pit of my stomach and a lost faith in preachers.

None of the mines in Bonanza worked all the time. The ore streak would pinch out or the money play out; then it was a 'shut-down.' For over forty-five years it has been a continual opening-up and closing-down of mines. It is the mine owner's dream to get some one to put up money to run his mine. And in Bonanza I am quite sure there has been much more money put into the ground than has ever been taken from it. The ore here runs in pockets and a few, a very few, have been fortunate enough to run into one of the 'glory holes.' Times are good when a mine is working and outside money is being put up, but very hard times came to our house, when there was a shut-down — Henry had to leave town to find work. He goes to Silverton, Colorado, where he gets a job on the North Star Mine, and when he returns, has wondrous tales of tough men, snow-slides, and wild women. I look back to this time of his absence as a happy, peaceful one, although we are very poor. Meal after meal of only cornbread and milk, but such cornbread as Mama made, so nutty-smelling, and brown and crisp!

She washed all this time, and Ed and I delivered the clothes, a big bundle each week to the Rathvons, who lived in Exchequer in the same house we were to live in afterward. This was a mile walk, but we liked to go as Mrs. Rathvon often asked us in, treated us, and, besides, we could see carpets, curtains, and pictures, and glimpses of other wonderful things. Then, too, we had clothes to deliver to the 'fast-house,' where one mustn't go in.

'Why not?'

'Just because.'

But we did, or at least I did. Ed minded better, or was not so curious. And this is what I remember: first, a strong sweet smell (strong perfume always brings back the fancy-girl smell), several pretty girls with lots of lace on their clothes, which were long loose affairs. One is sitting on the floor in a mess of pillows, two men (we wash for one of them), dressed and seemingly in their right minds, are sitting there laughing. They give me candy and I leave after having a very pleasant time. I tell Mama, and she is so interested in all details she forgets to whip me, but next time we go, she has me take a bouquet of wild flowers to pay for the candy they gave me.

Some of these miners' wives were afraid when left alone. It must have been just the wildness and new country, because I never heard of one being disturbed. One I knew, when her husband was on night shift, would fill the stove-boiler with tin things, put it on a chair against the door, feeling sure of awakening if any one came; another kept a can of coal-oil and a match near the door, intending to set any intruder afire. Mama wakened one night to see feet coming down the loft steps. She commenced to scream and call the man names, grabbing something to kill him with, and then found it was only a pair of old boots left on the top step the night before.

This is the summer before Frank is born (yes, I know I am having a baby in every chapter, but that is the way we had them!). Mama, keeping up her laundry work, still finds time to go after wild raspberries, four or five miles to the nearest patch. Here she picks all day, coming home at night so tired. One day in a bunch of slide rock she slips and falls, and in trying not to spill these precious berries hurts herself, and has a hard time getting home; but — the washing never stops, and she must do a pile of it, because when Henry returns home she has saved seventy-five dollars, besides keeping up all expenses.

In addition to the laundry, Mama sewed for the men. I remember one masquerade suit made of flour sacks, with Pride of Denver on the seat, which was a prize-winner. She also made some buckskin shirts which were almost the finish of us, as she had such a time in sewing the seams, getting in the extra piece across the shoulder and yoke, which later is to be cut in long fringe. She had only a plain needle, while buckskin needles are three-cornered.

The ceiling of our cabin was usually covered with canvas — in this dirt would collect, making it sag in places, and where the rain or snow had dried, there would be designs on the roof. Mountain rats also made their nests just on top of the canvas and this would make a big sag. Once a rat ran along the canvas and Mama saw the shape of his body and stuck a fork into him. The blood dripped through, and I cried, not because I was sorry for the rat, but just at the sordidness of it all. Then I go out on the hillside, throw myself down flat on my back, and stare straight up at the sky, with such a feeling of relief, knowing that nothing dirty will drop into my eyes.

Mama is a born doctor, going at the first call to any animal needing her help. One time she found a snowbird with a broken leg, brought it in and put splints on with twine string, but when it got well one leg was always twisted to one side. This bird lived in an old rubber boot, coming out at night and hobbling over the floor. We called him Hobscobble, and to-day when I hear a cripple coming I want to call him Hobscobble. When any one fell sick, the first medicine was whiskey, then came quinine and camphor (this camphor prepared at home from the gum and whiskey); then turpentine. One was pretty far gone when one or all of these did not bring him out of it! There was also a good deal of virtue in a chew of tobacco bound on a sore place. I have had many a chew on a cracked toe. Fresh cow manure was also considered good for this, leaving such a white place! For babies with bowel trouble Mama fixed brown flour of which I would steal nibbles, and if this did not help, rose-root tea would, and I would be the one to dig the roots. She was always brewing sage tea for some tenderfoot, who was getting ''climated.' Then there was Oregon grape root, brewed with rock candy, supposed to be fine for the kidneys, when juniper and a lot of whiskey were added to it. I have known men in Denver to send to us for the roots, supplying their own whiskey.

In these days one never heard of 'T.B.' — people had 'consumption.' One time a young man was dying of this. He was so sick, so homesick, too, and longing for his mother's cooking. Mama goes to him, doing all she can, and he tells her of a special kind of cake his mother made. Mama finds out just what it looked and tasted like, comes home and tries to make one just like it. He also wished for hominy. There was none in cans then, so she goes to all the livery barns trying to get corn, then works for days with ashes and the corn to fix this for him. After he died, she had Henry write and tell his mother of his last days, of the cake and all. I seem to remember more men dying than women; for one thing, there were a lot more men, and for another, I suppose the women had some one to do for them, while Mama would go and help with the men — washing, dressing, and laying them out — always shedding tears over them. She would come home and send us children after flowers. I remember one prospector who died in his cabin — little was known of him except that he was a Catholic, or at least one time when he was caught in a cave-in, along with other miners, he was seen to cross himself. Mama had heard that Catholics have candles at a funeral, so when the men came to 'set up,' they found the coffin (I have even known her to cover a coffin) resting on two chairs, miners' candles rigged up at the head and foot, and the top of the coffin almost covered with a huge white cross, made of wild tansy. We children all had a hand in the cross.

There was an old man, a sort of bum, who had been washing spittoons in Q. T.'s saloon. (This was the only name I ever knew him to have, and this was painted above his saloon door, 'Q. T.'s.') The old man fell sick and was allowed to go to bed in one of the back rooms. Not much attention was paid to him, but Mama heard of him and went to see if she could not do something. She took me with her and we went to the saloon, which was an unheard-of thing, as no woman ever went there unless she was crazy mad or a fast woman. We knocked on the door; it was opened a crack and the mustache of the barkeeper showed around the corner. He wanted to get the 'lay of the land,' as people not meaning trouble and having just and legitimate business were not in the habit of knocking on saloon doors. When he saw who it was, he said,

Q. T.'S SALOON

'Oh, howdy, Miz Levon. Brayton's sobered off, and gone to work.' (When Brayton was on one of his sprees, we took buttermilk to the saloon for him.)

'Yeah, I know, but I want to see Old Jenks; can't I?'

'Wait a minute; I'll see Q. T.'

The door is closed in our faces, and I don't get to see a thing — no pictures of naked women, mirrors, shiny glassware, wonderful hanging lamps, or any of the things I have been led to believe are in saloons! I get only a strong sickening smell, and feel my back burning with the eyes which are looking at us from across the street, where neighbors are wondering what Miz Levon is doing so long at Q. T.'s door! Finally, Q. T. himself comes to the door — his stomach getting there long before he does. He was the fattest man I have ever known — had to have his white shirts made to order and always wore one. His shiny stiff bosom might have started the expression, 'a skating rink finish.'

He said, 'All right, slip around to the back door, and I will let you in.' We do, and he does! The door opens and I peek under Mama's arm, and see a cot in one corner; on this a man, his face red and covered with whiskers, his eyes turned back in his head. Each breath is so hard and loud that it frightens me and I go no nearer, but Mama walks over to the bed, leans down, puts her hand on his forehead, looks up, and turns away as much as to say, 'There is no use'; then moistening her fingers in a cup of water sitting on a box at the head of the cot, she leans over him again

[45]

and trails her fingers softly across his parched lips. She does this time and time again; and I, watching around the side of the door, see a look of relief come over that drawn, tortured face at the touch of this woman's hand. Mama stays long enough to see the final shudder pass over this figure, then she closes his eyes, pulls the cover up over his head, and we leave, she wiping tears from her eyes with the corner of her apron.

It is spring, the snow water is running in little gullies off the mountain-sides, the willows along the creek are showing red, the miners coming from work all walk single file on the lower side of the road. Mama decides to clean house, putting all the bedding on the line, scrubbing the floor and washing windows. As she works, she sings,

'When I can read my ti-tul clear to man-shuns in the skies,
I'll bid farewell to every fear, and wipe my weepin' eyes.'

Then the curtains are washed, ironed, and put back; clean newspapers put on cupboard shelves and back of the stove; never a moment does she stop all day long. An old woman coming in in the evening remarks, 'Bet you are sick to-night, that is the way it goes'; and she was. We are wakened by whisperings — some one comes, asking, 'Is there whiskey in the house?' (This was the first thing to be got ready.) 'Is your bed ready, and where are the cloths, and is the cord fixed?' Yes, everything is ready. Some pieces of real linen from an old 'boiled' shirt — this has been browned in the oven, a package of safety pins, bands made of flour sacks, long, wide cumbersome skirts and pinning blankets, a bottle of vaseline, cornstarch tied in a cloth — these things, along with a pile of washed rags and other things left over from the last baby, are all packed in a box and have been ready for some time. Since we children are getting older now, we are hustled away, going to a neighbor's, where there are two old men who entertain us by singing, first one, then the other, then both together. This would make them dry, which called for hot toddy; and this brought forth more songs.

Now one would bellow forth, his chin whiskers wagging like a chewing goat:

> 'Now, all you young ladies take warning by me,
> Don't cast your affection on a young man so free.
> For if you do, he'll leave you, like Willie left me,
> To weep and to mourn 'neath a green willow tree.'

Then comes something less doleful, faster, but there will only be a few words of this — for they glance at each other, then at us, and end it by singing 'hun-h-h-hum.' Then they brighten up; of course they know songs fit for children to hear:

> 'Arouse, arouse, you drowsy sleeper, arouse, arouse, 'tis almost day!
> How can you lie there and sleep and slumber, when your true love is going away?
> In yonder wall there sticks an arrow, I wish the same were in my breast,
> Then I'd be out of pain and sorrow, and this poor soul would be at rest.'

[47]

But this was too sad, so we asked them to sing something with love in it.

'Out of her bosom grew a red, red rose,
Out of his grew a brier-er,
And they grew and they grew to the old church tow-er
Till they could grow no high-er.
And they twined themselves in a true lover's knot,
For all true lovers to admi-er.'

But we drop asleep.

After a good breakfast of pancakes (and they let us have coffee, too), we are sent home, only to find another baby. On April Fool's Day, too! The only thing that makes it bearable is the wine sent as a present to Mama. In those days this was the only excuse I could see for any one having babies.

CHAPTER V

When you hear a man bragging on being
good or bad, chances are — he isn't.
A. E.

AT this time I am half-past six, but have never been to school before. This first school was in an old 'false-front' store building, the upper side built level with the ground, a flight of steps on the lower side. Nice little girls sat on these steps with their arms around each other, and whispered; I never sat there, or if I did it was alone. When I started to school I was told where babies came from and I was disgusted. A little later, I decided that when I was married I was going to be a 'barn doe,' because it was explained to me that they never had little ones; they must have said 'barren doe,' but to me it was 'barn doe.'

The school seats were made of lumber, two pupils always in one seat, sitting on a bench. The blackboard was also made of boards painted a shiny black.

On the first day I went to school the teacher insisted on my taking off the bag of asafetida. In the backwoods where we came from, pantalettes were in order, but mine were laughed at. My talk must have been funny too, as the children would mock and laugh when I said 'cow,' and I would slip away and repeat 'cow, cow' (or I suppose it was 'caouw') to myself, and it sounded to me as though I said it just as they did. I never got over this terrible feeling of being made fun of, and I then took on a spirit of don't care and rebellion. I was hurt, then stubborn, to hide my hurt. This attitude I might have got over, but one day a dreadful thing happened. One girl, after eating her lunch, left a sandwich on a desk, such a luscious-looking one, the red jam showing with little pink streaks where it had soaked in. I watched it for quite a while, my mouth watering, then slipped over and got it. But oh, how I paid! The owner caught me. She had thrown it away, but since another had found virtue in it, she needs must make a big fuss, and I never heard the last of it — of starving and stealing to eat.

Children are so cruel. Jean Valjean did not suffer much more over his loaf than I did over my slice; no girl ever made a companion of me or put her arms around me, and even now when a woman shows any feeling toward me it embarrasses and thrills me. I could not be a leader and they wouldn't have me for a follower. I think it was partly my clothes, and in after years, although always poverty-stricken, I worked very hard to keep my children as well, if not better, dressed than others.

We never went by grades at school; you were either in the first or so on to the fifth reader, and to finish the fifth was to know all there was to know. I managed to finish it, but never got through fractions. The tears I have shed over arithmetic! But I can spell it!

I was once stood on the floor until I did learn to spell it. I concentrated by spitting on the leaves of the book, then rolling the paper up in wads with my fingers; by the time this word was mastered, the book was a wreck, and so was I.

I had an idea that learning came easier every other day, and so I dreaded the off day, and the teachers would try — in their way — to show me.

'Now, Anne, this is so plain any one can see it, and you have been over it so many times'; and so on; 'now that is plain, isn't it?'

And I, who had not understood, but was getting weaker each minute, with a big lump swelling in my throat, would lie and say, 'I begin to see.'

· 'Well, please remember. Now I will go over it once more, that it may be firmly fixed in your mind.'

I would watch her hands moving over the slate and wonder how she kept them so clean (mine were always rusty and sore), and would wish my hair grew down in front of my ears like hers. I would see that the ruching around her collar was getting dirty, and wonder if she really did live on just graham crackers as I had been told she did.

'Now, I am quite sure you understand, do you not?'

'You bet I savvie now,' I respond politely.

But I didn't, and with a final caution to 'please not use so much slang,' I go to my seat thinking, 'Thank the Lord, that is over for one more day.' Even now, when I want to divide anything in more quarters than there are in a pie, I am lost. Never did I get any help at home, as Mama couldn't and Henry wouldn't. He would say, 'Suffering blazes! are you only over there? I'll bet the Adams girl has been through that long ago.' Sometimes we spoke pieces, but I couldn't even speak well. I was told that there was no use trying, so I didn't. I have trained my children to get up and speak any place, any time, on almost any subject, or to have a try at it anyway.

Once the County Superintendent is visiting the school and, in talking on grammar, explains that there can be no sentence with just one word. I, who am only in the first reader and not studying that, jump up and say, 'Bet I can make a sentence of one word. If I see a dog coming for me and I yell, "git!" to him, he knows what I mean and he "gits."'

The Christmas following my tenth birthday, a miner who had eaten at our house left town, and sent, as a bread-and-butter gift, a huge box of candy, all in fancy shapes; I remember one in the shape of a cross with dents in it as though pressed with a waffle iron; there was also a tiny straw box filled with gum. All this seemed to inspire Henry to fix us a tree, and he did, making tiny candles by dipping string in hot grease, letting it cool and dipping again, till a dear little candle was the result. When these and our candy were hung on the tree, how filled the cabin was with light and gladness! Not a shadow, except one — and I tried so hard to avoid this, too! I had been told it was a sure sign that some one was coming into the family if a dog lay with his head in the door; if he lay with his head out of the door, some one was going out of the family. So I didn't take any chances, but kicked and pulled him away every time he lay near the door. But, in spite of all my trouble, didn't we up and have

A NEWLY ARRIVED EASTERN WOMAN

another baby on Christmas Day! Mama attended to the baby herself, then had the chicken which we were to have for dinner brought to the side of the bed and showed us how to stuff it.

A newly arrived Eastern woman (we didn't think her much force, because one night a jack brayed under her window and her husband had to call the doctor) thought all this terrible, and played Lady Bountiful, sending cake, wine, jelly, and some really lovely baby clothes.

This baby was named Gertrude Alice in honor of the woman who gave the things. She also asked to be her godmother. This was a fearsome word, and I think she had a time explaining to Mama just what it meant. I think, too, she insisted on the baby being christened, and I know that this question was talked over among us. If Gertie was christened, she was the only one of us who was.

Some time along here we moved a mile up the road from town to what we called the Rawley Gulch house. This was a three-room affair built in the hillside, the rooms all in a row; the kitchen quite low and dark; the canvas bulging off the walls with long torn places in it where the younger children would creep in and hide. A brother tells me one of his first remembrances is of being behind this canvas, thinking he was hid (he was frightened of a newly killed fawn Henry had thrown down on the doorstep), but in front there is a big bulge the shape of a very fat little boy, and Henry, who is eating, throws hot coffee on the head of this shape. The middle room was quite small, and had in it a trunk and a single bed; also a home-made desk kept under lock and key. Above the desk hung an Indian war club, the pride of Henry's heart. He would take it down and show it, explaining the carving and painting on it, and run his fingers along the notches cut in the side, saying each notch was for a person clubbed to death. I would look closely, trying to find hairs still clinging to it; and, to make it really worth while, one time I stole it out, and made notches all around it, then rubbed bacon grease in to give it an old look. Along here I must have been a sore trial. I expect nowadays we would call it self-expression, but then they said I was possessed of a devil.

In the front room were two beds and a stove. It was around this stove we gathered to hear Henry read Rider Haggard's 'She' and 'Allan Quatermain' to us. And the thrill of these stories! I believed every word of them. Soon I am reading on my own account. 'Swiss Family Robinson' and 'Arabian Nights.' Barrie writes that he was so disappointed on taking this home to find that it was 'Nights' instead of 'Knights,' but I wasn't, and while I thought some of the things were a little far-fetched, 'still they could have happened.'

Here, too, I have my first lesson in stealing or not stealing. (It never had to be repeated.) Mama wanted to make ice cream (freezing it in a bucket) and sent Ed and me after the ice. This we get by going to the mine, and asking the men to chop us off some from where the water in the mine has frozen. This day we climbed the hot road at noon, so as to

catch the men before they went down, after eating
their lunch. One of them took the empty gunnysack
and started down the ladder, and when his head disappeared from sight (we are hanging over the mouth
of the shaft), his candle light no larger than a pin,
we straightened up and looked around us. I spied a
little strap. I have no use for it, but steal it, anyway,
hiding it in the front of my apron.

After a time the signal comes to the man on the
windlass to pull the ice up, and we go to take it (I
stepping lightly so as not to shake the strap down).
When we are home, wet from the ice leaking on us, I
show Mama the strap, thinking she will be pleased,
but — she isn't, and, after slapping me a few times,
starts me back up this long hill, insisting that I return
the strap, and — this is the worst of it — tell the man
I had stolen it. This I do, my feet dragging the last
hundred feet, but — with my kind of a mother it is
easier to go forward than back — I hand it to the
windlass man, and how I choke and burn over this
part of it, 'I swiped it, and she made me bring it
back.' At this the tears will no longer stay back, although I bite my tongue very hard. He felt sorry for
me, and could only show it by giving me a dime. This
helps some.

Our spring house is built over the creek, through
which the water runs all the time, and here we keep
the milk on shelves. When we, Ed and I, come in with
our ice, knowing Mama isn't quite ready for it, we
take it into the milk-house and dump it in the water
to keep it from melting. During the strap fracas,

Mama fails to notice this, and by the time she cools down after starting me back to the Cornucopia (the mine's name) and goes for her ice, she finds only an empty sack floating on the water, and being 'plum outdone' swears, and this is what she says, 'Jesus wept, and Moses crept!' and how I shuddered.

It was the custom, then, for the women to go visiting and stay all day. Our place was a great hold-out, as Mama was a good cook, always glad to have them, very entertaining, laughing at and with them. She had such a clear, ringing laugh, throwing her head backward and just letting it gurgle forth (it reminded one of water running over a rock). Mrs. Rayworth, who was a frosty-nosed sort of a person, came oftener than most, and was given of our best; so one day Mama decided to return some of these visits, and taking the two youngest and her sewing she walked the mile to town, arriving tired and a little cross. Mrs. Rayworth does not seem any too glad to see her, but Mama goes in and, after getting the children settled, telling the oldest not to 'dare touch a thing,' gets out her sewing and prepares for a visit. She sits and sits, till it is time to start dinner, but nothing stirs; dinner time comes, still nothing doing (the children growing restless and Mama with her stomach clinging to her backbone); afternoon comes, but no mention is made of eating. Then Mama can stand it no longer, so bundles up her sewing and children and walks the mile home, hot, and hungry. The next day at ten o'clock who walks in the yard but Mrs. Rayworth, bringing a friend with her. She smiles hungrily,

but Mama's back is up, and as they come through
the gate she meets them, with blood in her eye,
saying, 'Stop right in your tracks; you ain't comin' in
here.'

'Why, Mrs. Levon, what can have happened?'

'Don't you dare talk mealy-mouthed to me! The
gall of you! Never so much as offering me a drink of
water, you, you ——' and she goes a step forward,
while Mrs. Rayworth backs off. 'If you don't hit the
trail pretty soon, my dander is going to raise.' At
this her chin begins to quiver, and she turns away so
they cannot see the tears coming. Never in her life
has she refused a meal to man or beast, and how it
hurts! And what will this strange woman think of
her? To the day of her death she regrets having done
this, because ——

Emma Botts, this 'strange woman,' was in love
with the stage driver, Hank Day. Hank was a Beau
Brummel among the ladies, with his long golden
mustache, his strong handsome face; very tall and
erect; a heavy gold watch-chain, with a horseshoe for
a charm, crossed over his vest; his eyes, under his big
hat, giving a woman the look that makes her drop her
eyes, then raise them quickly for more. Well, he had
given Emma Botts too many of these glances when
he would drive up to the hotel, his horses on a trot,
cracking his long whip over their backs; and she — a
waitress — gave more than glances.

Then, one day he 'goes back on her.' A married
woman — the mother of three boys, a tiny little
creature, combing her hair in black, slick, flat curls all

across her forehead, called 'beau-catchers'; wearing the close-knitted jersey so popular then, as though melted and poured into it, ever walking with a quick trip — trips into Hank's life, and he quits Emma cold. And she, going to her dreary room one night, prepares all her clothes for her burial, takes poison, and lies down to sleep and rest. Mama, when she hears of them finding her there, alone and dead, is conscience-stricken and mourns for days.

Another visitor was Lil, I suppose her name was Lily; such a cheerful, happy sinner, married when sixteen, very good-looking and attractive to men, and usually she had one or more lovers. But, I think neither her husband nor any one else considered her bad; many times at a dance, I have heard her husband — crying drunk — tell of his wife and what a fine woman she was. And, in a way, she was. She did far less harm than some of her more virtuous sisters. In the first place, she had a kind word for every one, was always cheerful and very generous, would leave her work (in fact, it was no trial to leave her work, as she was a dreadful housekeeper) and go to help a neighbor. She sang well, played the organ, and was a beautiful dancer. I think some of her wrongdoing came from the fact that she was so good-hearted; she just couldn't say 'no,' at any rate she didn't. My first job was with her — I got twenty-five cents each day, and this was far more than I earned, as I did little, except eat; she said she was afraid to stay alone; her husband was on night shift.

We put in the day stringing beads, working on

cardboard or anything except cleaning house; then at meal time I would be rushed to the store for a steak, canned corn, and gingersnaps. In the evening she would read 'Peck's Bad Boy' to me. Over this we giggled a great deal. Many nights I would be awakened by the sounds of a man in the house, but this neither amused, interested, nor disgusted me; my only thought was never to let Mama know, because she would make me come home. Mama was one of her best friends, and many the day she put in cooking for Lil and her children, trying to teach her to sew and keep house; then washing up all the baby's soiled clothes which Lil would forget to take home with her. Still, Mama was jealous of her; after a dance I have heard her say to Henry, 'You can't pull the wool over my eyes; I saw you squeeze her hand in that last quadrille.'

Once a woman who knew Lil before she was married said, 'They 'lowed to send her to the home for *encourageable* girls, but couldn't get the kibosh on her, because none of the men would stand pat.' Her lovers came and went, but there was one (Billy) who was ever faithful. He had a large, red, flowing mustache. He boasted of the fact that he had not had a bath in fifteen years, and said, 'My skin is as white as a baby's.' He was a great help to Lil in caring for her children — she always had a baby. One bitter cold New Year's night, Billy and some other men are sitting huddled in the snow, waiting for twelve o'clock to come, so that they can jump a claim; they pass the time telling what they most wish for. One wants a good hot square meal; another, a jug of Three Star Hennessey; then they turn to Billy.

'Say, pardner, what do you hone most for?'

'Just her,' Billy answers.

'Just who?' they ask.

'Just Bird.'

This was his pet name for Lil. He would be sitting in a poker game, stop, listen, and hold up the play. When asked the cause, he would say, 'I hear the pitty-pat of Bird's feet, going up and down the street.'

Once she had an affair with a Swede — for some reason she was arrested, and came before Judge Kenny. After he asked her name (he had known her for years), he said, 'Are yez guilty or not guilty?' and before she had a chance to answer, he went on 'Yez are guilty, I know yez of ould.' At this every one laughed, Lil loudest of all. To-day, should you ask any one who knew her, they would tell you that they liked her, and that she was her own worst enemy.

We always had a cage of canary birds, and at times, when one would escape or die, all of us cried at the funeral. Yes, they were laid away in match-boxes and covered with flowers. When one got out of the cage, any one coming up the gulch would think it the fire brigade. One kid in the lead looking up at the trees, keeping his eye on the bird, and woe betide him if he lost sight of it; then Mama running, a bucket of water in her hand (this to be thrown over the bird, bringing it to the ground without injury), then all the other

children with water, in case the first does not reach;
then several barking dogs circling the whole outfit.
We all parade home, wet and happy, if we catch the
runaway.

Once we hear a great commotion in the henhouse
and find a huge skunk there, but so far he has done no
damage, either to chickens or henhouse. Mama gets
the gun, but he doesn't wait to be shot, running behind
some loose boards, but neglects to get his tail out of
sight, and Mama, fearing he will run away, makes me
pinch on to the tip of it with a pair of fire tongs, and
hold him while she shoots. I consider this a brave
deed, as I was in danger of being shot by Mama, or
the skunk, but I gritted my teeth, closed my eyes, and
held on. After the loud report and the smell of powder
smoke had cleared away, everything is lovely, as we
are ahead a skunk, minus the smell.

We always invented our own playthings; made a
swing in the barn, fighting to see who would swing the
longest, it taking such a time for the cat to die. But
the end of this came when one of Pat's calves ran its
head through the loop, twisting round and round till
finally (its feet just touching the ground, its eyes
popping out, gasping for breath) it is discovered and
cut down by Henry, who declares he 'will thump the
living daylights out of the next varmint that makes a
swing.'

The mesa was our playground. This mesa is one of
the places I love. On top it is rather flat, the ground
covered with white daisies; a lovely grove of quaking
aspen, fringed on the outside with pines; the trail

winding up one side, across the top, and down again. In my time, at the head of the trail was a tiny grave, and very often I would stop and rest here, reading the baby's name; then pick a few daisies in a hard little bunch, placing them near the head board, and wonder. I had heard this baby's father had been hanged. He killed his brother and his brother's wife, and today old-timers will tell you of the Marshall-Clemmons hanging. Coming up the other side, the first honeysuckle was found, and seemed so bright and cheerful, hanging there where the snow had so lately been. Here, too, kinnikinnic grew all the year, creeping and spreading, such a soft carpet for tired bare feet; and here, too, roses and primroses bloomed. In the early morning when hunting cows, I have met miners coming off night shift, primroses in the buttonholes of their jumpers, on their faces yellow pollen mixed with powder smoke, coal dust, and dirt.

Comes now a tiny thread of love into this weaving which we will follow to the end, in most places a thin, sickly, little thread, but in some places it glows so much it makes a wonderful splotch of color. From the first day Jim came to school, a flat-nosed, stubby-fingered boy, his hair growing down the back of his neck, I was attracted to him. He was dressed in some sort of a grey uniform; was part Indian and may have come from an Indian school. He had very nice manners and was brilliant in his studies. One time he spoke, 'Over the Hill to the Poor House,' and never have I heard anything which thrilled me so much. I always worshiped him.

A TINY THREAD OF LOVE

We were asked to write a composition (this was my first literary attempt, and only once, till this, have I tried it since then), and I did my best, leaving it on my desk. Jim and some other boys stole it and sent it to the county paper to be published. Up to this time this was the worst disgrace I had ever known. I threw myself on the schoolroom floor and cried and sobbed. I must have been terribly hurt to let any one see me cry, for, according to my code, one must never show their feelings to the public. This was over forty years ago, and if I hadn't been so squelched in the beginning I might have written before this. There must have been some merit in this first composition or it would never have been noticed. Funny, I suppose.

Then we played 'pum-pum-pull-away,' and how hard I would run, how hard I would try to get away from him, and how pleased when he would catch me, not caring how hard were the three slaps on the back! The old skating rink was just across from the schoolhouse and here we skated at noon and recess. Most of the time I had no skates, and very seldom partners that I cared to skate with, Jim always skating with Winnie Adams, whom I admired and envied. One morning I asked to be excused from school, went to the rink, stole one of her skates, climbed into the loft, and hid it. I expect it is there to-day. She was the one who rode on the back of his sled, her hands on his shoulders, swaying so gracefully with the swing of the sled; while I, heavy-hearted, smiled at them as they glided by. He never paid any attention to me, but both he and Winnie were clever, and I am sure they made fun of me, and, I will admit, there was plenty of cause.

I am going to school barefooted, and one day in a game of hide-and-seek, I almost cut my toe off on a broken beer-bottle. It bleeds a great deal, and, several children with me, bringing up in the rear, we parade into the drugstore, leaving a bloody trail. Jim demands sticking plaster. I am so swelled with pride! This is worth having my whole foot taken off! Billy Hannigan pokes his head out of the post-office window and raves at the way his floor is being messed up. He drives us out, and I go home and get a chew of tobacco on it. This scar is a symbol of a very happy time; Jim had taken some notice of me.

Above my bed, wrapped in newspaper, hung a straw hat trimmed all around in pink roses, which looked much better off than on. Very often I would climb on the bed and pull a tiny place in the paper to admire the contents. One day I wear it, and, going around the Turn, I meet Jim. At this time we are having a family feud over a large thin book, Will Carleton's poems. We both claimed it, and in the end I think we got it, or at least half, like King Solomon's baby. We passed without speaking, glaring at each other, but I felt I had the better of him, because, as he went by, he glanced at my hat with the roses. Summers he worked in a store, and long before I would reach the door, my heart would beat a tattoo in my throat, and how thrilled I was if he waited on me, giving me the quarter's worth of oatmeal or sugar. He had a grey suit which smelled sweaty, but I loved even that odor.

I would see the other girls with an apple, which was cut so carefully, the seeds saved and counted, a formula something like this being said over them (I straining ears and eyes from a distance), 'One I love, two I love, three I love I say, four I love with all my heart, and five I cast away, six he loves, seven they both love,' but I never learned any more. I tried it alone, but, like other games of fortune, it is no fun if one is alone and lonely.

CHAPTER VI

There was an old geiser and he had a wooden leg,
He had no tobacco; no tobacco could he beg.
He went to a miser who lived among the rocks
And kept his tobacco in his old tobacco box.
Said the geiser to the miser, 'Will you give me a chew?'
Said the miser to the geiser, 'I'll be damned if I do.'

Old Song

THE miners I knew were so different from the miner of to-day, being of American, English, Scotch, and Irish birth. Most of them came from good families and were well-educated young men, who came West for adventure.

We had a colony of Englishmen, all educated, and with some money; I knew some of these were remittance men. I would hang around their cabins, and they (especially the Englishmen) would lend me books, and treat me with their food sent from England. Here I first saw chocolate, orange marmalade, and Worcestershire sauce. These men always expected to strike it rich, and lived from year to year on hope. They 'borned' (we always said this) the next generation of agitators and strikers, but now were satisfied with the wages received, two-fifty or three dollars per day. Sometimes they took a lease, when they could clean up a little extra, or a contract where the men would work very hard, sometimes making a pile and other times losing.

One of these, Butterfield, looked like a member of Parliament, or a first-class butler. (No, I have never seen either, but they should look like him — so clean, with snow-white side whiskers.) Once in an old cabin, after he had left, I found the most beautifully written letters, full of love, from his wife in England. Butterfield once had, in the old country, over a million dollars, and spent it in France gambling. He lived among us for years, leading a useful respectable life, but all at once (when he was quite old) he started to drink, and to visit the house on the hill. He got lower and lower, as time went on, finally doing odd jobs around the saloon; then sickness came to him and he was sent away to die alone.

One day, as we children were going home from school, we found two small tents pitched just below the Turn; alongside of them a hard-looking wagon, with two much harder-looking horses feeding near by. We went over to investigate, and found a coarse, red-faced woman, her straw-colored hair hanging in her eyes. She was one who had fallen so low that she drove from one camp to another, plying her trade in these tents.

Another Englishman, Spencer, very tall, quiet, and queer, never being 'broke' between payments from home (as most of them were), started to visit her and ended by marrying her! They made a trip to Denver and came home with all sorts of things, and lived in one of the best houses in town. I once sneaked in to visit her, finding her very rich as to conversation. She showed me her new diamonds, her very red plush furniture, and her very pale blue and bright pink tea gowns; also a parrot and a cage of parrakeets.

Another of our Englishmen, a hard drinker, the regular English type, tall and thin with light eyes and mustache, named Alex Harence, is always waiting for some relative to die. For years they are accommodating, and Alex and his friends have a big time on the proceeds. Finally, there is a long lapse between deaths. Alex has gone 'on tick' as long as possible, and it looks as though he might have to sober up, when word comes of another aunt having passed, a rich one, who should have gone long ago. Such a time! All his friends were invited to the blow-out, each saloon-keeper urged Alex to buy of him, and letting him have the best in the house; finally, when the money should be coming from England, word came instead that it was the wrong aunt who had died!

These are some of our neighbors:
Uncle Pomp was no relation. His name was Pompeia Howard, and he was a jolly, fine-looking man with a black beard. Mama washed and mended for him; in return for this he would stay with us children when she was away from home. Then we had big times, if he was not too bossy. If he was, we called him 'Pompey-eye.' He would sing to us in a loud, roaring voice, 'The Hat Me Father Wore.'

'Oh, it's ould and it's beautiful, the best you ever saan,
'Twas worn for more than forty years in that little isle of grann.'

And so on.

Then, 'Oh, Susanna, don't you cry for me, for I'm Bound for California-e with a wash bowl on me knee.' This had to be acted out, with hands, eyes, and feet.

Sometimes little brother Frank would get an ear-ache, and at these times Uncle Pomp would stop singing long enough to light his pipe, and between verses blow large mouthfuls of smoke into the aching ear. Then he would return to his stories of wild Indians he had killed, and finish by singing,

'Don't go to that city, they call it Cheyenne,
For if you do, the Chanitin Bills [it sounded like this]
And Old Sittin Bull, will take off your scalp
In them dreary Black Hills.'

Then, in another song, some one went 'up the flume, in the days of June, in the days of Forty-Nine';

'Oh, the days of old were the days of gold, in the days of Forty-Nine.'

By now, I was commencing to read and thought every one should be married, or at least have a sweetheart, so I asked each 'old bach' why he was not married. Pomp answered me thus:

'Well, Sis, you see I am hard up; when I do hitch up for life, I want to be able to keep a pretty man around to amuse my old woman. I bank every woman ought to have a husband to bring in the grub, and a purty one to entertain her, and I can't stand the racket yet.'

He was a spiritualist, and he and Mrs. Smeltzer often thought they heard her brother trying to give them a message. In his time this brother had been a great fighter. He would say, 'Now when I get outside of a few drinks, I am spoiling for a fight.'

For a long time, our family and Uncle Pomp were friends and neighbors, but finally, relations were strained. Four of the younger children decided to go in swimming; there was a good hole near Pomp's, but they found the rocks on the creek bottom too sharp, so went into Uncle Pomp's house, took the quilts off his bed, put them in the creek, and pressed them down, to cover the rocks. They were really enjoying themselves when Pomp came along and discovered them. He got a long willow switch and ran them home without giving them time to dress; they arrived all breathless, and soon all four came down with scarlet fever. Uncle Pomp was put out over his bedding, and Mama was 'plum mad'; in fact she was 'outdone' to think he would run them so hard when they were just coming down with scarlet fever. They were over it quickly, however, and with no bad results, except that Uncle Pomp ever after kept his eye peeled for us.

J. Frazier Buck is a man whom some one with more power than I have should have known. They might do him justice. He came from a prosperous Southern family. He said, 'The only mark left of it is a scar on my forehead where I fell down the marble steps'; but it wasn't — he was a well-bred gentleman always, although an artist at swearing; this was his only bad habit, as he never drank or gambled — unless one would call prospecting gambling and a bad habit. I am sure Mrs. Buck did. Sometime I am going to write a story of her — she was so different and worth while. Each day you would see him, a knapsack on his back, a red bandanna handkerchief about to drop out of his hip pocket, going to dig more holes. I hate to think of all the dirt he has thrown over his shoulders and behind him; he always had a smile for us children and always something snappy to say. He did own a very good mine, and when the worse came to the worst, could work it and ship enough ore for a grubstake, then go on prospecting. We used to call these holes 'Buck's graves.' He had a violent temper. One time he was on the road to the mine, his horse loaded with provisions. Among other things there was a box of blasting powder. In going up a steep grade, the horse commenced to pitch, threw the load off, and ran away. Buck jumped up and down on the box of powder and screamed,

'Christ, blow me into a million pieces, put four legs on each piece, so I can run down that damned horse!'

Once, when going to work, he slipped on the ice and fell very hard; he jumped up spluttering and swearing that he 'didn't see why Jesus Christ couldn't make the slippery side of the ice down.'

One time Jose, my sister, looked down where he was working in one of his endless holes, and dropped sand and rocks on his bald head. When he discovered where it was coming from, he looked up at her and said, 'Female, Hell's death-traps are yawning to receive you.' In speaking of some one who was considered stingy, he said, 'His heart is harder than the cold chilled steel hinges of Hell.' Once he started for the mine with his partner, who outwalked him. Buck came in panting, his handkerchief flying in the wind, 'And so he beat me, did he? May the Devil absorb him.'

He was on the election board once when his wife came to vote. She was given a ticket and, after disappearing in the booth for a time, she poked her head out and asked for help. Buck said, 'Madam, one can only help the blind, or of unsound mind; which class do you wish to be classified under?' He kept us entertained for many years. Around the stoves, in the store, saloons, and barber shop, where the affairs of the nation were cussed and discussed, each evening some one would start, 'Here is Buck's latest; ain't it a dandy?'

Eli had lived and worked in Leadville, during the boom time there. Conditions were so hard he had pneumonia — every new camp has its pneumonia victims; following this he had consumption or lung fever — never tuberculosis in those times. Some one who knew, even in those days, told him to live outdoors; then he bought a mule team and went to Bonanza prospecting, always sleeping under the trees or his wagon. He was one of the first men in camp. Each week Eli made two trips to Salida, bringing in freight with his mule teams. Once he had six barrels of Missouri moonshine whiskey for Pike Moore, who had his saloon in a tent. A man whom Moore owed tried to take this from Eli, but Eli stood him off with a gun and delivered it. The first price on this whiskey was about two hundred dollars a barrel; a barrel held about sixty-two gallons; this sold for twenty-five cents a drink. Eli was a tinner by trade, and also one of the best cooks I have ever known. It was from him I learned that one decorated food. We always held him in awe because his cabin was so clean, so scrubbed and polished. This was the one cabin we approached with respect, wiping our feet carefully, before even stepping on the porch. After we were in, we sat quiet and did not prowl through his cupboard or books; and if he did open up his heart and give us something to eat, it was worth waiting for; cakes with rose flavoring; I did not know there was any kind but lemon extract or lemon and whiskey mixed. (Try it, it's good!) He was always dressed so trim and clean; for that matter, these old bachelors are the cleanest, best-mended, and pressed men I have known, and Eli stood at the head of the class. He had the best garden; things seemed to ripen earlier and frost came later to him. He did not eat at our house as often as other people; Mama was afraid to cook for him; and when we saw him coming, what a rushing to straighten up! — things were thrown under the beds, and the kids rushed to the washpan, the dogs were chased out of the back door, so when he arrived he would find us quite out of breath. Then, 'Annie, get Eli a glass of milk, and you need not mind flipping all the cream back.' I would get a tall schooner — we had several — wash it in front of him and go to the buttery and return licking my fingers where I had flipped the cream, have Mama frown at me, and move her lips in a formula, which meant, 'Young lady, I'll tend to you after he is gone.' Most men gave us nickels if we stood around and hinted long enough, but Eli was sensible and gave advice instead.

Before our time a family of French people drifted to town; going away, they left their things in Eli's care. After a long time (he must have known they were not returning), he doled out some of their things to us. Now I watched for his coming! There would be little rolls of pale blue ribbon, about an inch wide, which he had carefully washed and wrapped around a bottle to dry; there were yards and yards of this, which they must have used to tie back curtains or draperies. Then there was a black straw hat, with the most wonderful silk flowers on it; and Mama got a pair of shoes — much too small for her, but on occasions she squeezed into them. They had extra high buttoned tops, and were red silk-lined, very high heels, with little metal hearts for heel plates; we always swelled when we spoke of Mama's French shoes.

Never did I know Eli to pay attention to a woman in any way, and think he considered it a weakness in any one who did. This, he told me, was the romance of his life: once when quite young he was standing on a street corner in St. Louis; a carriage passed, a very beautiful woman looked out at him and smiled; he gave his heart to her, and had been looking and waiting all these years to find both lady and heart.

In these years he had made a few good strikes, and sold his claims, but used the money searching for others, and now is one of the old-timers who is still there, getting his wood for each winter, all piled just so, each spring planting his garden anew; doing odd jobs; and whatever it is, you may be sure it is done the best ever. His cabin and his clothes are as clean as when he was young and hopeful. Besides never running after women, he neither drank nor gambled; I wonder if this is why he is alive to-day while most of the others are gone? Last summer I saw him. The first thing he said was:

'Christ! Annie, no wonder you're sick — half dressed. Why don't you get some clothes on? Do you know what I call you wimmen? Shinshiners, that's what.'

He told me of an operation — he had an eye taken out — and that when he was under the ether he prayed so wonderfully that the doctors and nurses stopped and listened.

I said, 'Why, Eli! do you pray?'

'Hell! yes, I pray every day; don't you? Try this, it will be good for you — "Universal and eternal flame of life of which my soul is but a little spark, grant me, I beg of you, a little part of yourself, which is strength, resistance, and health."'

I thought, 'Too bad these glimpses of another's inside workings come so seldom.' We all hide better feelings than we display. The fear of being laughed at is such a strong fear.

We lived in this place till after Moosie was born, the only one of our numerous babies I ever cared for when they were babies; but she was so quiet, pretty and good; never any trouble, always looking so well in her clothes, from the long-dress stage to the putting-on of the first short dress made of small figured red calico. Mama's babies never had shoes till they commenced to walk, and only then when they went out. Moosie always refused to wear them, crumpling her toes so that they would not go on. When she went coasting, she went barefoot. Her golden curls were the pride of the family. One day she slipped out to the barn and sheared off one side, in a very calm manner. Her mad spells were also calm as far as noise went; she would go without a cry and bump her head on the wall until, about three feet from the floor, is a spot on the wall where she bumped till the blood came. We used to say this was the Indian cropping out.

One day Frank and Jose are gone a long time. Mama knows they are up to something, and she is right as usual, for soon smoke is boiling up over the hill. She goes to investigate, and meets two singed, smoky, tear-stained kids, their eyes popping out of their heads. It seems they are playing Papa and Mama in a vacant house in Exchequer, and when it comes time for Papa to build the fire, he does — on the floor at that, enjoying the tiny curls of smoke! Shortly it is beyond them, and they creep out through a broken pane in the window, only to find Jose has forgotten her sunbonnet, so she shuts her eyes and creeps back into the flame and smoke, groping about till it is found. Just after passing the window the second time, the roof falls. She gets a whipping in spite of having saved the bonnet. Adventures were nothing new to these two. People dreaded to see them coming.

Once Jose is dressed for Sunday School in a bright pink outing flannel, the skirt gathered full on a tight waist (very tight for Jose); her feet and legs newly washed, the scratches and mosquito bites showing up, and as a last touch, a handkerchief pinned with a safety pin on the front of her dress. But she is not quite satisfied with the result, so she sprinkles some vanilla on for perfume, and steals Mama's hoopskirt, slipping it under the pink skirt. Of course several wires hung beneath. Then, thinking she might as well go the whole hog, she steals the long watch-chain, draping it about her neck. She prances off the mile to town, arriving at Sunday School without a doubt in her mind till she starts to sit down, and the hoops flare up in front. But it takes more than this to faze a Levon, so she presses it down, hooking one of her big toes over the bottom wire to hold it in place, and sits there, very self-satisfied, as others will do to the end of time when they are dressed as foolishly as she.

Down the gulch a short way in the old town of Exchequer is a vacant house, covered on the outside with slabs, a rustic porch in front. To this we want to move, but Mama objects; she never liked changes. I dwell on how much better it would be, so much more room, being able to see every one who passed either up Rawley, Squirrel, or Sawmill gulches. Still no move; till one day Henry and I decide to move, anyway, and do, on a hand sled, taking all the furniture and putting it in place, Mama just sitting and 'sulling.' Then all the children come down. It is getting evening; still no move from Mama. We prepare supper, one of us being stationed at a window to watch for her. What if she wouldn't come and we had to move back again? Dark comes, and now the lookout reports he thinks he sees her coming around the Turn. Soon she is among us, tears in her eyes, her head held high, the family cat under her arm, and said if it wasn't for us having the baby she would never have given in.

Now we felt we were coming up in the world. Four rooms, a summer kitchen papered with fresh newspapers each spring, and the buttery, which as I remember smelled mousy. In the kitchen was a long oilcloth-covered table, a stove which would not draw and left things doughy; behind this stove, a bench, on which the bread was set to raise or cream to warm for churning, or a small keg of vinegar in the making; above the table, a long shelf, loaded with any and everything. At one side of the door is a box; this holds the water pail and dipper, we being cautioned, 'Ain't you got any manners? Don't drink over the pail.' Above this box a small mirror hung, and here, besides drinking, we washed, combed, and Henry shaved. When more than one is getting ready at the same time, it is necessary to look over the first one's shoulder. In the front room are two beds and two rocking-chairs (one with a patch, where I worked it over).

In what should have been called the parlor in those

days, but as we didn't have the nerve, was called the best room, is Mama's bed with the feather tick, and it is a great favor to be permitted to sleep with her. If an older one, this is accomplished by getting sick. The two last babies always slept with her. Our center table was a round poker table, a drawer underneath and a slit cut in the top. I used to wish I had all the money which had been dropped through this slit. The table was covered with a checked tablecloth and on it was the family Bible (right over the slit), a lamp — not a fancy one, we couldn't afford it — but later, oh, joy, Q. T. gives us a hanging lamp with lots of brass, long glass pendants, and above this, bright-colored jewels all around it. When the brass on this was cleaned with salt and vinegar, each pendant washed and polished, and a ray of sun shining on it, what splendor! No, it didn't give any light; that's why Q. T. gave it away. By now we have two or three pictures (Henry made the frames), 'The Challenge,' 'A Stag at Bay' by Landseer, and Rosa Bonheur's 'Horse Fair.'

And then — this was something to brag about — Si Dore goes to the boom in Creede, strikes a mine, and makes a sale. When he returns to Bonanza, he just sifts his money around. We wonder if he will remember us, and after several days he does come to see us. We all act *so* pleased to see him (all visitors should have money), each kid stepping around on tiptoe, Mama cooking the best meal — no sparing the cream now; taking the egg from under the old black hen while it is yet warm, to build one of those thick custard pies; each of us hanging on every word of his adventures. He tells of seeing Bob Ford shot down in his tent dance-hall; of the man with a barrel of whiskey and a cup, who opened a saloon in the lee of a rock, and many others; but no mention is made of selling a mine or of money. After dinner Mama and I are in the buttery. I give her a questioning glance, and she says, 'Now you hold yore horses; bet he has blowed it all in'; and my heart sinks.

We go back into the room where he is; then he reaches in his pocket and pulls out a buckskin bag, and after running through it, gives each child, except me, a dollar, while Mama smiles, telling each child to say, 'Thank you.' I stand there, heavy-hearted. Now he counts out some bills and hands Mama twenty-five dollars, 'To get you something to remember me by; you have been so good to an old stiff.' Still I am left out, my only hope, 'Bet I get part of Mama's. What's the matter with him anyway?' He asks for his hat — in those times you asked for a man's hat when he came in, and laid it carefully on the bed, especially if he had just sold a mine — and gets up to leave, shaking hands with each one. I come last, just as he is going out the door, and, after giving my hand a squeeze, he goes through the gate in a hurry. There is something in the palm of my hand; I look and find a shiny yellow dollar. It is a twenty-dollar gold piece!

There must have been many things Mama longed for (we never had any carpets or curtains), but after talking it over with Henry, she decided to get something we could all enjoy! Their choice fell on a picture. The next question was, what picture? I am quite sure Henry made the final decision, 'The Battle of Waterloo!' The twenty-five is turned over and the picture sent for. After what seems a long time it comes, taking three men to unload it. We children all gather around; the crate is removed, and it stands forth in all its glory. I was disappointed, and think Mama was, too, but neither of us ever admitted it. It is about five feet long and two and a half wide, in a heavy gold frame, we repeat it, 'a real gold frame.' The army is drawn up as big as life, and, if one cared to, one could pick out individuals; the sunken road in the foreground, horses and men falling, others piling on top; plenty of blood. After much driving of big spikes and heaving, it is hung, and can be viewed either close up, or one can back off and squint at it. Still I didn't like it. It is very heavy and I always hope one grand day it will fall. Back of it are hidden papers and things of all sorts, and if things were not found on the 'Safe,' they would be behind the 'Big Picher.' Under this, and running the full length, is a shelf with a lambrequin of green felt, painted in water-lilies; tassels hung from it every now and then. On this shelf were all kinds of specimens, which were a nightmare to dust.

The middle room was for the rest of the children to sleep in. Our bed ticks were filled with hay, and when freshly filled smelled so minty. They scratched your arms when stirring them up. In the spring when they are emptied the hay is a fine dust, and smells far from minty.

THE LIFE OF AN ORDINARY WOMAN

The end room is Henry's. Here he can lock himself in and read, away from the uproar of the family. Here the gun-rack was kept, and I hated it, because it seemed to me that we never needed anything but there was a shotgun or Winchester, twenty-two or double-barreled shotgun, cartridges or reloading outfit to come first. The same desk, always locked, is kept at the head of his bed; in which he would lock any book he happened to be reading, to keep it from me, but I pulled the staple out and in this way read Hugo's 'The Miserable Ones,' and Eugene Sue's 'Wandering Jew.'

Evenings, when the day's work is done, the cows in and milked, wood off the hill and chopped, water brought from the creek, the chicken-house fastened (Mama doing all this, with the help of some of the children), Henry in his room; the rest of us gather round the heating stove, Mama always with sewing or mending. She made all our clothes, dreading the boys' suits, making underwear from flour sacks — never enough to go around. Besides this, she would hook rugs and piece quilts. She would often drop her work and cry, and when asked the reason, would say, 'Just blues.' I wish now that I had read to her, but I was young and selfish, only reading to amuse myself. There was one, Jose, who would slip to her side, lean on her, and cry with her. There was never any affection shown, except that I have seen her love the latest baby, or gather the one next to it in her arms, deploring the fact that he had to be weaned, 'and only a little un yoreself.'

[82]

HENRY'S SONGS

There were other evenings (so rare) when Henry would get the fiddle from under the bed and play, bringing forth wailing notes which made the dog howl. Then sometimes, when he was in the right mood, he would sing:

'"Twas better by far we lived as we did,
The Summer of Life together,
And one of us tired, and lay down to rest,
Ere the coming of wintry weather.
Oh, the beautiful, beautiful daisies,
Oh, the snowy, snowy daisies;
'Tis but a handful of dust in a coffin hid,
And a low grave crowned with daisies,'

or,

'Long ago, sweet long ago,
On the golden shore of sweet long ago,
There are buds and blossoms rare,
Bound with threads of auburn hair.
There are crowns, there are scepters fallen low,
There are kisses fond and sweet,
Pressed by lips no more to meet,
On the golden shores of sweet long ago.'

I have never known how these songs affected the other children, but I, sitting huddled on the floor back of the stove, have a lump in my throat, and think, 'Guess I won't tell any more lies, and guess I could help Mama better, and bet I am rich some day, and I'll get things for all the kids, and Mama ——'

CHAPTER VII

Wake up, Jacob, day's a-breakin' —
Beans in the pot and a hoecake bakin'.

Old Song

ONE big day we have our pictures 'took'! How I would like to see this real picture, after so many years, and see if it is like the one I have in my mind. It was the first time, that I know of, when we all left home at the same time. And how did Mama ever get us ready? I expect I dressed myself in a checked outing flannel — you see we are coming on — made with a yoke; on this a piece is gathered, both back and front; this in turn is gathered into a tight narrow belt, then a full skirt is gathered on this belt. Of course she had to button me up the back, and comb my hair, which was loose with a narrow ribbon slipped under the back and tied on top with long ends hanging in my eyes. It seems to me Ed would have his hair trimmed (you sometimes put a large bowl on their heads, and cut what hung below), and be buttoned into his home-made waist and pants. Such a time, when you are making them, to get the pockets and the little flapper in front to go as they should! Both Frank and Jose would have tight-waisted dresses with pleated skirts; boys didn't get into pants as soon then as now; and I remember all of them had on home-knitted stockings. Jose's hair would be standing straight out, as Henry said, 'like a thatched roof.'

Ed and I are ready first and go on; I expect I want

[84]

to get out of helping. After this Henry dresses, Mama having laid out his things, after sweating so, doing up his boiled shirt. The bosom is so stiff she cannot get the studs in, nor his tie on the high stiff collar, so gives up, and he puts on one with a 'lay-down' collar. Now she finishes Jose, Frank, and Gertie, who has curly hair, and takes longer — but, how fine this will look in the picture! Gertie and the baby have on boughten white dresses, and, for this one time, we all have on shoes and stockings, except Moosie. After a while Henry comes on, bringing three with him. Now Mama gets herself ready, combing her long hair smooth, and pinning the braids in a big coil in the back, puts on her tight basque, the buttons touching all up the front, and the long skirt, dragging the ground. I must mention a little stand-up collar on the basque, with a whip and horseshoe embroidered on it, then inside of this is a stiff starched one, little tails flaring out inside the waist to hold it in place. She then picks up the year-old baby (another is on the way) and comes on down this mile of hot dusty road.

In the mean time Ed and I are at the photographer's tent; we had wiped the dirt off our shoes and waited. Then she comes, but — where is Henry? She leaves the baby with us and goes to find him. He had stopped to gas with some of the boys, who gave the kids a nickel, and they all leave him and buy red candy. About then Jose and Frank decide they don't want their 'picher took' and that they will 'sull' if they have to, so they run and hide. Mama, getting madder every minute (she is so tired), rounds up Henry and finds Gertie with her white dress all ruined, takes her to the town pump and washes her the best she can, then begins the search for the hidden ones, but gives up and comes to the tent. Some one has found them and they come, creeping on all fours under the side of the tent, and oh, the looks Henry gets!

Finally we are fixed, and this is the result: Mama sitting bolt upright, Moosie on her lap with her bare feet sticking out; Mama's eyes drawn together in a frown; Henry, sitting beside her, his hair roached back and his mustache sticking out fine, a sheepish look on his face, knows she is just waiting to haul him over the coals; has Gertie on his lap, whose curls add a lot anyway. At their feet are the two wild ones, still 'sullin' with their mouths in a pout; in back, Ed is standing looking very solemn, he was ever quiet. There, too, I am standing, feeling sorry for Mama, yet enjoying it all; always like to show off, had pulled my hair over my shoulder so it would show, and as a sort of a 'blest be the tie that binds' effect, I put one hand on Mama's shoulder, the other on Henry's. A Family Group is the result!

Our clothes were not a problem then, as they are to-day. A new dress twice a year, Christmas and the Fourth of July, Mama usually making them out of three yards of calico, purchased with a quarter you had 'boned' one of the boys for. The first nightgowns I ever remember having were made from some old canvas which I ripped off an empty cabin. They were made with a yoke, high neck and long tight sleeves,

A FAMILY GROUP
The author in the rear

the sleeves made in two pieces. In putting them in, I got the short seam over the elbow, but wore them out without changing. In addition to Mama's ladycloth dress which Nellie Smeltzer charged ten dollars for making, was a pair of hoops, and how fine the puffs and ruffles hung over them! The tapes, running from one hoop to the other, were clamped together with little gilt buttons, and at times, when I thought I needed one of these for anything, I swiped it by prying it loose with a fork. The next time she wanted to wear them the hoops all sank in a pile.

Mama had two really good pieces of jewelry — a long watch-chain with a pearl slide (to-day each girl has a piece of this chain; I don't know where the slide is) and an amethyst ring set in pearls. I begged to wear this, and ran after the pigs, swung myself around the gate, caught a nail under the ring, and pushed the stone out. We could never find it.

I was built straight up and down; never needed a corset and refused to wear one, which was a disgrace. I was coaxed, hired, and finally ordered to have one, and consented to some kind of a corset waist, never wearing this except when forced to. When I was sixteen I was engaged. He came for me to go to a dance, and, gosh, the corset waist is lost! We looked everywhere, while he waited; the kids were called in and questioned, and again we went through the corner cupboard, the clothes press, and under the bed. Still he waited; by now we were slinging things right and left, and it is finally discovered back of Mama's big trunk.

THE LIFE OF AN ORDINARY WOMAN

Then, too, I must have a bustle — everybody did. Ellen Jack, a woman I knew in Gunnison — we called her 'Cap.' Jack — told me that when she came to Denver in the early days she filled her bustle with money and Government bonds. She also told me, when she was staging it from Denver to Gunnison, on the same stage with her was Alva Adams, afterward Governor of Colorado. His brother, Billy Adams, is now Governor of Colorado. Alva Adams was going into Gunnison to start a hardware store and had as his first stock two valises of guns and cartridges. They were held up on the road and armed themselves from the contents of the valises. Cap. Jack shot right along with the men, only better, as she could and did clip a finger or ear off at will.

Mama made her bustle by folding a thick towel over a string, then tying it around her waist. But never would I carry any extra weight for beauty's sake; but I must have a bustle, and not a heavy one, so hunted up an empty tomato can, punched a hole in the bottom, ran a string through it, and had a lovely bustle. Of course there were a few sharp corners, but you can't have everything.

The older people wore their hair in what they called a French twist; the younger girls combed theirs straight off the face, braiding it in a braid which was turned up under and tied with a bow of ribbon. This was called a Cadogan knot. It was years later that we had the Psyche knot, and then came the dreadful pompadour and rats. These were the days of the fascinator, made of wool in all colors; sometimes beads were woven in, and on moonlight nights how they would glisten! There was something about a fascinator; much more than about the toboggan cap which followed, a wool cap fitting close to the head with three large pompons in front.

Forty years from now, I wonder if the clothes of this generation will seem as foolish as did the tight basques, long skirts, the many starched petticoats, and the bustle and the tiny shoe of that generation.

Nellie Smeltzer was the town dressmaker and milliner. As a girl, she had money and some of the good things it brings; such as education and breeding. She always boasted of going to a private school. When quite young she married a mining man in Georgetown and had followed him from one mining camp to the other. Finally they came to Bonanza; here she planted herself and said, 'No more moves.'

She has often told me of how she shocked the 'natives' when she first came to town with her lovely and daring clothes. I think a low-necked, black tarletan dress was the knock-out. I know she must have been beautiful in those days, as she always had very good features, and such an air; talked with her eyebrows and shoulders. The first thing I remember of her was the enticing colored pictures in her windows. She could twist a scarf around a hat and give it *that* look. These pictures in the window attracted me, and I paid her my first visit, finding a fairyland, mirrors, flowers, hats, Japanese parasols, furniture, and pictures. For many years, her house was a stopping-place for me, always warm and pleasant. She was a good dressmaker and considered very expensive. Once, when we were flush, she made Mama a dress and charged ten dollars for it; this seemed awful, but in spite of shirrings, ruffles, pinkings, and puffings, a big howl went up over it and it was shown to all of the neighbors.

In those days you never held a dress up so that your friends could see the outside, oh, no! It was the wrong side which was turned outward and examined to the smallest detail. How it was lined, and interlined; how bound; how the seams were finished; the smallness and evenness of the stitches; how the steels were put in — there was the test of the dressmaker's art: they should be put up and down every dart and seam, with fancy stitches in bright colored silk thread; from fourteen to seventeen were required for the usual basque.

In this dress of Mama's, which looked very stylish, the lining in the overskirt was pieced and patched. This ruined it, and many times I have seen it held at arm's length, and have heard, 'Now, I just wish you would cast your eye over that; the nerve of a woman to charge me ten dollars for making a gacy thing like that; it takes the cake, that's all I've got to say.' Nevertheless, we children bragged a good deal over the dress that cost ten dollars to make.

Mrs. Smeltzer got her spring millinery just before the Fourth of July, but this was soon enough, as it was never warm before this, and the Fourth was the event of the year; and if one had a new hat it would not be worn before this day, anyway. I had many new hats of her, some paid for (in small 'dribs,' depending on how the washing came in or how much milk was sold) and some given me. Always, when I visited her, she would give me good advice, none of which I remember. Only once was I asked to eat with her. The linen napkins and the egg cups of silver filigree impressed me very much. She would tell of Paris fashions, the lack of appreciation in Bonanza, of her girlhood, of balls she attended (I only knew dances); of a dead brother she had loved dearly, and of how she tried to talk to him through the spirits; of her stepmother beating her out of her money; of (when I was older) my love affairs, or rather the lack of them. She would say: 'Now, Annie, aren't you mashed on any one? Do you know why you haven't as many beaus as the other girls? Your breasts are too small; you should eat more butter and eggs.'

For many years she would go on the mountain-side, cut huge pine trees, and drag or carry them home and put them in holes in front of her house, where they would last for months; strangers wondered why she had such fine shade trees. She always got her own wood off the mountain, hauled it home, sawed and split it. If you think this is an easy job, you should try it once.

The years pass, each day she looks for the return of her husband. But he never comes. She has no intimate friends, neither women nor men, and never seems to feel the want of them. No relative ever came to see her.

She is never talked about, although many men

have tried their luck with her, and have left sadder but wiser men. One was told to come late at night; he went, tapped gently on the door; it was opened a crack, he stepped eagerly forward and had his eyes filled with red pepper. Another was also told to 'come ahead.' When he tapped, a sweet voice whispered, 'Come,' but a bucket of cold water had been left hanging above the door which tipped, drenched him, and cooled his ardor. There was another one whom she enjoyed visiting with, as he was clever, a good talker, and more one of her own kind. By now she was washing, as the sewing had played out, and when this man would come for his washing, he would slip out the back way if he saw any one coming. I expect he wanted the other men to think he had a clear thing. She never said one word, but at the back door was a steep step; this she loosened and slipped so that the next time her friend sidled through her bedroom, so that he could go out the back way (our houses always had the rooms in a row), he fell, heels over head. She lost his washing!

She was one of the proudest persons I have ever known; she would never allow any one to help her or give her anything. When she would be out hunting her cow, dressed in gunnysacks, maybe one foot in an old rubber boot and the other wrapped in an ore sack, if you could coax her in, wanting to give her something to eat, you had to make an affair of it, and drink tea along with her. One Christmas people knew she was hungry. They filled a sack with groceries, and put it on her doorstep. When she found it, she took it by the bottom, and dumped it first to the right, then to the left, threw the sack over the fence, went into the house and slammed the door. She held on to one blue velveteen dress, which she wore on election days, when she dressed for the occasion; for years she wore gunnysacks, and sometimes these were very scant, but whatever she wore, she wore it with an air. She even walked with a tripping sort of strut, and each day of her life powdered, white as snow, with flour; in later years she was very dirty, but always powdered thick over the dirt.

Once, when a woman whom she disliked very much left town, Mrs. Smeltzer slipped over and hung crêpe on the door. Once, while pulling a bale of hay up the snowy, icy street, a young miner, coming off shift, stopped and offered to help her. She peered up at him, and said, 'Young man, I don't want to get you talked about!'

She carried her money in her mouth and the store kept a glass of water to drop it in!

She was honest to a degree; I have known her to walk to Saguache to pay her taxes, seventeen miles over a high mountain pass. Once she borrowed our cart, piled it high with millinery, put herself in the shafts, and hauled it to Villa Grove, fifteen miles away.

A year or two ago, she was brought to the county seat on an insanity charge, and after the jailer's wife had washed her hair, it was lovely. Then they got one of those cheap straw garden hats, and she insisted on a piece of cheesecloth to trim it, and finished with a creation. She and I laughed over the charge; one of the complaints was, that she kissed her cow! The cow had come to be her only means of livelihood, and she said to me, 'She's the only creature who loves me; why not kiss her?' It was at this time she gave me this advice: 'Annie, don't ask people their business. If they want you to know they will tell you, and if they don't they will lie.'

During all these years there was never one word of complaint at an unkind fate. She died, as she lived; proud and alone, asking no odds of any one. At the last she was with the only things on earth that loved her, the cow and chickens; these chickens roosted on the foot and under the bed, and were blinded by the light when brought out. But, even to the end, there was a sign creaking above the door, 'Fashionable dressmaking'; and ladies, yellow and fly-specked, dressed in beautiful colors, with tiny waists, big sleeves, and long trains, looked and smiled at you from the fashion sheets in the bay window.

CHAPTER VIII

Oh! ever thus, from childhood's hour,
I've seen my fondest hopes decay.

MOORE

WE now get our first cow, paying seventy-five dollars, which is a lot of money in these days. Henry goes to the valley and drives her home. How we watch for his return, thinking of having a cow of our own, and all the milk we can drink, and buttermilk and butter! 'Then, too, you know, we will have to sell enough to feed her'; thus we plan.

Finally Henry comes, with a wild, big-horned, raw-boned cow, which doesn't look much like seventy-five dollars, but after Mama makes friends with her and they seem to have a secret understanding, Pat (as we named her) comes through and does her duty nobly; is a member of the family and we demand that she be treated as such. She could and did open any gate or door in town. On these occasions she would eat till she choked herself, then come home for help, which was given by Mama running the broomstick down Pat's throat! Times when she was not able to come home, any one seeing her would come on the run —
'Miz Levon, come quick, yore old cow is down again.' Times when there was no broomstick handy, Mama would unbutton her basque, slip it off, and reach down with her bare arm.

Once Pat is lost for several days. Finally, on a high mountain back of the house, we find her feeding, and

[95]

close by is a little new calf, all legs, and so tottery on them. I take my apron and make a sort of sling; and thus we go home, the dog in the lead, his tail high over his back, we next, bent double with our load, old Pat coming behind, bawling every step. This time it is good news we bring; it is a heifer.

Our living was plain and cheap, plenty of milk, and, in the summer, a garden planted with lettuce, onions, radishes, and mustard for greens. The summer is very short in these high altitudes, and I am quite sure the garden was always more work than help. In a paper I read how easy it was to grow peanuts, so I sent for some, planted them, digging them up each day to see how they were coming, and when the frost came, there were really tiny little blisters growing on the ends of strings. Mama said, 'They would call them goobers, back home.' She waited till the moon was right to plant. I think things bearing above the ground are planted in the light of the moon, and things bearing in the ground in the dark. We carried all the water for the garden in buckets, from the creek, and it was an endless job; I think she would put one of us at it, and finish by doing it herself.

Summers we had lots of fish, Henry and the boys catching them where no one else could. I have gone with Ed and we would have a lot on a willow twig (I went along to carry the fish and keep the dog back), caught with a bent pin. We would meet some one with all the fixings, but no fish, and they would wonder how Ed did it; and I wonder, too. Henry read of some new-fangled way to keep fish in a brine, so a five-gallon keg is prepared, Mama doing the preparing, while he reads the rules. But — something must have slipped a notch, as they have a very peculiar taste, and none of us can eat them except Henry, who downs them and declares them good. There is one word in the English language which I never use and shudder when other people do; it is 'stink.' It may be I have a hang-over from that keg of fish.

In the fall we would lay in the winter's grub, all of twenty-five dollars' worth at once. This came near filling the buttery; sugar, codfish, beans, flour, cornmeal, oatmeal, dried apples, and salt side were the mainstays. Sometimes, when the cow is dry, we can hardly wait for her to 'come in'; then there is the three days' wait for the 'beeslings' to get good.

In the winter we usually butchered a pig Mama had raised during the summer. Mama butchered it, too, by knocking it in the head; then she scraped and cleaned it. Once Henry is going to do it; he always had new ways which seldom panned out, and this time it was to shoot the pig. After loading up and fooling around a lot, he was ready. Mama, in the mean time, had a fire going and plenty of hot water to scald and scrape the pig; also the knives are whetted. She cautions him to be sure and get it in the head, so as not to spoil the meat, calling to us to stay out of range of the gun; then she helped him corner the pig. He drew a bead on it, and let go. Afterward Mama said Henry had 'buck ague'; anyhow, he got the pig in the leg. Then it broke out of the pen and started running, Henry after it, reloading as he ran,

Mama after him, yelling, 'You can't kill a pig unless you get him in the head.' The two dogs now join in; Henry shoots again and misses it clean. By now it is really exciting, and we kids join in, some screaming and some crying. (Such a way to use the Barth boys, the pigs, when they had been so good as to meet you when coming from school and let you ride a way on their backs. They were named after two very dark-complexioned men; the pigs were of the dark variety also.) By now Mama's hair is all down her back and she is frantic. Henry, Mama, two dogs, and six kids, run that pig all over Exchequer, till finally we get it, and what a bloody mess! It was never good and the grease would foam in the pan. Mama said, 'If you kill a pig when it is mad, the grease always foams.'

We almost always had venison. Henry was a good hunter, and as soon as the boys were big enough, they also brought home rabbits, and finally deer. Ed killed his first deer when he was nine years old. When he started, he insisted on a knife to bleed it, so Mama gave him an old rusty case knife, knowing he could not cut himself with it. This day he was gone a short time and came running, all out of breath ——

'Mama, Mama, I have killed the biggest one you ever saw!'

'Yes, I bet you have.'

'Honest Injun, I have! Awful, awful big!'

She pulls up his sleeves — 'Look at the blood!' Now she is frightened. 'Bet you have shot a cow.'

'No, no, it's got deer horns.' He convinces Mama

enough so that she goes with him and they do find a big one, weighing over two hundred pounds, its neck sawed a good deal where Ed had got in his work with the old rusty knife.

The berry-picking season brings back some of the happiest times in my life. I loved to get them. Straight up the mountain-side in front of our house, was a small patch in the burned timber. I would take a five-pound lard pail and go after them, never having to be driven, as I was at other tasks. First up a steep pitch, then on a trail where wood had been skidded down, on up to where I can see the first bushes. There is no finer sight than to see a wild raspberry bush from below, hanging full of ripe berries. Then the climbing over rocks and logs, squatting near each bush, the sun warm on your back, everything so still and peaceful — how you could dream and enjoy it! After the bottom of the pail is covered, it seems to go slower, and — when you are within an inch of the top, it seems as though it could never be filled. Now you step so carefully for fear of spilling them; going downhill is much harder than up. At last you are home, tired and satisfied. Mama makes a cobbler of them, and, oh, the smell when the oven door is opened! The odor of raspberries cooking, and of a geranium leaf, can take me in a moment back forty years; and I love them both.

From farther away people were bringing in jack loads each day. It was impossible for Mama to go, so I coaxed her to let Ed and me go; at this time I was ten or eleven, he two years younger. We were to camp, and fill a five-gallon keg. She arranged to have Picnic Jim take us, packing our grub and bedding on his burro. She bet she 'wouldn't find him sober long enough to make the trip'; but she did, and we started this seven miles over the range and down the other side to the Spring Creek. Picnic unpacked our things at a miner's tent, where we were planning to make our camp. Just now our things are thrown on the ground under a tree — no time to waste on camps, we want to pick berries. Picnic takes us down the trail about a mile into the patch, and we are frantic, so many berries one could not see the end of them. Each of us had a ten-pound pail we wished to fill at once.

Here Picnic left us, telling us to pick away, and he would come for us in the evening. We started, working hard and fast, never looking up, and when we do, all the trees look the same, and the trail has vanished, but we don't care, berries are what we want. At last the pails are full and mashed down till the juice rises to the top; now we know we are tired and hungry and want Picnic to come. We try to find the trail, but are confused in that forest of dead timber; then we know we are lost, and run from tree to tree, calling and calling (but never once letting loose of the bucket of berries). Ed starts to cry, he is so little and tired, and I want to, but know it won't do.

Then dark comes, and we are at an old tunnel, the timbers partly caving in, but anything is better than those naked trees on every side. Here we set the berries inside, and while doing this I find part of an old mattress left there. This I pull out and go on exploring, peeking in every corner, and am rewarded by finding part of a box of matches behind the lagging. These were lit very carefully, part of the stuffing from the mattress was used, and how wonderful when it blazed up! I drew myself up and told Ed, 'No fear of lions now, they were skeered of fire.' (I don't think there were any lions in miles.) So we slipped under the mattress and he fell asleep. I was awake, planning on walking to the valley the next day; it seemed such a short distance from where we could see it from this mountain-side. This was our first glimpse, as we had never been out of the gulch since coming in, but — it was ten or twelve miles away.

After a long time, I think I hear a call — my heart is beating so I can hardly listen. Then again, and yes, it is a call. I jump up and answer, and soon hear some one running and jumping through the slide rock and fallen timber. It is Picnic, who, after leaving us, had a chance to pack berries back to town. He took the job, went over, got drunk, and forgot us.

Some one in the course of the day asked him, 'How you servin' the Lord nowadays, Picnic?'

'Oh, havin' a picnic' (he always was). 'Packin' to Spring Creek.'

At the mention of this he remembered, and was sobered at once, got his old patient jack, which probably had not been fed or watered all day, made it 'get a move on,' feeling very guilty when he passed our house, came on to camp, getting the miners up and asking if any had seen us. None had. Then he started running and calling; when he heard my first answer, he only ran the harder, coming up to me with a bound. 'Are you all right? What a brave kid!' Here he pulls off his coat, putting it on me, then his vest is wrapped around Ed, and, taking us in one hand, the berries in the other, we just plough up that hill, meeting the other men looking for us. We all return to camp and Picnic makes up a batch of biscuit and we eat. It is now near morning. After we ate, Picnic said, 'Annie, before you get in bed, don't you want to go and look at the stars?' I did. (And he was supposed to be, and was, a drunken bum!)

After a time we are 'set up' over having an organ for the front room. I think a cow was sold to buy this, price sixty dollars, and we surely had our money's worth. The lace work on the lower part, with red cloth under that, was ever a temptation to children, poking their fingers in to see if it would stand the racket. Then, too, the plugs were found amusing, either pulling out to make it thunder, the shivers running up and down one's back, or pushing in, when it made it soft and low, reminding one of the creek around the Turn, the smell of roses, and the cows coming home at night chewing their cuds.

No, none of us played, but — it gave such an air to the Front Room; the music on the rack open at 'In the gloaming, oh, my darling,' as though some one had just finished playing. Henry intimated that if I had any 'get up' I would learn to play by ear, but I didn't even know what he meant, as I could never tell one tune from the other, only when·dancing.

Now, when I think of it, we had several things to

be proud of, the 'Big Picher,' the 'Norgin,' and last but not least, the 'Caster.' This, in the middle of the long oilcloth-covered table, was something all families did not own, even in those days, and something which very few have now. Ours cost six dollars and was silver-plated. The center of this turned, and had holes in it; in these holes glass bottles fitted; these were filled with salt, pepper, and vinegar. I think one was for oil, but we only used this 'sweet oil' for earaches; instead it was filled with red pepper, and — oh, the burning of eyes and mouth when it was filled.

Days when we would 'redd up' the house, we had throws made of meal sacks, drawn work across one end; these were snowy white from washing, and were tied on the backs of the two rocking-chairs. Newspapers were notched for the shelves; this was a pleasure. You folded them over and over, then trimmed the lower edge, either in a point or scallops, then notched these all around. In the top of this (if you had one spark of sentiment or artistic ability) you cut hearts — first, a good-sized one, topped off with a row of smaller ones. All the specimens on the big shelf must be either washed or dusted.

Times when we would run out of coal-oil and candles, Mama would fill a bowl with melted grease, then braid or twist pieces of rag, putting one end in the grease, lighting the other, and thus making a very good light. She called it a 'slut.' It looked like the lamp the Wise Virgin carried. We never had a screen door, but did have flies. When they got too thick at meal time, one of us was delegated to wave a willow branch over the table, and when they were just swarming, as a last resort the black dishrag was put in a tin pan on the floor and set afire. When it was smoking good, you said, 'Flies, all go,' mentioning the neighbor you cared least for.

It was a mighty poor specimen of a man that couldn't raise a mustache, and one of the horrors to me was to see one (after drinking buttermilk) suck first one side in his mouth to clean it, then the other. We had a mustache cup, made with a little shield across the top to keep the hair from soaking up the cream, before the drinker had a chance at it. This particular cup had a rose on one side, and the word 'Mother' on the other. I often wondered why.

Times when we would have company, Mama would spread it on, by pointing her little finger out straight from the cup, and say 'thum' for 'them'; and I thought it all fine. Henry would entertain them by telling his stories, usually hunting adventures; of a mother grouse sitting on a limb, with three young ones, he shooting at them, missing them all, but is surprised to see none of them fly; goes up, and finds he has split the limb, which has caught all their toes and held them fast. Another time he was duck hunting at a small lake; goes early in the morning and sees the lake just covered with ducks; shoots — and is thunderstruck to see all the ducks rise at once, taking the lake with them, it had frozen in the night around their feet. And many others which they listened to and pretended to believe, but never did.

We had a big family Bible — it must have been

made to sell, certainly not made to be read; it was too heavy unless one laid it on the floor. It had designs all around the leaves, places for photographs, also places for births, deaths and marriages. Mama's and Henry's was the first marriage, and the births of one or two of the first children were recorded, but not all; I expect they came too fast, and it got to be an old story. I always resented it that I wasn't there. Once or twice I tried to read it to Mama. One place it was Rachel weeping for her children, and at this my mother cried so, Jose joining in (she always cried when Mama did), that I decided to get something more cheerful and read to myself. This Bible was fine to press flowers in, but they left rusty marks in it, so I was made to stop, 'because it must not be spoiled, it cost ten dollars.' But — there were a few flowers resting between these leaves which had a divine right there, a lady's-slipper and some ferns from Mama's old home, and some taken from a dead baby's coffin — there was a lock of hair twined with this bunch. Once Frank hid a nickel between the leaves, and never again could find it (I expect I saw him hide it). Instead of opening to look for it, he slid a knife along between the leaves, and cut a lot out. This was a great mystery — where those leaves had gone, and Mama wondered if it was a warning of some sort. Once, in reading it, I found the dire things that happened to one that called his brother a fool, and I was frightened, because of calling Ed that so often. I wonder if this book is in the world to-day, or if some one burned it long ago? But no one would ever burn a Bible. The most I used it for was to shut my eyes tight, and open it at random; this was for luck, and, if the passage sounded good, I believed it, and if bad, I didn't think it would come true anyway.

Though we grew up in this saloon-keeping and whiskey-drinking atmosphere, none of us ever cared for it especially, one brother, who lived and worked among the roughest miners and cowboys, never taking a drink up to the day of his death. We used it for medicine, for cooking, in putting up jam, after making our jars from beer bottles. This is done by heating a harness ring till red hot, dropping it over the neck of the bottle, then dashing cold water over it. When the jars are full of jam, you dip pieces of paper in whiskey, put these over the top, and the jam will never mould. Then, when we picked the berries, they were packed and brought home in an empty five-gallon whiskey keg; if some of the whiskey was left in the keg, it gave the berries a better taste.

There were good and bad saloon-keepers and good and bad saloons. As I remember now, Q. T. ran a high-class place, having no drunken men around, getting his bouncer busy as soon as a fight was started; his fixtures were the best — the goldenest, heaviest frames on his pictures, his carpets the reddest and thickest, his glassware the shiniest, his mirrors the largest. He made his money honestly (?), never rolling the men when they were too drunk to protect themselves. Across the street from Q. T's was Uncle Sam's place, and quite different in every way. Once when I saw in it, I wondered what drew the men to a dirty place like this. Farther down the street was 'The House of Lords,' surely a good-sounding name. I think there was a lot of gambling went on here. Once when sent to town in a hurry, I stopped there and had my picture taken with a bunch of miners. There I stood, my shoes unbuttoned, my drawers hanging below my apron, looking as though the outcome of the artist depended on me. To-day, this is one of my most prized pictures. Across the street from 'The House of Lords' was 'The Miners' Exchange.' This has always appeared to me to be a sensible sort of name for a saloon. When men would come home drunk from some of these places, declaring that they had been given knock-out drops, and their money taken from them, often the wife would threaten to have the saloon-keeper's license revoked, or inform on him so that he could never have it renewed, but I don't think any of them ever did.

I have known Henry to be drunk only once or twice; one time in particular we all remember. It was the occasion of one of the largest weddings ever held in Bonanza — dresses and dress suits from Denver, flowers being bought for decorations, invitations sent out by the dozen, cooks hired days ahead, guests from all over the valley, afterward long columns in the county paper of costumes and presents, and woe betide the printer if he had confused the giver of a silver caster with one who merely gave a sugar-shell. Well, Henry and Mama receive an invitation (I bragged a good deal); she, as usual, is 'expecting' again, and cannot go. I don't see how I managed it, unless she let me go to watch Henry, but anyway I do go. I think I just wore my usual apron, and expect I was not to show up with the crowd, but I remember her pressing Henry's 'other suit' and ironing a 'biled shirt.' She had such a time when ironing one of these stiff bosoms, trying so hard to get it stiff and shiny without scorching it, and when the iron would stick, or the starch roll up, or a wrinkle come in it, how she sweat to get it out, running the iron over salt, then over a candle. At these times we children stepped lightly, and usually outside and away. Then she hunts up studs and collar buttons for him; a necktie comes next which takes a tug of war to get around his stiff standing collar; his Masonic pin must be fixed just so (although he had been suspended long ere this for non-payment of dues); his shoes have already been carefully blacked. Finally, when all are worn out with the struggle, he is dressed and off, a last dash of hair oil on his cowlick, some cloves in his pocket — in case.

I must have gone ahead or behind him, as I have no recollection of him at the dance. For a while I stand around in corners, taking in all the sights, goldfish in a bowl, a net on a woman's head with a tiny stone at each cross-section, these glittering with every move so that I thought I was seeing diamonds. Finally I grow bolder and slip in where they are dancing and am sitting huddled in a chair when a young man (he was surely making fun of me) asks me to dance. I don't know how, but I want to so much, so say I will try. He says he will be after me the next

I HAD MY PICTURE TAKEN WITH A BUNCH OF MINERS IN FRONT OF THE
HOUSE OF LORDS SALOON

quadrille, and I sit there nervous, not knowing what to do (never think the poorly dressed child doesn't know and feel it), so bring my hair over my face, part it in tiny strands, then braid these strands in tight little braids which stick out and down my face. He comes for me before I have time to unbraid them, drags me out on the floor, and, while trying to follow the directions of the call, how ashamed and weak I am!

During this time Henry has been helping with the music, drinking quite often; not because he likes it, but to be a good fellow. Some one complains that a polka is too slow, and Henry brings the fiddle down over his head — I hope it was the head of the one who asked me to dance! Every one thought it was the whiskey, but he may have caught a glimpse of me with my hair braided in front instead of behind; at any rate, he goes hog wild, striking to the right and left. One-Eye Thompson says, 'Let me to him, he is a brother Mason,' but even this has no effect, as he knocks 'One-Eye' down. Some one suggests they send for 'Miz Levon; bet she can handle him.' This they do, dragging her out of bed, and she goes; she has only to step to the window and look in. He sees her, and, as she afterward said, 'coiled' down at once and goes out quietly with her; but when about half a mile from home he backs up, and sits down on the high bank on the upper side of the road, braces his feet, spits, and looks at her, her eyes drawn in toward the corners, her forehead wrinkled in a heavy frown.

'Old woman,' he says, 'do you love me?'

She snaps back, 'The gall of you! I should say not. Come on.'

But he leans back with a sigh as though preparing to spend the night. She walks on a little way, and, seeing he makes no move, returns.

'Singee, don't you love me?'

She answers, 'Not by a long sight, and you cutting up this way, and getting in such a rucus.'

She is so tired and sleepy that, although it is a bitter pill, the next time it comes, 'Say, don't you love me?' she answers unwillingly, 'Yes, come on to bed'; and she, who never does things grudgingly, takes him by the arm and half leads, half carries him home, while I bring up a long way in the rear.

CHAPTER IX

What a lot of wear and tear, trouble and disappointment could be avoided, if we quit expecting others to do for us things we would not do for them.
A. E.

YOU dude wranglers, think of this outfit! A fourteen-year-old girl, never strong, and always skinny; a twelve-year-old boy who was puny; a little girl of eight; and a baby of six, although he would have kicked and cried had you called him a baby. I suppose it was the call of the wild in us older two, and maybe just in me; anyway, I coax Mama to go goose-berrying. She would not hear of it, was afraid, and now I can see how she must have worried about us; but then it seemed so foolish and I coaxed on. She knew 'nothin' ever happened' and I would be care-ful, and, besides, 'Think of all the fish and berries we would bring home!' This brought her; we were al-ways needing so much. Still it was a half-hearted consent she gave, and I learned very young if my mo-ther was not for anything it never seemed to turn out well.

We got ready an old wagon sheet, which a man, describing afterward, said 'had six holes to the square inch'; a frying-pan and a few tin plates, a couple of cups and some old knives and spoons. We didn't use forks, anyway, and none of us drank coffee. We took a piece of salt side, which we called 'sow-belly,' a few loaves of bread, home-made of course, as in these times we knew nothing of baker's bread, a little flour with baking powder and salt mixed in it, in case the bread ran out. 'Don't forget matches, and carry some in two old cartridge shells fitted together, in case you fall in the creek.' We also had salt and a small supply of sugar to make jelly, which I did, straining it through the dishrag! 'And don't forget the onions — anybody can make a fine meal on bread, fish, and onions.' All this is packed in pails in which we will put the berries later. Then there are the gun and fishing tackle, and a roll of old bedding — not much, as we would all sleep together. We take an old jenny (we are going to slip away from her little colt — needn't think we will fool along with that!) which we put the pack-saddle on and part of the load, leaving the saddle free for one of the smaller children to ride on; the other is to perch behind him. Then we round up Old Tony, a miserable, pot-bellied horse which we own, but can use very little, as he has spells, and you never know just when one is coming on. He throws himself from side to side and sits down on his rump, also on any one who is in sitting distance, and goes backward instead of the other direction. We don't call it balking or bucking, only one of Tony's 'spells.' We saddle him, throwing the bedding on behind, telling Mama we are going to ride when through town. We know we are not, as Tony has the Indian sign on us.

We are off, with a dog to take care of us, Mama calling after, 'Be good, be careful, look out for fire.' And when we come to the Turn, I looked back and saw her standing there (a baby on one hip), shading her eyes with her hand, and, I now know, thinking a prayer for us. On down through town (Jose has since said I made them get off going through town, while I climb on, spreading my skirts over the side of the burro to make it look like a riding-skirt. Maybe I did, it sounds like me!), the men laughing at us and our way of packing, the women saying, 'Them Levon kids is off again; they'll come to some bad end, I bet.'

On we go, one leading Tony, the other driving the jenny. The dog runs in circles around us and we all are happy except Old Tony, and he is always sad. Everything is fresh and cool; the birds so friendly, and the chipmunks sitting up and calling to us. 'Come back here, Turk, you know you mustn't kill anything except to eat. Now, if you see a rabbit, that will be different.' On past some cattle — 'They say, they never take after any one on horseback'; of course two of us are walking, but then Tony is near, and can't they see the kids on the jenny? Here we leave the road, and start over Simmons Trail, across a creek — 'Darn a burro, anyway; they hate so to get their feet wet. Well, hold tight now and I will prod her from behind.' On up this trail, so quiet, the tall trees on either side, uphill, and we go more slowly; besides we are getting tired and hot. I change the kids on the pack-saddle, as they have begun to quarrel. 'Well, get off and walk, then, it is so nice along here. I am not going to have fighting, and will lick the stuffin' out of the one who begins it.'

We talk of the Indians who may have come up this trail, making it so real we would not be surprised to see one come from behind a bunch of juniper. We tell of the Ute Indian who had killed his wife with an axe. When asked why he did it, he answered, 'She seek, she no get well, she no die, I keel her.'

Turk, the dog, goes in the lead, turns around, his tongue hanging out and waits for us to come up to him. I tell the children he is the pathfinder. Now we come to a place which drops down toward the stream; the kids are riding again, and one of them must have kicked the jenny in the flank. They said that Turk ran up behind and snapped at her heels, but I didn't believe this of him; anyway she humped up, and Jose flew off, running a rock in her head. (Mama didn't want us to come this trip, anyway.) The blood pours, but I am not going to get excited over this; she bleeds at the drop of the hat, anyway. She is crying at the top of her voice. I take her to the creek and wash it. 'Yes, it is pretty bad, but I am not going back, anyway. We might as well eat here.' To eat would quiet her more than anything else. So we do, Tony and the jenny eating along the creek banks, and Turk biting pieces of grass.

Now Jose gets sleepy, but I will have none of this; they say, 'sometimes when they have had a bad bump, and go to sleep, they never waken.'

'Let's go on before a bear smells us and comes.'

'Do bears honest eat people?'

'They say they do, and I am not going to take any chances, with you so nice and fat.'

This wakens her, and we are off again up the cool trail. I have tied her head in a piece of flour sack —

what if there is flour on it? It will stop the blood. Now I commence to worry, so haul her off and chew up some tansy (I wish I had a little turpentine) and cover it with this. She is getting so tired of this pack-saddle.

'Ed, you have just got to get up on Tony and hold her. Oh, well, he is tired, and going uphill he will be all right; I thought you always claimed to be a cowboy? 'Fore I would be afraid to get on an old plug like him (I wouldn't have got on him myself at any price!) I would go and soak my head. Come on, now, give me the gun. Now, old Tony, keep still. There, I knew you could. Bet it feels nice up there; wish it was me.'

Tony is good, and we go on, I hoping it would be all right. I will have to watch the cut, and look out for proud flesh (we never heard of blood poison), and if I see any coming I will heat a fish-hook and pick it out. It is six or eight miles to Ford Creek, the place we are bound for. The only one who lived there was an old bachelor, said to be a woman-hater; also said to have the picture of the one who disappointed him hanging over his bed in his cabin — I intended to slip in sometime and see.

Finally we came to the place we were going to camp, about a mile above Sam's; the kids are unloaded, then the packs, I making Ed do the most of it. I'd rather boss than work; besides, he had been riding anyway. We hobbled Tony, or at least Ed did — 'He is more usted to you, you know' — picketed the jenny — 'If she once gets loose, she won't let any grass grow under her feet till she gets back to that colt.' We take the wagon sheet and spread it over some bent willows, staking the ends in the ground. 'Now I will do the rest; I expect you better get some fish for supper.' Ed likes this, gets ready and leaves, I yelling after him, 'Look out for rattlesnakes!' The rest of us break pine boughs for our bed, and carry the bedding and grub in, being careful to see that everything is covered from rats and mice, except the onions — they are safe anywhere. Now we get wood to make a fire — too late to get berries to-day. Soon the shadows are lengthening, and I know it will be night before long.

Ed comes with the fish; we clean them and I get supper at once. The fish double up in the pan, and the fire smokes whichever side you are on, as all camp-fires do. We all squat and eat, being careful to throw the bones in the fire so the dog can't get them — 'We'll try and get a rabbit to-morrow, and he can have the insides.' We rub most of the dirt off the dishes, picket the jenny in a new place, and then get ready for bed, or at least go to bed, Ed having such a time with his boots — always the stiffest, hardest things, almost impossible to get off. This night we all have a whirl at them; then he goes to the crotch of a tree and uses it for a boot-jack.

We had only the clothes we had on. Our shoes and stockings were taken off and put under our heads for pillows; besides, it kept them dry. We spread a rope on the ground all around the tent; this was supposed to keep the snakes out — we had heard they never went over a rope. Long afterward I discovered it must be a hair rope; but none came, anyway.

Soon we are all settled for the night — the two largest on the outside, the dog on the foot of the bed. I waken only a few times, to rearrange some of the boughs; in some places they make huge lumps. Then every noise is so loud; Tony and the jenny make such a noise feeding. I always worried. What if the burro should get tangled up in her rope and kill herself? (She was borrowed.) What if Ed didn't get the hobbles on right and they would burn all the skin off Old Tony? And — I never believed these bear and mountain lion stories; but — I don't know, when it is dark!

Soon it is morning and the sun shining. This day we pay a visit to Sam Calvert, who is making wild gooseberry jelly; and I don't think much of him, because he leaves the wormy ones in. He says, 'They are just like a gooseberry and you don't know the difference, anyway, when they are strained.' We see dozens of his yellow cats that he is raising for their hides; but — I do not get a glimpse of the picture. He gives us some potatoes, which I put to bake in the warm ashes that night, and the jenny comes and paws them out and eats them. But — we have come for berries, so must get busy. When we came to the patch where they grew thickest, I made the kids all walk along the fence, so as to keep up out of the rattlesnakes, and I had forgotten this, but Jose says, at one time she is just stepping over a log, and we hear that warning rattle, like seeds in a blueflag pod, and I grab her and throw her back of me. Finally the pails are full and we return to camp and pass the night much the same as the other.

In the morning it is drizzling rain. Now, rain pattering on a tent is music, if you have a tent, but we had but this old wagon sheet. We get breakfast the best we can — 'Darn the jenny, anyway, for stealing the potatoes!' The rain comes harder — we wish we had dug a ditch around the outside of our camp so the water would not run under the bed, and try now to scrape one with a rock, but do not make much of a job of it, and so we huddle there. By now it is coming in torrents, and the wind has risen, and we have thunder and lightning. 'Hope Old Tony doesn't come any nearer. Mama says to keep away from rocks, trees, and horses when it lightnings.'

Have you seen the blinding flashes of lightning we have in these narrow gulches? First comes the thunder which will lift you off your feet in its heavy crashes; now it will rumble, then bellow, gaining in strength; every nerve is tense, waiting for the final clap, which seems to split things wide open; then the holding of breath, waiting for the flash, then the relaxing and getting ready for the next one. I am not afraid of storms, in fact rather enjoy them, but Jose is almost frantic, and cries so hard. The wind has blown one end of the sheet from the ground, we are all wet and the dog has crept in, whining. I am on my knees trying to hold a corner of the sheet down and hear a sound behind me (a new sound in all this uproar), glance over my shoulder, never letting loose of my grip on the sheet, and see Jose down on her knees (where did she learn? — or was it just instinct?) praying,

'Oh, God, stop the thunder, and, God, I'll try not to be afraid if Annie ain't.'

You can know then how I would grit my teeth and put on a bold front. And those prayers were answered. Soon now it is over, and all of us, dripping, creep forth, and are unable to get a fire for a long time. Now Old Sam comes, his slicker all dripping, his horse splashing each step.

'Say, you kids, come to the cabin. This has been a hell of a storm, and it ain't safe for you.'

It must have been a bad one to make this woman-hater ride through the storm, wanting to take these dirty wild ones in. I would like to see that picture, but — refuse. 'No, thank you, Mr. Calvert' (now I am being nice, we call him Old Sam to ourselves), 'I think it is about over, and we want to pack up and go home in the morning. You know we have all the berries we want.' (I'm not going to have him think a storm could scare me!)

He turns his horse. 'Well, you are foolish, better come and dry anyway.' And he rides away.

Then the sun comes out and we get a fire, drying both ourselves and bedding, and we decide the rest of the day we will hunt. So, Ed in the lead, with the gun, telling me, 'You make me tired,' because I am afraid of guns and caution him each moment to be careful how he carries it. I don't want the darn thing pointing back at me, and he doesn't want the stock toward me either — 'Can't shoot quick enough in case we should jump a deer.' So we compromise by his carrying it over his arm with the barrel sideways. Next come Frank and Jose, and I bring up the rear. We make too much noise to suit Ed, till finally he gives in, and we all talk, we older ones telling bear and mountain lion stories till we frighten even ourselves, and we brag on what we would do in case we did run into one — and it is plenty!

The dog has left us and — here he comes, growling and almost creeping, his hair turned the wrong way; then the most dreadful shriek. Have you ever heard a lion scream? I think that when the eagle carries off the mother's baby, she must have shrieked in the manner 'that cut like blades of steel the air.' There is such a deep feeling of despair, such a ripping out of the heart, in it. We stop in our tracks, wild-eyed and trembling, then turn and start for camp. 'It wouldn't be nice to kill a mama lion, anyway; then what would her poor babies do?' We step lightly and fast to get away from there, making all sorts of excuses except the one of fear.

After supper (and now you see how really ornery I am) I think the jenny and Old Tony need a good feed before their journey home, so tear out a panel of Sam's fence and turn them in on his oats (not long enough to make them sick), and how they mow it down! Next morning we make the homeward journey without trouble, till we come to town. I am leading the jenny, the rope wrapped several times around my arm. She sees her colt and runs for it, and nothing on earth can stop her; so drags me with her, and the rope burns the skin off my arm from elbow to wrist. A mile to go now, and we are home, to a good cooked meal, and somehow the rooms all look larger than when we left.

CHAPTER X

I am as full of knowledge as the best of them. They do not know where we come from, nor why, nor where we go. Neither do I. Education is having read other men's opinions on these three things.

A. E.

THE greatest influence in my life has been books, good books, bad books, and indifferent ones. I started in by reading what we called 'Nick Carters' — everything, of course, borrowed. How wonderful they are! I am just reading 'Wild Bill,' deep in his adventures, when I am called to 'go see if the calf is with the cow.' As I move slowly toward the barn, the book in my hand, almost finished, much to my sorrow, I pause to have a look around for that blamed calf, see a big saw-log lying there, and wish the book was as thick through as the log is long.

I claim it is better to read 'Nick Carters' than nothing. Then there was what we called 'The Yellow Back,' the 'Ten-Cent Novel.' I think E. P. Roe, the Duchess, Bertha M. Clay, E. D. E. N. Southworth, and others came in this class, and while there was a lot of fun made of these books, still they were a Godsend, as many read them who would read nothing else. One always felt better after reading one, as they ever had a fine moral, the villain getting it handed to him, and the lovely maiden and brave hero living happily ever after.

Some of the bachelors I borrow from — mostly the Englishmen — have other books, and I start to read

[122]

them; then, too, people are reading Dickens, Scott, and some of the better writers, and when they would mention something from one of these books, I wished to be able to say something about it. (It is a trial for me to keep out of any conversation.) Finally I came to enjoy only this class of reading. To-day Charles Dickens is like a fine friend I have known. We had a few books at home, a truly fine set of Plutarch's 'Lives,' leather-bound and very old. I found it hard to read them because the *s*'s were all like *f*'s.

Then there was 'Don Quixote' — I knew him by heart; and while I wasn't fond of the Don — did not get the irony of it then — I did love Sancho Panza. Then there were Moore's poems, and, starved though I was for reading matter, I could never go them, and now only remember 'Lalla Rookh.' Most of the books were borrowed, 'The Wandering Jew,' 'The Count of Monte Cristo,' 'The Three Guardsmen,' and 'Twenty Years After'; and ('Your mother may not want you to read these!') how carefully I kept them hid from Henry, and how tame they were after all, 'Camille,' 'Nana, and Nana's Daughter.' Then, too, there was Amélie Rives's 'The Quick or the Dead.' I didn't know what the 'Quick' meant. When I was in the Bertha M. Clay period, one of my loved heroines would so often have a 'headache' — I pronounced it 'headitch' and thought that was what it was — and I think she fell in my estimation because she didn't do something for it.

Somehow I get George Sand's 'Society' and pronounce it 'Sowshety,' and never do find just what it means. An Englishman, Hubert Poole, once told me to select two hundred books, ten-cent ones, and he would pay for them. How I do revel in that selection, choose about one third of what I want and the rest of what I think he wants me to want, but — he was only joking. Bill Nye is very popular now, and when we have company they have to sit and listen to Henry read him. He never seemed to grow tired of this. It might be a beau of mine who was the listener, but he had to sit and take his medicine, and laugh at Bill Nye's latest.

A man lends me his precious Christmas gift, a beautifully bound and illustrated book, called 'Grey Eagle.' I dance all the way home, anxious to get into it, and promise myself that I will be very careful of it. I just get fairly started before night, and decide to take it to bed with me. We have candlesticks made by driving three nails into a piece of board; I put in a new candle and fix it on a chair at the head of the bed, wait till all are asleep, then light up, and am soon lost in my book. I reach out once in a while and snip off the burned end of the candle. Finally I am sleepy, reach out and drop the book with a sigh, but — oh, the morning light shows such a tragedy! The hot candle grease had dripped on the cover — a midnight mouse had eaten the candle sperm and on into the book. I wonder what excuses I made why it was never returned!

In the books I read, the characters, in their conversations, always spoke of or alluded to happenings of people in mythology, so, against the time I am going to be with educated people, and wanting to join in their conversations, I get all the names and myths down pat, and have never yet had a chance to use them. Sir James Barrie writes that his mother, Margaret Ogilvy, learned a few sentences of Latin to use when she felt the need of it, but she would break into a laugh before finishing.

There was Ella Wheeler Wilcox's 'Poems of Passion,' and that word 'passion,' said right out, was going pretty far. I read them and was disappointed. I didn't understand then, as I do now, what she meant by 'a heart rusted with tears.' Rudyard Kipling was also a favorite. We waited each year for Rider Haggard's latest book. Then there was 'Samantha at Saratoga.' Her mistakes were supposed to be funny, but were not so to me, because they were just the same sort of mistakes I would have made. You knew you were on safe ground when, in front of people, you read 'The Hearth and Home,' Harriet Beecher Stowe, Editor.

There was 'The Cosmopolitan,' very much dog-eared by the time it got around to us. The cover then was always the same, two worlds supported by two columns; wound around these columns was this, 'To every man according to his needs from every man according to his ability.' No doubt the policy of 'The Cosmopolitan' is just the same; it is the 'needs' and 'ability' that are different. Lately, I saw an old number of 'The Cosmopolitan' — my sister keeps her gay embroidery thread between the leaves — published just after the San Francisco fire. There was but one automobile advertisement in it, and there was an editorial saying automobiles never will be practicable on account of the roads. But there are many ads of whiskey, beer, and corsets; especially corsets. On the same page would be a whiskey advertisement and another of something to put in a man's coffee to break him of the habit; of tobacco, then of something to use in place of it. I have known men to have a chew of tobacco in one cheek and a tablet of No-tobac in the other.

Our chief amusements were discussing our neighbors, school entertainments, and dances. If times were good at all, we had a dance every Saturday night, and, oh, how fine they were! The Prairie Queen, the Fireman's Dance, and the Military Lancers were beautiful in their changes. This was one of Butcher Knife Bill's calls: he would yell, 'Gents to the right, don't you know enough to pass behind your pardner? Swing the one that looks so sweet — Now the one that dresses neat — Now the one with the little feet — Now the Belle of the b-a-l-l-room! Come on now, step lively! Ladies to the right — Swing the one that looks so shy — Then the one with the red necktie — Now the one that kicks so high — Now the best in the ball-r-o-o-m!'

There were two young fellows who came to camp, went broke, and gave dancing lessons to keep them on their feet, as it were. I hung around taking in all I could; learning just the proper distances to stand from one's partner; how to bow gracefully; just how lightly to bear one's hand on the 'gent's' shoulder; that the man should always have a large silk handkerchief in the hand which went around the lady's waist, so as not to soil the back of her dress; that one should dance first with the one he brings, also the dance after supper. This done, he was free to dance with all other ladies in the hall, till the 'Home, Sweet Home' waltz, and it showed he was peeved if he failed to dance at least once with every woman there. If he danced with the same one more than three times, it showed, if it was his girl, that he was pretty badly gone, and if it was some other fellow's girl, that he was looking for trouble. We thought it dreadful then for a man to smoke in the hall. If one was drinking, and lit his cigar before leaving the room, he was invited out by the floor manager. Some of them, most, I guess, drank at the dances; but you weren't supposed to know this, and when they go outside and pull a bottle from under the porch, and all in drinking distance take a swig, then return chewing a clove, or numerous cloves, they act as if, and you are supposed to believe that they were only taking the air. I learned the waltz — there will never be a more beautiful dance, especially the 'Blue Danube,' when danced smoothly and gracefully — and the Military Schottisch, Newport, Polka, Rye Waltz, Minuet, Breeze, Rockaway, and many others. One-Eye Thompson taught me the Varsovienne. He was one Mama did not care to have around. I couldn't see why, he had such a hearty laugh, so full of blarney, and good nature.

THE LIFE OF AN ORDINARY WOMAN

My heroes were Lincoln, John L. Sullivan, and Frances Folsom Cleveland. We had a lovely picture of her we got with coffee wrappers. She was beautiful and sweet, and my idea of a lady, and when I practiced being a lady I used her for an example. Yes, I practiced. I read somewhere of a woman who, one time at a dinner party, when a wasp flew down her dinner dress, stinging as it went, was so well bred that she smiled and never moved. I thought, 'If that is all it takes,' and caught a yellow jacket — pinching him a little to get him in good working order; then sat down before a flat rock, opened my apron at the neck, and slipped the yellow jacket down inside. He did his stuff, and I stood the test, and smiled at my only guest, a serious-looking dog.

We never tired of hearing of the wonders they were to have at the World's Fair. This was in 1893, and how I wanted to go, and hinted to every man in camp! Each one promised to send me, provided he could sell a mine in the mean time. Each day I inquire what the chances are for a sale, and go over the talks I am to have with Mrs. Potter Palmer, and rehearse backing away after meeting the Infanta Eulalia of Spain; but this is also the year of the slump in the price of silver and when the bottom fell out of the mining business. No mines were sold, so I never walked down the Midway.

Along about here I have been getting a few scattering letters from my father, who is living in Joseph, New Mexico. He was digging and selling the prehistoric pottery found there. One letter causes a great deal of excitement — he writes that if I care to visit him, he will send the money to do so. Mama feels sure that this is 'only a flash in the pan' and gives her consent, thinking the money will never come; but after watching the stage come in for weeks, being numberless times turned away from the post-office window with a shake of the head, one day the postmaster beams on me, and there is a registered letter. (The first I have ever seen and how I tremble as I sign for it!) On opening it, I find fifty dollars in bills. Think of so much money for my very own! Travelling must have been much cheaper than now, as this fifty paid for some clothes to start with, and on arriving in Magdalena, I had in the neighborhood of ten dollars left. I remember paying seventy-five cents for a meal at one of the Harvey Houses, and thinking it terrible, although how lovely, having so many wait on you, and think of having some of each dish. We thought a quarter enough to pay for any meal!

Mama has Nellie Smeltzer make me a black sateen princess — in this there were many gores, and from the waist up it was tight-fitting. It just came up under the arms and was kept in place by many steels stitched in each seam. Nellie got it too tight to start with, and where she let it out, the machine stitches always showed. She declared that I looked so dreadful, having no bust, that she was compelled to make cotton pads and fit in. With this I wore a white waist. The day comes when I am to leave. Mama has told me a hundred times to be a good girl, which doesn't even go in at one ear. The morning I leave they all kiss me — the first kiss I recall having from Mama — and as I am turning from her she gives me three pats on the back, which have always stayed with me. In these pats she conveyed so much love, so much mother worry, so many blessings to me, that I seemed enveloped in protection. The stage-driver adds his advice to that which has already been given me.

Charley Eat thinks I ought not to go, 'Coz youh muthah don't want you should. My mothah died when I was a little shaver' (tears always come in his eyes). 'Youah's has done a lot for you; I knew her in Bassickville, when youah fathah left.'

When we come to the train, I feel I am really seeing life. This little narrow-gauge train, consisting of a dinkey engine and two spitty, dusty cars, seems lovely to me. After this glorious ride, we come to Salida, and, oh, such crowds! I had been cautioned to look out for my pocketbook here, and did clutch it very, very hard. It was a round one with what we would call to-day King Tut figures pressed in it. It had no handle, but I tied a ribbon in for one. I have no hat, but, crossing the streets carefully, find a store, and get a little sailor, which sits up on top of my head. I look dreadful in almost any kind of a hat, but this sailor sitting on the back of my head must have been the limit. I think I had a gingham dress on — am saving the sateen to dress up in — and know I had a wide belt with a large buckle, and a striped coat which tied in front with cords — this was called a blazer. I think it was sort of a grandmother to the Norfolk which came later for sports wear.

MY FIRST SHOW

A boy I know has gone over with me, and we discover there is to be a show that night and decide to go. Now I had heard and read of theaters, and knew what was expected of one who was attending. Of course he should have sent me flowers, but I doubted if he knew what was done in the best circles; but I knew, and intended to have flowers, so I walk along the street, see a woman in her garden, and going boldly in, ask for a bouquet. She gives me one, and I fix it to wear, pin it on, also the sailor on the back of my head, and go to see my first show, 'The Black Crook.' We sit in the gallery, and I don't know whether to take my hat off or not, and while I was thrilled at the big (to me) theater, the way the curtain goes up, the crowd, and the acting, still I am disappointed in the show. It isn't like the ones I had read of, and, besides, I didn't see any one else with flowers on.

After many adventures, such as hanging off the train as far as I can going through the Royal Gorge, and being yanked in by a conductor; making my bed by putting two seats together; visiting with every one on the train, telling them who and what I was, and where I was going; I confided to one man, who looked oily around the eyes, that I was almost starved. He thought this dreadful, and suggested we get off at the next station and eat, says he will stand the treat, and that I am much too pretty a girl to go hungry. I agree with him, and am planning to get off; it is in the night, when my ever-faithful Guardian Angel takes a hand, and I tell the man to bring me a lunch on the train. He seems very disgusted, and although, after coaxing, consents to do so, I never see him again.

My father meets me in Magdalena and we take a stage for the three days' trip to the Tularosa. As we travel along through the sand under the hot sun, the mules going on a fast walk, I enjoy every minute of it, talking constantly to the stage-driver. Especially, I like it at night, when we stopped at Mexican ranches. The third evening we came to Joseph — just a post-office. The woman who kept the office, a Mexican married to a white man, had her house built on an old ruin, and much to my surprise, pieces of human bones were in the yard, where they had been dug up and left. One thing that impressed me was a skull, just the white line showing around it, where it had worked up through the hard-packed yard, and each time I came near it, I was very careful not to step on it.

Here we intended to stay, as my father was working in the ruins near by. After a supper of tortillas and frijoles, I am put to bed on a porch with two little Mexican girls. It is a very clean bed, but smells dreadfully, being made of the raw wool. We are wakened in the night by the mother coming and turning the covers back and shooting fine powder over us. It is for fleas, and the bed is full of them, coming from the near-by sheep pens. For three days I am here, enjoying it all, except the menu, which never changes; then I think it time to move on.

My father gets me a place to stay at a white man's ranch about three miles from there. These people have very little to get along with, but still are considered better off than most people here. There are a daughter and five sons. I am very popular with the sons — which, of course, pleases me. We have blessings before each meal and prayers at night, and I like it. The mother dips snuff, chewing a little stick, then dipping this into the snuff, then smearing it over her gums and teeth. Here I spend a very happy two months, thinking about Jim, dreaming, as all girls do, I expect, wondering if he would ever come to care for me. Some time before this, one day in school he is playing mumbly-peg and dares me to let him pitch his knife at my hand. At once my finger goes down, and almost as quick is split wide open by his good aim. When the blood runs, he looks so startled that I consider cutting my little finger off and sending it to him, to show how really in earnest I was. I am very glad to-day that I only considered it!

On moonlight nights, when I am homesick, I look at the moon and stars and am comforted by thinking that it is the same moon shining down on the folks at home. I will watch very carefully for the first star; when I see it I say, 'Star light, star bright, first star I've seen to-night. I wish I may, I wish I might, get the wish I wish to-night' — always wishing the same wish, that he love me.

Mama insists that I return home, and I make the return journey out with just the stage-driver and a Mexican who is on the road to prison in Socorro. It was on this trip I had the worst fright of my checkered life. At one of the stage stations, there is a sort of bar in the front room, around which are Mexicans, miners, and cowboys, most of them carrying guns. After supper, a Mexican girl shows me my room — just off this front room; she has evidently been sleeping here, because, before leaving, she reaches under the pillow, gets her gown, and takes it with her, telling me 'Good-night' as she leaves. At once I drop asleep, and some time in the night am brought wide awake by a heavy body against me, a still heavier arm across me, and still heavier breathing in my ear. I am stiff with terror, and know one of the cowboys has wandered into this dark room and is sleeping off a drunk beside me. I scarcely breathe — am perfectly willing to let 'sleeping dogs lie.' Thus I lie there till morning, expecting to see my hair snow white. When the first streaks of day come, I raise myself slowly to find the Mexican girl beside me.

CHAPTER XI

'They loved, but the story we cannot unfold.
They scorned, but the heart of the haughty is cold.
They grieved, but no wail from their slumber will come.
They joyed, but the tongue of their gladness is dumb.'
From 'Oh, why should the spirit of mortal be proud?'
(Jim spoke it at school.)

MY trip away seemed to help, as people said of me, 'She has quieted down and uses less slang.' While away, in trying my luck, besides wishing when I saw the first star, I would drop an apple peeling over my shoulder, trusting to fate that it would land in the shape of a *J* or *C*. Then, too, I would try this on the chair rounds, fence posts, or various things, 'He loves me, He loves me not'; always trying to pick the right number to make it come out 'He loves me'; and this may have helped, because Jim does pay a little attention to me. At Christmas time he sent me a rose-colored velvet workbox, fitted with 'footie' tools, which bent at the slightest excuse. I have the box after forty years. (No, sentiment never dies in a woman — I don't know how it is with a man.) At Easter came a booklet in the shape of a butterfly — on the first leaf was written:

'Had I the wings of the morning,
Would fly to you to-day.
But now can only whisper,
Soft whisper, hope and pray,
That in your heart for me,
There lies the same affection as in my heart for thee.

I thought this the finest thing ever written.

[135]

THE LIFE OF AN ORDINARY WOMAN

When at school, Jim sang, grinning,

> 'My Annie's eyes are blue,
> They'll be black 'fore I get through,'

I did not notice the sentiment — it was the first pronoun that thrilled me. When we were all locked out of the schoolhouse for punishment, how he wrenched at the bars running across the windows; how he threw his shoulder against the door, then bared his arm to show the welts; and how he could swell his muscles out! Of course, this was for the benefit of Winnie, but I take it all in, being disgusted with him, and all the time loving him in spite of myself. When we played Pum-Pum-Pullaway, on skates, I was so quick, so skillful, and fearless that Jim always chose me for his side. The girls called me the Amazon. I learned that these Amazons were women fighters who slashed their breasts when they interfered with drawing their bow strings.

Just to get to see Jim, I would make all sorts of excuses. It was in the spring. The creek would freeze each night, melt in the day, and run over the roads, and the mile to town was every step mud and slush, water and ice. I would begin, 'Say, Mama, why don't you go and see Mrs. Chipman?' (Jim's mother.) 'You haven't been there in a long time.'

'The roads are too bad.'

'I know, but I could go along and carry the diapers and sewing.'

'No,' she said, 'I don't want to leave the kids alone. I might go sometime and leave you with them —

anyway, the sign's not right.' She believed in 'signs,'
and would often not do a thing till the sign was right.
When anything did not turn out well, she 'guessed
the sign wasn't right.'

'Now, you know them kids are getting big enough
to stay alone, and we fight more when I am here.'
(We did!) 'And I will carry the baby some of the
way' (I knew she wouldn't let me), 'and Mrs. Chipman will think you are getting stuck up; and, besides,
she hasn't been well, and you might help her.'

This brings her, and I hauled this tired woman,
carrying a big baby, over a mile of dreadful road,
just to get a glimpse of a flat-nosed, thick-lipped
boy, with a look in his eye I could never resist. And,
if I remember right, Mama had the grippe over it,
too.

Now Jim begins to dance with me more often, and
I, although I am not looking at him, can tell across
the full length of the hall when he starts toward me,
and my heart almost chokes me. One day he is going
home from school with me, and we loiter by the cliff of
rocks below the Turn. He scratched our initials on
one of the rocks, where it stayed many years; and I,
if I should pass this place a million times, will always
glance at this rock and think of these happy times.
How innocent our talk! I call to mind now only a few
things he said. Once I said I wished I was a boy; my
heart thumped so when he said, 'I am glad you are
not.' Once he said, 'If there is a saint on earth, you
are it.' You see, I had him fooled. Then he said —
and I thought he was cussing — 'In this world there

is fools, damned fools, and God-damned fools.' I believe him.

One night we stopped where the primroses grow. Any one who has never seen or smelled one of these primroses has missed something. They grow on steep hillsides where it is dry, and seem to love an old mining dump. (Maybe they are the buried hopes coming forth!) They are as large around as a saucer, pure white, till they start to fade, then a delicate pink. Blossoming at night, many times a miner, coming off shift, will stop, tired as he is, and take some to a wife, who loved them, or, if he had no wife, stick one in the front of his dirty jumper. And the smell was like — well — like a primrose, and there is no other like it. This night I had been teasing Jim, leading him on, pushing and slapping, yet daring him to lay a finger on me. Then (of course, this is what I wanted all the time) he picked me up in his arms. I am afraid I hung over in no graceful manner, as I am tall — he saying he will hold me there till I kiss him. Oh, the gladness of that time! Of course, I struggle and kick, but he is strong, and I am held there till there is a kiss planted somewhere back of my ear (I think he is growing tired too), and my feet are on the ground again. And we go on, quite quiet now, only talking of the weather.

And the day we spend up Squirrel Gulch, our initials, and a heart, of course, carved in an aspen. Is the fluid one afterward sees coming from these old carved places — tears, shed, perhaps, for these innocent travelers on the road of life? We walk these few miles talking and laughing — no, no word of love — and finally come to a fallen log, where we rest. He decides he wants a lock of my hair. (Now this is getting interesting, and something like!) I make him coax awhile — don't see what he wants a lock of my hair for, and so on; then I say all right, but he must promise never to show it to any one. Now, how to get it off — we have no scissors, and only his jackknife. I unbraid my hair (feeling kind of naked) and we pull out a piece. It is long, yellow, and beautiful. He saws away with the knife, and while I am bubbling over with happiness, still this pulling is more than I can stand. We must think of another plan. We do. I kneel on the ground, my head against the log, he, on the other side, separates a strand from the head, pulls it over the log, and cuts it off with his knife. If some one had seen us, I wonder what they would have thought. We tie it with a piece of ribbon, and he puts it in his shirt pocket. Long afterward I bet him he hasn't it, and he opens a pocketbook and shows me this yellow curl lying there, and my jealous eyes see others there also, brown and black; but I have the satisfaction of thinking none so pretty as mine.

There is a Fourth-of-July celebration in Villa Grove. Times must have been extra flush with us then, because we are all to go. It must have been a job to get ready, as we were to stay all night, and there were never enough clothes to go around, so Mama must have made an extra supply. The Levons were going in style for once, in One-Eye Thompson's two-seated light wagon. Of course, I would have to make some excuse to go the day before, the real one being that Jim was in Salida and I hoped to see him before he went on up to camp. I get a ride down in an ore wagon, sitting in a chair, which is placed on the bottom of the wagon bed, back of the spring seat. I stay all night with a woman we have known before, and am so excited I never sleep a wink, telling this woman it is a headache that is keeping me awake. She comes to the bed and puts a wet cloth over my eyes.

Morning comes and I dress in my white dress — a lace scrim. It is made with a round yoke and a little stand-up collar — underneath this collar, and showing above it, is tied a narrow lavender ribbon, the bow and long ends hanging down my back, and, yes, with this dress I had a really lovely sash, lavender watered ribbon. When I was going to town for the money order to the Boston Store (using some of my Si Dore money), I stopped in at Eli's. I had not yet decided on the color I wanted — and asked him for his advice. 'Don't know how you would think an old fossil like me would know, but I've always liked lavender.' This was new to me, but I sent for it, and ever since I opened that bundle lavender has been my favorite shade.

The folks do not get in till about ten o'clock. I am at the hotel to meet them, and never before, till they commence to pile out of that wagon, do I realize there is such a mob of us. Frank and Jose are on deck at once, looking for trouble. They soon come running in to Mama, sitting there with two babies on her lap.

THE ODOR OF A GERANIUM

In the parlor is another woman, also with two children pressed up close to her.

'Oh, Mama, come see the drunk man, down on the ground, out by the backhouse, and a girl has just throwed dishwater over him.'

She calls to them to 'hush,' but not before this other little woman has heard, and grips her hands into the arm of the chair. Mama feels so sorry for her. She does not realize then that this drunken man will take the gold cure, and come to be one of the richest men in the country, leaving his children and his children's children well heeled.

After a while I see Jim. Yes, he does smell of whiskey. He borrows a cart and takes me out to the race-track. This is the happiest moment of my life, but on our return to town this is soon put a stop to. Henry — I don't know why this sudden burst of virtue — decides Jim isn't good enough for me to go with; but I am a convincing talker when on some subjects, and, after Mama has her cry out, she consents for me to go and have ice-cream with him, provided Jose goes along to keep an eye on me. The rest of this day I am followed by a fat little girl, in a bright pink outing-flannel dress, even when we go to a house for flowers for me to wear to the dance, geranium blossoms and leaves. (All my life the odor of a geranium brings back many memories; and times when I have been nervous and tired, cooking all day for boarders, or finishing a dress for some one, just to pin a rose geranium leaf on my dress has soothed and rested me.) At this dance I met the tall, slender boy whom I was years afterward to marry; but in my memories he has no connection with the geraniums.

Any one coming to see me had his courage with him, as there was no place to entertain except in the kitchen or the front room, and Mama's bed was here. Then if Henry wasn't in a good humor it was disagreeable, while if he was pleasant he read Bill Nye to them. There were always the children, and they were never quiet children; instead, with the exception of Ruth and Ed, each one had to have a hand in the conversation.

Once when Mama is sick, Jim is there. I am doing the cooking and feel very full of business. I have him stay for supper, and cook everything the house affords, call the kids out and threaten their lives if they don't perform as they should. Everything is going beautifully till Jim takes his first sip of tea, and (why can't things ever go right with me?) we both discover at the same time that I have made the tea in the same bucket that I had cooked onions in.

One day at school we are telling how strong we are. I have nothing to brag about, but am very thrilled to hear Jim say, 'Her strength is as the strength of ten, because her heart is pure.' He advised me what to do in case a man ever insulted me — and, oh, dear, I have never had occasion to use it — 'Don't cry and take on. Most of them do. It's a sign you are weakening. Don't get indignant; if you do, you have already weakened. Just walk away from there.' He really, I think, founded and built my moral sense, as

[142]

all my life I have wanted to be and do good in his sight. He objected to my running with Picnic Jim and especially going to Lil's. To please him I tried to forget the slang, and to-day I know he was instrumental in making me a worth-while woman, although any one who knew him would tell you that he was no good, a menace to all women — a drunkard. But a great deal of the good I may be able to do in this world, or any which I may have tried to give my children, they in turn to theirs, has come from the influence this boy had over me.

Before this time there was the boom in Creede. A good many from our town went. Dore was the only one I knew of who struck it rich; he discovered and sold the Commodore Mine. N. C. Creede, whom Creede was named for, at one time prospected near Bonanza and located the Twin Mine on Tuttle Creek. Prospectors reported that the ore in Creede was 'plumb lousy with native silver.'

Mrs. Adler was another who went from Bonanza. She was a large, dark-complexioned Frenchwoman; strong, good features, and dressed — this was a queer thing to us then — in a long, dark, tight-fitting skirt worn with a man's white shirt, no collar, the bosom starched and shiny always. Her hair was twisted on the back of her head, but she wore a man's hat on top of it. She was our barber, and, from what we could gather, a very entertaining one. Sometimes we would have thought her a man if it hadn't been for two beautiful daughters she had. She smoked cigars, and one would very seldom meet her when there wasn't one sticking from the corner of her mouth. She moved her barber shop to Creede and lived and barbered there till her death.

Jim borrowed five dollars from us to go to this new camp. His father had known N. C. Creede, and Jim thought he might get on the inside. I think he walked over the mountains, and this five dollars was to keep him till he made a raise, but it didn't work out this way and he came home again. There was a good deal of talk at our house as to whether he was trying to beat us out of that five. He didn't.

Next summer there is a scare of scarlet fever in town, and Jim and I urge his mother to go camping for a while, or till it blows over. We go to Ford Creek, the same place we children went the time it rained. Now I step lightly and happily, because I am to be with him for a time. We two do the dishes, snatching the towel from each other. When he seems to grab me roughly by the arm, it is only a caress. Always before there had been something mocking in his eyes; now this is gone. He shows me how to clean the frying-pans without washing them (and I think, 'Oh, aren't you wonderful!') by putting them on the fire, then, when they are hot, pour in some cold water, give it a swirl, and, see — they are clean.

I suppose every girl's new love is such a bright warming affair, but this was really my only love, except for Moosie when she was a baby (the only one I ever cuddled) and an affection for one dog, and I do not remember up to this time any one showing the least feeling for me in any way. I believe this is one reason why many girls go wrong — they are so hungry for love. (Not love as a man terms it, but love!) I went to bed that night with the wonder of it glowing in my heart and stomach. (I think I really feel more with my stomach than my heart!)

The next morning after breakfast we start up the creek, some with fish poles and some with pails for berries, I with a big bandanna handkerchief folded around my waist over my calico dress, and wearing some light gray stockings — cotton, three pairs for a quarter. As I came to each rock and log I pointed my toe, I thought, in a very graceful manner, being careful to show those stockings. (Yes, we were the same, thirty years ago, now, and will be to the end of time!) Jim and I never look at each other all morning, but, somehow, we are separated from the others. We go on filling our pails, talking of the most ordinary things, only to me he never said anything ordinary. (I wonder if he was as clever as I thought.) Too soon those pails are full.

Now we come to the foot of a high cliff and decide to climb up the face of it. He goes ahead, putting his fingers in the smallest openings, swinging by one arm to another foothold. I follow, sometimes hanging on to his hand, other times he can only reach a foot down to me, till, by struggling, resting, and going on, we come to a small opening near the top, just a narrow ledge. We are like two swallows up there. We drop breathless, and lie there for a time, far up here from the world; no one could see us, no one find us. It is warm, and we are tired, and think it would be fine to have a sleep. We do curl up, never touching, and he sleeps, but I dream, looking far up at the sky and far down the canyon, with a fear in my heart, not of him, but of what he would think of me. I must have been born with a complex against doing wrong, not through any fear of punishment from God or man. In these young days I wanted Jim's good opinion, and since have wanted my own.

Finally Jim awakens, rolls over, and looks at me — we were never so silent before — slips over and lays his arm across my shoulders — my heart beating so — and I can hear his. He bends over to kiss me. I object — then he coaxes, till finally I nod my head; this is too much for words, and he does kiss me — but even the joy of this first kiss is dimmed for me. Here comes my complex again. In all the books I had read, they first told you they loved you, asked you to be their wife, then kissed you, or rode or strode away. Nothing of love or marrying here, and — these torturing thoughts — I had heard such stories of him, drinking trips to Salida with other men — he was nineteen now — 'to have his teeth fixed.' (This expression came from Chippie McDonald, I think maybe he earned the title. He was, at home, a virtuous old gentleman with white sideburns, false teeth, and one glass eye. Once in Salida on Front Street, where he went 'to have his teeth fixed,' he got drunk, raised a rough-house, and the girls threw him out. Those who found him had quite a time finding the teeth and glass eye, he having lost both in the shuffle.) What if all these stories about Jim are true, and this is the way you go about it? Anyway, we sit there by the hour, not saying much, but — I am troubled — so is his mother.

She sends a younger son to hunt us, and he comes up the gulch (so small from our roost), calls and calls, and at last we answer, but do not let him see us. He knows we are hid in the cliff, and draws up his gun and takes a few shots at us just for luck, then turns and goes back toward camp. We now see it is evening. We have perched here a long time, and decide we had better move toward camp. Jim tries to find a way out. (We can't go down.) He gives me a little white stone, with petrified bugs on it. (I have it to-day. Aren't we women foolish?) We have to go up and struggle and fight again to get out. (Some day I am going back, and last year, after I was home from being sick, the first trip into the mountains I slipped away and tried the face of a cliff to see if I had lost the art of climbing. I hadn't.) We go down the gulch, a sobered pair. His mother meets us and says, 'We start for home in the morning,' and we did; but stop down on Saguache Creek to fish. I am more friendly with the other boy (as I have always been) than Jim. It is he who carries me across the creek, he, who, when I am combing my hair (there is such a pile of it), offers to help and I let him, while all my heart's yearnings, beatings, and burnings are for Jim. While we are around the camp-fire he never notices me, but somehow we are alone again, on the creek bank, in the thick willows, and I am in his arms. (The mosquitoes are devouring me alive, but I couldn't slap mos-

THE LIFE OF AN ORDINARY WOMAN

quitoes now, besides, I never felt them. But you should have seen my legs days afterward!)

Now he tells me we will be married some day. He seemed to know I was willing, and I was, and very happy now he had mentioned this marriage question, although I would have liked it more romantic. The delight of thinking he cared, and the thrill of his arms is with me yet. We stayed there by the creek a long time; so did the mosquitoes. I wonder if any pleasure is unalloyed? Well, no sorrow is either.

We come on home, getting into Bonanza before sundown. No telephones in these days; still Mama hears we are home almost as soon as we arrive. I have supper with the Chipmans and Jim goes to my home in Exchequer with me, to carry the berries. It is coming night. On the road we talk only of ordinary subjects. It is quite dark when we come to the old Kelly smelter. After picking our way across the slag dump, we come to a place where a board is torn off the building, and we slip inside, find some old timbers, and sit on them. I feel no fear. Aren't we to be married? We crowd closer together, his arms around me, and really have a lovely time, or at least I do. Now I kiss in return and enjoy it. He commences to shiver and tremble. I say, 'Let us go on, you are cold.'

'No, I am not cold, am burning up — but we will go on.'

And although afterward there were stories of a trail of women from Colorado through New Mexico and on to South America (one a Governor's wife!) all honor to this boy. He did go out through the opening in the wall, helping this foolish lovesick girl after him.

But — her little hour is almost over. I wish there were more of them. On we go through the dark, hand in hand. On the upper road we see some one coming through the trees. (A dropping of hands.) We come up to them, and oh, Lord, it is Mama with the buggy whip in her hands. Jose is trudging at her side.

'Young lady, I'm going to tend to you. If you think you can rampse around all night, why, you're off your base, that's all!'

I begin to talk very fast to head her off, and turn to Jim. 'Give me those berries.'

This 'those' is the last straw to Mama's burden. 'I'll "those" you — trying to talk high-toned! Now, you come home, and you go home, you low-down ——' but he has gone. A good thing, too, as Mama didn't mince words when started. Jose is the only one who got any enjoyment out of this. I am a good talker, especially when my heart is in it, as it is this night. Before we have gone the last mile, I have her crying, she was so tender-hearted; and, somehow that night I convince her she need never give me another thought in her life, I would be all right always.

Next day Jim is seen fishing below the house (not a fish along there in years), and Mama goes out and makes her peace with him and all is serene again; but alas, never the same. He never asks me to go to a dance with him, and pays very little attention to me. I have such a heavy heart, although no one ever knows. One day I meet him on the street and start to speak. He says, 'Don't you dare speak to me'; and I pass on, troubled and wondering, feeling brave because I 'never told my love, but let the worm i' the bud feed on my damask cheek.' I was able to laugh at my other admirers, but never him. One night we are at a party, and he and I are alone for a minute. I (poor simp) lay my hand on his arm; he throws it off, and this evening is spoiled. I did not shine at parties, anyway; I did not have enough concentration to play either whist or euchre, and could play no instrument, nor sing.

If I were going to a dance (he had stopped dancing with me even), I would sing over and over, 'I'll be all smiles to-night, love, I'll be all smiles to-night. Tho' my heart may break to-morrow, I'll be all smiles to-night.' At one dance we are dancing a set called the Prairie Queen. In it you take your places as for a quadrille. It is danced something like the lancers (those beautiful old lancers, I wish now the folks could see some of us who knew how, go through with them), only some of the changes were waltzed, and some were a polka. In changing, I come to Jim, never saying a word, but looking all I felt, I imagine, as he held me tightly, putting his cheek down close to mine. The evening was brighter after this.

CHAPTER XII

Of all sad words of tongue or pen,
The saddest are these, 'It might have been.'
But sadder these we daily see,
'It is, but hadn't ought to be.'

AND now a man comes to town who has been horn-swoggled into buying one of the mines. For fifty-seven years there has always been some one to stake his money on a mine in Bonanza. He had made money in Ouray, had met a girl there, sent her away to be educated, then married her. He brought her to Bonanza, and with them a sister and her husband from Pennsylvania. They, too, had money when they came, but all left dead broke. They got one of the largest and best houses in town, moving in carloads of furniture from the East. (It soon commenced to crack and draw apart with the dry climate.) With them also was a brother — now we are coming to it, very good-looking, well dressed, and brave enough even in these days to go smooth-shaved.

The first time he saw me, he fell in love with me, arranged a meeting, and asked me to marry him at once. He came up to and surpassed the lovers in any of the books I had read. Of course, I was pleased, but not especially thrilled. He was a very intense and passionate lover. I learned this word 'passionate' from him, and what it meant — in fact, learned many things that he tried to explain to this simple girl, all perfectly regular, things that boys and girls talk on every corner now, but which were never mentioned then. It is all right, we are engaged, yes, we are, and planning a wedding.

These are the first things I fix for my future home and life: little bags of pieces of silk — those I had seen had bangles on the bottom; I had no bangles, but made some by boring holes in pennies and sewing these on. These bags of different colors were quite the thing to hang from the corner of a picture; little balls made of milkweed silk, colored, and tied with baby ribbon, were supposed to be very effective for this, too. If you didn't have a 'throw' over the right-hand corner of each picture, well — you just weren't in it, that's all. Throws were used, too, on the corners of stands, letting the long-fringed or hand-painted ends hang down. It would be held in place either by a shell, a specimen, or a piece of glass brought from the World's Fair with a picture of one of the buildings on it. In addition to the little bags, I made a crazy-work lambrequin. Wasn't it awful?

His sisters are not any too well pleased, and I don't blame them. Any of our tribe going to or coming from town passed their house. When they see he is in dead earnest, they hold out the flag of truce by sending word to me to come and let them dress 'that wonderful hair.' He discovered I had 'beautiful hands, legs and feet, and wonderful blue eyes'; in fact, 'If your teeth were closer together, and I will attend to them as soon as we are married, you would be a raving beauty.' (You see he was in love and blind.)

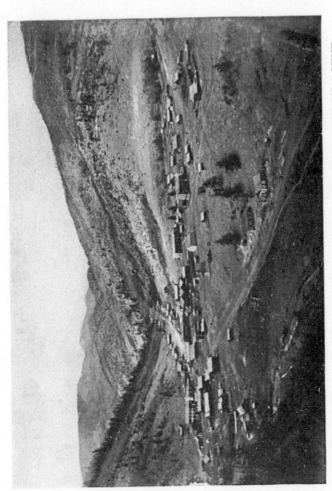

'THERE HAS ALWAYS BEEN SOME ONE TO STAKE HIS MONEY ON A MINE
IN BONANZA'

ENGAGED

He showed me every attention, getting a top buggy to drive me to the dances in. One night he upset us, too, but no harm was done except that my knees were mighty weak for the first waltz. The first time I was ever in Saguache he took me to a dance. On this trip he bought me a large black satin fan, and gave me a stickpin with a small diamond in it that his sister had given him. Some of the men who knew us both thought it a joke to dope a drink for him. (I know we usually say they are doped when it isn't straight goods.) This was done, we understood, by dropping cigar ashes in the whiskey. This knocked him out, and a friend had to walk him for hours to bring him out of it in time for the dance.

I am really having the best time in my life and look forward to being married, and do have my wedding dress made — the Si Dore money still holding out. It was a sage-green cashmere, made with a gored skirt and lined and interlined with goods called fiber chamois; on the bottom was a circular flounce headed with a narrow silk braid. The tight-fitting waist was made with a puffed silk yoke running down in points; around and over this was the braid; the sleeves had three puffs in them held down by the goods and braid. It was quite the best thing I had ever had. As hard up as I am to-day, I would give a hundred dollars to have it. I take care of the dressmaker's children for making part of it, and Mama gives her the balance. No, Nellie Smeltzer wasn't going to get a chance to whack into this.

Now Jim sees how popular I am, and starts to pay

[153]

attention to me. He can make me tremble by looking at me, and so weak by touching me. (I can almost believe that Ben Bolt business.) Jamie (his name was James also, but I couldn't bear to call him this, so invented the other) was frantic with jealousy, but through it all he never said one cross word to me or blamed me in any way. (I think he was the only man who ever really loved me.) These are troubled times at our house. Mama (so good-hearted) cries over the one who happens to be talking to her at the time. (She really knows Jamie ought to have all her sympathy, but Jim has a way with women.) Jim explains the cause of his coldness. He said that the boy who was out berrying with us told him a story about me which he believed for a time. I have always had my doubts of this; as I think Jim soon grew tired of any one woman.

Jamie wrote this acrostic in my autograph album ——

'Annex all graces to this gentle name,
Nor fear she will at all truth put to shame.
Nice is her sense of what pertains to good,
In virtue's brightest light she aye has stood,
Enshrined in all that is best of womanhood.'

While Jim simply wrote, 'Best wishes for your future happiness.' He was never one to wear his heart on his sleeve.

Sometime along here my father comes to Colorado and arrives in Bonanza to see me. He stays at our house. One day while he was there, Mama has a session of the all-day visitors so popular then; among them a jolly fat widow, a very worth-while woman. She and my father hit it off at once, are in love, engaged, and married in a few weeks, and I, as usual, spoil my chances and 'break my plate,' in her good opinion, by writing my grandfather — not a word of truth in it, I just wanted to be romantic — 'They are to be married, but am sure his heart is with Fan' (his second wife).

When they leave Bonanza, Jamie has my father get our engagement ring in Salida and send him, but Jim says our engagement still stands. I recall leaning on the window and thinking, 'Did ever such trouble come to a girl before?' — and run over in my mind anything I had read of a girl being engaged to two men at once and how she handled it.

Mama, trying not to play favorites, asked both to a Sunday dinner, killing one of her precious chickens and making ice-cream. This was no small job, as first the ice had to be got from an old mine or prospect hole where the water had dripped and frozen. After she has sent one or more children after the ice, cautioning them to 'get it clean, no rocks or talc in it; don't be afraid to get plenty, and get home before it all melts on you,' she has in the mean time made her custard and it is now in a ten-pound lard pail, in the creek cooling. Once we had the dreadful misfortune to have it upset. When the ice comes, it is pounded fine and put in a tub, a good deal of salt sprinkled in, the custard is brought from the creek, the cream added (and how carefully that precious cream is poured in and measured with the eye, thinking of the butter it would have made, 'pint a pound, the world around'), the lid then put on the bucket and placed in a nest in the ice. Now the real work commences; we take turnabout twisting that pail with one hand, halfway round, then halfway back, and it seems endless; you grow so tired even with the reward of icecream in sight. When it grows harder, it is commencing to freeze, then Mama comes and opens it, scraping it off the sides, and, if you are not complaining too bitterly, she lets you lick the spoon. It seemed to take hours to freeze it this way; still I have known this tireless woman to freeze enough for a dance in this manner, freezing one pail, then emptying and packing it, and going after another.

To this Sunday dinner Jim comes early in the morning. Jamie knows of it and, not to be outdone, soon follows. The chicken is not on yet, and Mama, so confused, puts the chicken on without cleaning the gizzard, and she cries into the bread. Jamie gets so wrought up that he goes out and paces the yard. Mama goes to console him. He says, 'To think of him in there talking to my wife,' and at this, through her tears, Mama has one of her big laughs. Then dinner, gizzard, rocks, and all are served; but I remember no more of this day.

I can come to no decision. (I would like to have them both, one to love and one to love me —wonder if this is not the cause of a good many triangles?) I want Jim so — but know all the time he doesn't mean it — and Jamie wants me. They get together and have some sort of an understanding, and Jamie gives

BIDDING JIM GOOD-BYE

Jim one evening to tell me good-bye. (How Jim must have laughed in his sleeve!) I heard afterward Jamie walked the hills raging. Jim comes, and what a wonderful night! He finds I have learned all the arts and graces of love-making (he was born with them). We say good-bye — dozens of times — and he leaves, after having me promise that if ever I am in trouble and he could help me to send for him and he would come from the ends of the earth. This old, foolish, and dear promise, always given and never used! Had I sent for him each time I have been in trouble, he would have had a steady job. I hear he is making preparations to leave town, but am too heartsick to care much. I do go to town and parade up one side and down the other. He sees me, but never turns his head.

A day later, just as it is getting light, some one is in my room. I am wide awake at once, but never speak. It is Jim come to tell me good-bye for the last time. He leans over the bed, takes me in his arms, kisses me, and walks out. And to this day this brings a lump in my throat, that I have no night dress on, or no sheets on the bed — am sleeping in my undershirt, a gray cotton long-sleeved affair with gussets in front, which I did not need. I never see Jim again, but — there is never a day in all these years I do not think of him, never a day, up to nine years ago, that I have not dressed for him, thinking and hoping he might come.

And — I thank the Lord for this love; I have been able to understand life so much better. Many people have said to me, 'Do you think there is anything in

this love you read about?' I say, 'I don't know.'
They would not understand. But — I know there is.
This is the first time I have ever written or spoken of
this.

Just the other night I dreamed that it was my wedding day. I am very happy and run eagerly forward
to meet my lover — Jim — thinking, as I run — because of the great love I have for him — of our life
and the wonderful children we will have. When I
reach him, he is holding out both hands to me. I
awaken to find myself a very sick, almost old woman
with grown children. The man I ran to meet was not
their father — still, mine are wonderful children.
Romance is not nor ever will be dead, not in the heart
of a woman, anyway.

I go on getting ready to be married, half-hearted,
but I want to leave home. Henry is making it disagreeable for me, and we both make it disagreeable for
Mama. By now Jamie's brother-in-law's mine peters
out, so does the money, and they leave. Jamie stays
on; there is no work and he is hard up, but intends to
marry, anyway; the old story, 'If I had my little woman to give me courage, am sure things would break
easier, and two can live as cheaply as one.' He has
the cabin picked out where we are to live (the one-
room one where Jose was born). One night we write
the invitations and get them ready. Lil has whispered
to Mama that if she gets one she intends to give us a
tablecloth. We hadn't planned on her, but we needed
the tablecloth, so her name is written down. For
some reason they are not mailed — Mama saying it is

bad luck to postpone a wedding — and now times are getting harder. The mines have closed. Whoever has been running them goes out to try and raise money (usually leaving one or more paydays due). The stage is watched each day for their return; the people who are supposed to get mail from them are followed to the post-office and their mail examined over their shoulders.

This is the first question that is asked of another — even the children — 'Have you heard anything of the Bonanza?' — Sosthenis, Rawley, or whatever mine it happens to be at the time — 'starting?'

'Not exactly, but Poole — you know he is on to everything — was overheard telling Eli that he heard Long John tell Paul and I-Say Jaques to keep their teams up — there would be more ore to haul.'

Nine times out of ten the man who went to raise money never returned, and for forty years a group of these people have lived on hope of 'things opening up in the spring.' How they would get in their winter wood, bank and daub their houses, do their own assessments, each one having one or more prospective mines — or maybe try to lease a mine, paying a royalty on each carload of ore shipped! Ore in Bonanza runs in pockets, and while all the leasers made fair wages, if they were fortunate enough to run into a pocket of ore there was a chance of being 'well heeled.' The Exchequer, Empress Josephine, Revenue, Cornucopia, and others were good leasers.

Just now Jamie gets a lease on the Little Jenny, but makes nothing. He said he was so lucky in love that he could not expect much in a mining way. Somewhere along here a leaser who has taught school gets a catalogue from a summer institute to be held in Cañon City, and thinks it would be fine for me to go. He must have been joking, but I wasn't, and made up my mind to go. The catalogue reads fine, says it will cost very little, many advantages to be derived, and so on. First I spring it on Mama; she can't see why, and, 'Where would the money come from?' But I enlarge on all the benefits I would get from it (lots of times it stood me in hand that she could not read) and finally convince her. But still, 'Where is the money to come from?' Now this shows a woman's sense of honor, or the lack of it — I know Jamie would let me have it, only it isn't 'nice' to take money from a man, so I talk Mama into asking him for a loan (knowing it could never be paid), and this gullible mother — we all are — asks him for it, gets it, and never ceases to worry about it to the day of her death. But I (youth is so selfish) go blithely on — Mama so full of fears, and Jamie hating to see me go.

He was very fond of children and would grow enthusiastic over 'our' baby (in these days it was dreadful to talk to girls of babies, but he did). It was to be a girl (I never let on I was to be a 'barn doe'), with my hair and eyes. (I think she was to take her teeth after him!) My first child did have my hair and eyes and looked as he pictured she would. I wonder what my life would have been, married to him? In better places, over smoother roads, I imagine, but one doesn't develop much strength on a smooth road; besides, they are tiresome.

A SUMMER INSTITUTE

I start with forty dollars for tuition, railroad and stage fare, room and board. This is to do for the full term of nine weeks. I arrive, get a room and a place to board (it is much higher than the catalogue says), and start to school. So many girls and few boys, I am afraid it will not be interesting; and it isn't. While I have been having the pick of all the boys in camp, no one looks at me here. I don't know how I ever get by to enter, or how they ever place me, but they do. I am sure they are appalled at my spelling and arithmetic, but I am bubbling over with good humor and high spirits, and I expect I was a relief from the usual serious teacher type. Perhaps if the forty had held out, I might have got a certificate, but it doesn't. One day on the street I tell some girls my money is gone and I will have to go home.

One of them asked, 'Why don't you go to work?'

'How do you get a job?'

'Why, I'll go right in this house, get you one, then get me one in the next.' (The confidence of this girl! I bet she has gone far.)

I have such faith in her, and know we both will have a place to-morrow, but in the mean time, 'Let's have a hot tamale.' We do, and it is the end of my higher education — makes me dreadfully sick, and I have to go home. (That tamale may have changed my career.) To-day all that remains in my mind is a trip to the penitentiary. They are having an entertainment; the seats are all taken, and I climb on top of a radiator and am very corrugated when the entertainment is over. One prisoner sings 'After the Ball,' the first time for me to hear it. The boy murderer (only nine, he stayed till twenty-one) does a turn; also Parker, the man-eater.[1] (I don't think he ever did, only had it with him 'in case.')

When I arrive home I find that Jamie is sick and has had to leave camp, expecting to return for me soon.

After a time I make a trip to Monarch, another mining camp — a very picturesque one, the mountains rising very high, and so straight it seems almost impossible for the miners to keep a foothold going to or coming from work. Down in the gulch, far below the mines, but in sight of them, is a little camp running along either side of the small stream. Most of the homes are log cabins, as it is very cold here in the winter. My father was working on the Mary Madonna Mine. I was interested in a play that the school teacher was giving for Christmas, in which I was to be an angel with large scrim wings.

One day, not long ago, I ran across a letter Jose had written for Mama. I can almost see them gathered around the long oilcloth-covered table, Mama looking up from her sewing long enough to tell Jose what to put down. 'We want you to come home. Brother' — the name they all called Jamie — 'is home and is so sick, he can't lie down in bed — sleeps in one of the

---

[1] There seem to be several versions of this mountain idyl. According to the most picturesque the man Parker or Packard was found wandering about, far from civilization, carrying a human leg. He and two companions had been missing for some time. He was convicted and sentenced to life imprisonment for having killed the other two men for food. (*Ed.*)

big chairs. Mama rubs his heart. Mama says she has saved some on the forty dollars she owes Brother. He needs it. She says if you will come home she will get you a new dress, not a cheap one, a good one. She says she knows you would make a pretty angel; come home and be a good girl.' (The pity of it all!)

I do go home before Christmas, too. Jamie is better. He gives me three books, beautifully bound; on the fly leaf of each is written, 'From Jamie to Anna.' He never called me 'Annie.' One is 'Pilgrim's Progress.' (Think of it, you flaming youths of to-day!) All that I remember from it is:

> 'He that is down, need fear no fall,
> He that is low, no pride,
> He that is humble, ever shall
> Have God to be his guide.'

and,

> 'I am content with what I have,
> Little be it, or much:
> But, God, contentment still I crave,
> Because thou savest such.'

A copy of 'Lucile,' which I liked, and Byron's poems, which I did not like at all. Too Don Juany!

I do not remember when Jamie left again; our parting, and everything in connection with it is vague. (I expect it is because I like to forget things not to my credit. From him I learned that a man can feel a good, unselfish love for a woman, and that it is an honor, and something to be proud of, to have had such a love.) He leaves to be with his sister. I am happy to get his letters, but as each one is handed me by the postmaster, there is a feeling of disappointment that it isn't from Jim.

This spring was the first I knew Easter meant anything more than to eat all the eggs you could get or hold. A woman had a Sunday School and was giving an entertainment. We had new hats, and, best of all, she sent out and bought a few cut flowers. These meant so much to us, as our wild flowers do not bloom till late in June. We were very thrilled to carry home a Shasta daisy — at least this is what I drew. It was to this woman I confided my feeling for Jim. She was very religious and thought she knew him, so was duly shocked and explained to me, 'It couldn't be love — must be animal magnetism.' This sounded dreadful, so I said no more. I knew, whatever it was, it hurt, and I would never recover. I never have.

I am too full of my own troubles to think much of other people, and fill the days in longing and dreaming, looking at the same mountains, the same trees in the same places, and thinking, 'Is there no end?' (How I longed to look at these same things in a few short months!)

All this time Mama is sick, but no attention paid her. Another baby is coming. If it ever enters my head that she is not so well, I think this is all the trouble — and am afraid that I had a feeling of disgust that she would have so many. For a long time she complained, not doing as much work as formerly, resting more, her laugh coming less often; still we do not pay much attention, she has always been so strong. Now in her lighter moments she would not sing ——

'Oh, darkies, have you seen Old Massa with the mustache on
    his face?
He sta'ted down the road this maunin' lak he gwine to leave
    the place.
Ole Massa run away, the darkey stay, ho-ho,
It must be now the Kingdom's comin' in the year of jubilo.
He's six feet one way and seven feet the odder, an' he weighs
    six hundred pound;
His coat is so big he couldn't pay the tailor, an' it won't reach
    halfway round.
He saw the smoke way up the ribber where the Lincum gun
    boats lay,
He put on his hat an' he left mighty sudden, an' I spose he's
    runned away.'

We never heard her sing again.

She thinks she has a cancer or a tapeworm; finally decides it is a tapeworm, because when she eats a bite of something she is relieved. We really thought she was feeding that worm — why didn't Henry do something? We others were so ignorant, all selfish — I do not remember trying to make it any easier for her. (No wonder I have had to work so hard since!)

This fall, when school starts, I coax her to let me take all the kids of school age and live in town in Eli's house. (He is away.) I am seventeen that spring, the rest all younger. Finally she consents and we go. We get things from home to eat each week. I fix our meals — quite nice ones, as I remember — dream of Jim, and read Shakespeare; reading and living — almost — in those old forgotten times. Each day when I

dress, I think, 'To-day he may come.' I had a black
lace basque with a tiny V neck, but this I thought too
low, so wore a black velvet band around my throat. I
was very careful of this basque for fear it would wear
out before he returned, and I wanted so much to have
him see me in it.

One day Mama walks down to see us, and, as soon
as she gets in, lies on the bed. This frightens me, as
she is not one to lie down in the daytime. After she
eats she is rested and drags this weary mile home
again, probably carrying one or both of the children
with her part way. When Dr. Melvin is in town, she
does say something to him, and I think he puts her on
a diet, but she is like Buck, thinks, 'You might as
well let the moon shine down your throat' as to eat
some of the things you are supposed to.

Now it is just before Christmas. We are all in a
play; this is one of my excuses for staying in town, to
practice.

One day Charley Eat comes to the cabin and reads
the riot act to me. 'By gracious, Annie, don't see
what you mean. Yo' muthah is sick and you, by all the
rights in the case, should be home.' (Again she has
had the doctor; he has pronounced it diabetes, but
this has no meaning to me.) 'By gracious, I thought
better of you.'

We all go home at once, but it is too late. She is up
and down. This wonderful spirit will not give up to
go to bed, but the day before Christmas she does go to
bed and soon is unconscious. A man is sent — no, he
volunteers — to go to Saguache for the doctor. It is

seventeen miles over Ute Pass — the snow in dreadful drifts, but he makes it, sometimes riding, other times leading his horse and breaking trail. He is all night, then starts the doctor, who has a horse and buggy, on his forty-mile trip around by the Grove.

We are alone with her this Christmas Eve. The children are all in bed, Henry is reading, I am jumping every moment to wait on her who breathes so dreadfully, in gasps, and tries to talk — both hands on her side where this unborn child is knotted up. Her hands never leave this place; I never knew whether it was because of pain or trying to protect it. Dozens of times she would get up, I trying to help, then back to bed again. Henry reads on, but we disturb him. He says, 'Oh, let her alone; she don't know what she is talking about'; then he goes to bed, and I am alone with my regrets and fears. How I haunt the window, watching for the doctor's team to come around the Turn! After ages he does come, and many others with him. (Nowhere on earth are neighbors so good as in mining camps.) This dreadful breathing never quits, till I wish she would die and get away from the struggle of it. It beat on my brain so that I heard it, waking and sleeping, for many days. Henry is in bed yet. The women talk over his unfeelingness, and one goes in and asks him how he can sleep and his wife dying, but this does not faze him. He was born without any feeling.

This day she dies. What a relief not to hear the breathing! The rest is confusion, people coming and going; the smell of carbolic acid; I with the most dreadful nosebleed — quarts, it seems, and I hope it never stops; people bringing clothes for the funeral; others cooking; the Christmas things sent us from the tree; people talking in whispers, 'What will become of them?' Then they dress her. I always hated that dress, but she had it because Henry liked plaids. This did not button now, but a white lace fichu was arranged in front.

The next picture is of us standing around her coffin, seven of us, the oldest seventeen, the youngest but three. It is the baby and the fifteen-year-old boy who 'take on' the hardest. I suppose they both realize that it is they who will need her the most.

Then the men carry the coffin up the steep hillside through the deep snow, to a place under a pine tree on the mesa, the mesa which she had loved so, from its carpet of kinnikinnic in the shady places to its white friendly daisies in the sunny spots.

How many, many times crossing here, going to or coming from town, she had longed to stop and rest under the whispering quaking asp, but must always hurry on to do for her children. She has rested here many years now.

On the stone it says, 'Rachel Levon, age thirty-nine.' Oh, the pity of it! A brave soldier killed on duty.

CHAPTER XIII

I could never tell if it was Opportunity or the Wolf knocking.
A. E.

I AT once insist we move to town, taking the stand that it is easier for Henry to walk this mile through snow to work than it is for the children to walk it to school. (Then too, I want to leave the sound of that dreadful breathing.) Now my wishes are considered, as I decide to stay home and take care of the children. And so we move, Henry and I burying the hatchet. He works, and I do my duty nobly, cooking good meals, and keeping house. And how I do sew those children up, making all Mama's things over for them! I remember one dress for Jose, which in one place refused to come together, so I made a bow of ribbon and sewed over it — it was in a mighty conspicuous place, too. People are very kind and helpful to us.

I have many beaus (don't like this word, but it was the one we used, or 'fellows,' and I like that less) since they find I can do something besides dance. There was one — one of the dancing teachers — who wrote poetry to me, one poem beginning, 'In the springtime, gentle Annie, when the sweet-scented flowers cast their fragrance about you ——' Another he had typed and I am copying it. (Yes, a woman keeps a lot of junk!)

> 'Dare I murmur the name of this being,
> Man's rescuer, his heaven, his all?
> Nay, not yet awhile, I am dreaming.
> Nay, not till I outlive my fall.

[169]

THE LIFE OF AN ORDINARY WOMAN

'On earth, 'tis man's greatest blessing,
To guide him aright, so to speak,
Though he be vile and deceiving,
This light doth his heart ever seek.

'Ah, man, will you never awaken
And bless this bright, shining light?
'Tis love, 'tis woman whom you have forsaken;
She would save you from sin and your miserable plight.'

No, I never quite got it, and never appreciated the
giving of it, because it was the cause of too much fun
being made of me in the family. Henry would say,
'Wouldn't it jar you? Willie I. writing Annie poetry.
Bet he's woozy.' And — for once Henry was right.
This boy, who was such a fine dancer, a good singer,
and had lovely manners and morals, afterward lost
his leg, and his ambition seemed to go at the same
time. He lived a lonely life in an old tunnel, sawing
wood for just enough to exist on. For many years he
has been in the State Hospital for the Insane. If Henry
were alive he would say, 'I told you that long ago.
You can't fool your Uncle Henry when they start to
spout poetry. There's a screw loose somewhere.'

Another one, our school teacher, I did not care for.
He rubbed up against you when you walked, and was
an ardent lover. One night, in a very tense moment
(the kids are having their baths, and are quarreling
which will get to bathe first — in a little tin washtub,
the water heated and carried upstairs, they get in two
at a time — all in the same water, so the last two
find it rather cold), Jose is knocked downstairs, and
rolled out on us, back first, naked and unashamed.

One night I am at a dance later than Henry likes, so he locks the door. I come home, find it so, go to the woodpile, get the axe, and chop a panel out. We neither of us mention it again.

That spring or the next I am at a neighbor's house. They have been especially good to me; in fact, Rosie has been one of the best friends I have ever had. For some reason I am lying on the floor, and look up and see in the doorway, filling it from side to side and from top to bottom, it seems, a remarkably startling looking man — coal-black hair combed straight back (in these times men parted it on the left side bringing it down over their foreheads in scallops), high arched black brows over very dark eyes (nothing soft or merry in these eyes), a scar running across one cheek. He was beautifully dressed, in a tan suit, shoes and tie to match, the best manicured nails I had ever seen on a man. He said nothing, just stood and smiled (he said afterward he was noticing what good hips I had), and right there he had the Indian sign on me.

He was always a silent, brooding sort of man. I started in at once to show off. He was a cousin of Rosie's whom she had not seen in years, had not even known where he was. We never do find out. 'Where did you get that scar on your side?' 'British Columbia. Was knifed.' 'And the one on your leg?' 'Just a shooting scrape.' He had scars all over him, and I gathered, not from him, however, that he had led a rough, tough life. At this time he is thirty-two. He starts coming to the house at once, never saying much, only sitting and brooding; but this gets us women,

I think — we give them credit for thinking, when they are merely lazy.

Now comes news of a strike in Gunnison County; free gold, plenty of it, just waiting to be mined. George (this man's name) and Rosie's husband grubstake two men and send them over. Good reports come fast. The Cunins have sold the Lucky Strike for twenty thousand dollars and people are rushing in and have started a town at Iris, just on the boundary line between Saguache and Gunnison Counties. Here was and is an old mine, the Denver City, and to-day men pay taxes on it. We are all enthusiastic. John, Rosie's husband, is going over and start a livery barn. The news comes that the Gilbert boys have made a strike. (They are the grubstaked ones.)

Now, since George has a mine in view, he is more interesting than ever. He is leaving soon, and, I don't know whether this was my own idea or not, but expect it was — I had always had an urge to see a booming camp — I decide to go to this new camp, taking all the children with me, also the cows. I plan to make our fortune selling milk, and Henry lets us go. I expect he was glad of the rest. Ever faithful Charley Eat comes down and tries to talk me out of it, but George, John, and Rosie want me to go. They must have had lots of faith in me to fool with this mess of kids; anyway we load in John's wagons, the oldest boys driving the cows and horses. We camp two or three nights on the road, and finally arrive. The mine is showing up better all the time.

Every man you meet has a piece of quartz, which

he licks with his tongue and passes on to the next one (this makes the specks of gold show up better), who licks and looks in his turn. In Iris town lots are selling, but we intend to have a town of our own, so we go a mile and a half over the hill where there is a spring, and stake out Chance. The name of the new mine is The Only Chance. We pitch our tents and start in. I don't know where I got that tent — I expect I borrowed it, as I ever had my gall with me — and we started to peddle milk at once, poor faithful Ed doing most of the work, milking and carrying it to Iris.

People pour into camp, starting to build cabins, and it looks like a sure-enough boom. There had been no real lovemaking between George and me, not that I remember, anyway. There could not have been much in this small tent with six children watching. I do recall him on a load of ore starting to Gunnison, leaning over the side and saying, 'Good-bye' — now almost a whisper — 'Darling.'

Two things stand out in my mind. One morning I go outside to look for a ham left hanging on the back of the tent and find it missing. This is a calamity. Then I am taking a bath in a tub much too small; the tent flaps are all tied, but I look up to see a man pulling them apart and looking in.

'Go away,' I said, 'I'm taking a bath.'

'Yes,' he answered, 'I see you are' — and goes.

The Gilbert boys sell their share of the mine for ten thousand dollars and George and John could have sold also, but wanted more. The Gilberts (that

sounds like R. L. S.) had almost lived at our house
and Mama had cooked endless meals for them; but,
even though they know how hard up we are, they
never treat one of us — never even give one of the
children a dime. This was unheard of in mining
camps; when one made a sale he treated, but never
mind, Fate paid them back.

Along here Joe Sampliner, whom George had
known years before in Ouray, asks George to visit
him in Grand Junction, and to bring his girl with him.
(Think maybe Joe had been putting up some cash
too.) George tells me, and I am crazy to go, but —
'Know it wouldn't be right and have no clothes.'

'Of course it's right, or Joe wouldn't ask you; he is
having some people from Silverton, and one of them
is a girl.' (I found afterward she was to marry Bert
Sampliner.) He goes on, 'And we will get you some
clothes in Gunnison.'

I am conscience-stricken at leaving the children,
but — 'Rosie says she will look after them.'

So we go, I knowing it wasn't the right thing to be
running around with a man, much less to let him buy
clothes for me; but this was my first time to really see
anything. We are off on an ore team to Gunnison. I
think I am wearing the sage green that was to have
been my wedding dress; I do know that he buys me a
hat. It is the tail end of summer and not much choice,
the winter ones not in yet, so we choose a white lace
straw loaded with pale blue flowers.

We stay at the La Veta, and I am staggered at so
much elegance. I am shown my room, George, in a

[174]

very gentlemanly manner, only coming to the door. On this whole trip he is more than discreet; but I never feel right inside. I start to get ready for bed, then remember a light burning in the hall, and think this unnecessary, so go and blow it out, and return to my room. It is gas, and soon some one smells it and several come running. Then I open my door and stare out, but knowing enough for once to keep still; I return to my room and turn mine out. In spite of the worry in the back of my mind, it was a lovely trip; but just a few things remain with me: a new hat as soon as we arrived in Grand Junction — a flat, black felt with a big bow of blue ribbon next my hair; a blue suit with an Eton jacket.

Bert's girl and Mrs. Schlattery made huge Alsatian bows of velvet to wear on the back of their belts and collars. I expect they sized me up at once, and wondered what Joe Sampliner was thinking of, but I have always had a warm place in my heart for him because of this trip. To-day I have as souvenirs of this time a Chinese platter, and my photograph — a picture of rather a sweet-faced girl, a lace scarf around her shoulders, just a suggestion of bare neck showing. She has wistful eyes and a sensitive mouth. Once I was showing this picture to a friend of mine, a fast woman (yes, I have had all kinds!) and she said, 'Bedroomy eyes.'

When we return, I think the children feel this is the beginning of the end, but I honestly do not think I will marry him, though I know I can. We are having more of a struggle each day, and if it weren't for the

[175]

milk, very little to eat. It is getting cold weather, too, and I worry how the cows are to be fed. When Mama was with us, we watched for the Little Dipper to be in a certain position in the sky, because 'then the cows will lie down at night, full and chewing their cud.' This was fine for us, and the cows also, because they were fed mighty slim all winter, the hay doled out to them. It was with a feeling of richness that we would cut into a bale of hay, the 'ping' of the broken wires making music. To-day I never pass a small bunch of hay lying in the road that I do not have to restrain myself, wanting to take it home with me.

Then one day we hear Henry has been in Iris, and never even come to see us. This is too much. I say I will marry the first man who asks me, and soon have a proposal.

Many houses are being built, and we have our usual number of stores and saloons. There were, I expect, twenty or thirty log houses — some of them of two stories. To-day, thirty years later, not a vestige of this town remains; even the foundations dug in the hillside are smooth and grass-grown. I have a cabin almost built (or they say it is mine, but I know and fear it is ours). The mine looks better all the time.

One day we go to town on the ore teams. Even now I don't know it is my wedding day, but it is. Jamie is back in Bonanza, and afterward I heard when the news came he acted like a wild man. As we are nearing town, some one says (not me), 'Why not have this wedding over with?' My first thought, of course, 'I have no clothes'; but, all of us laughing, it is decided we will have it in spite of clothes. Rosie lends me a nightdress, and we go to the justice of the peace. It is night, and all stand around a table, and it is done, everything so cheap and common. I am choking inside. Where are all my dreams of romance? My dress was a white outing flannel that had been washed several times; around the neck, sleeves, and bottom is a frill of Oriental lace. I suppose we eat, but I don't remember now.

We go to the La Veta Hotel and are shown into the big parlor, or at this time it seems large to me. George leaves me for a time and I think, 'What have I done?' — but such thoughts do not add any to my happiness. Finally we are shown to our room and by request he leaves till I am safe in bed. I pray this first night is not such a horror to most girls as it was to me. And I thought, 'Is this being married?' Had there been a place in the world for me to run to, I would have run.

But back in my mind is the worst hurt of all — what to tell these brothers and sisters at camp; and the guilty feeling, knowing I had deserted them. Now there was no one they could depend on. I have never told them, but this was a dreadful hurt, and I did not feel at all pleased with the way I had played my part.

And soon these children — deserted now — are bundled up and sent back to Bonanza. The cows go with them. I wonder what cows we had. It would not be Old Pat, because in my early cooking days I made a jelly roll, a flat failure, and I hunted Old Pat and fed it to her, not wanting Mama to know. Old Pat died and I felt guilty and owned up. Old Spot fell into a prospect hole and killed herself, so we did not have her. We probably had Mulie, a very dignified cow which we took no liberties with — she could and did knock one stem-winding with her hornless head. We might have had Old Hene, who had to be driven into a chute before milking — running one bar in front of her hind legs and one in back.

Long afterward I heard that on the road home Ed took a short cut through the timber with the cows, taking a little grub with him. The horse bucked and ran away and they lost everything except a can of tomatoes. They camp at night, but good, careful Ed won't let them open the can. 'You can't sometimes tell — we might have to be out another night.' It gets toward noon the next day, and Frank cannot stand it any longer, and refuses to go farther if they don't open the can, so they do, with a sharp rock, having no knife, and find it pumpkin.

Henry gets a house for them and leaves them, telling the store to give them ten dollars' worth of groceries each month. Jose is housekeeper (twelve years old), and with the help of the neighbors they do get along somehow. Ed has the typhoid fever that winter, and their joys and troubles and sorrows would make a story in itself.

This winter was the end of Plutarch's 'Lives.' In their fights they used the volumes for weapons till they were falling apart, then combined forces and got on the roof, hurling the pieces at Mrs. Smeltzer as she went by. The top of the cupboard is a diving point, lighting on the bed springs. While the neighbors like and help them, still they are leery of them. I copy a letter of Jose's written at this time:

BONANZA, COLO. *Feb.* 31, 1895

DEAR ANNIE,

I received your letter the 29 and will answer it to-day, I don't know what to write, for Bonanza is as dull as ever. We had a party last night at Mrs. Robar's. I got the lovely box of paper and envelopes to-day. I have got Jick's mittens done and I have started another pair for Moosie. I have been out coasting all day and it is six o'clock. I am going over to Mrs. Cole's this afternoon so she can take off the thumb for my mittens, I think it is fun to knit. Moosie and Gertie are fixing rags for a rug. I am teaching Gertie how to sew and cook. Second Hand has given us Five dollars in all. I can't think of anything else so will close.

With love from JOSIE

And I? I am a bride, and when I look back over my life, though I hate self-pity, my heart aches for this poor girl. Nothing to do with. Joe sends us a pair of wool blankets and a set of knives and forks. My furniture is all home-made, table, bed, and shelves. The tiny stove is set up on blocks of wood; there is a shelf for the water bucket; my plates against the wall; the knives and forks where they will show; the Chinese platter brightening up one corner; the pansy picture doing its part; white sugar sacks hemstitched for a table cover; and we are started. I have always wanted things, but never so much as then. It was a hard, dreary time. From the first I am pregnant; married on the fourth of October, my baby is born on the Fourth of July. Ed Howe says, when he comes to this place in a woman's story, he lays the book down. I suppose he doesn't like it; neither did I.

One morning George is peeved (only we didn't have this word then — we would have said, 'on the prod') at our little stove, which refuses to draw, and he kicks the door off; the fire burns just as bright, still, there is a coolness for a few days. I find it is hard to keep him in a good humor. The time goes, cooking, cleaning, washing, and ironing; no amusements except planning what we will do when the mine is sold. They take out ore all the time and it is good, but not enough to pay.

In the spring I am given thirty-five dollars and go to Gunnison to buy furniture. With it I get a bed and mattress, a rocking-chair and two other chairs, a mirror, lace curtains, and have three dollars left. With this, I intend to feed my soul, and spend it all in house plants; they do make a brave showing in the windows with the new curtains. I color some gunny-sacks red (it always rubs off) for a rug, sew little pieces of silk in circles and make a lambrequin for the shelves on which my books and pictures are placed, and drape an old box for a dresser, hanging the new mirror over it and am quite 'decked out.'

This old mirror has done faithful service and has always played its part like a lady. It has been placed upright and the long way over dry-goods boxes, lending an air to every cabin, tent, or house it has been placed in, and has ever been a cheerful companion for over thirty years. New babies have been held up to see themselves in it, although it was considered bad luck for a child less than one year old to look in any mirror. Also, when, by a good deal of effort, you have twisted a little curl on the baby's head — you have stood off and looked at it from all sides — then you hold it up to the mirror that it, too, may see. Then there is the first short dress and new shoes to be looked at; also I remember a tiny pink sunbonnet. Later there is another baby held up to you, Old Mirror, this one with big brown eyes. After ten years of laughing into your face each day, she is gone, and I know how you missed her. Before this a wiggly boy with yellow curls comes to you. Each day the man combs before you; even though he is just coming off night shift at twelve o'clock, his hair is carefully combed and parted before going to bed. A mother hurriedly dresses before you each day; ofttimes you are an old flatterer to this tired one and give her hope to go on. Now school children hurry to you for one last glance, and a twist of the neck to see if it need washing — always decide it does not. A youth has his first shave right before your face; be sure no one else sees him. This same smiling youth turns from you and says, 'Look pretty good, don't you think?' — knowing beforehand the answer will be, 'If you act as well as you look, you will be all right.' At this a face is made at you which the one behind isn't supposed to see, but does. She is glowing with pride at what you are reflecting and hastens to the window to get one last glimpse of this boy or girl. Brides have dressed before you and you have looked on many happy occasions, more funny ones, and a few sad ones, but, thank God, no disgraceful ones. Many have gone to you with a frown, the corners of their mouths hanging, and left with a smile. So good luck to your faithful old shining face; splotches on it now like those on an old lady's face.

All this first winter, George is trying to train me. I find men who have led a wild life are more exacting of their own womenkind. I expect they have seen so many tough women they have lost faith. One day we have a time over my saying 'darn.' He didn't intend to have his woman swearing. To-day I have an enlarged throat. It may have come from swallowing, or trying to, the lump which would rise in it. It would have been better had I quarreled, but, when a small child, listening to Mama and Henry and seeing how foolish and useless it all was, I decided there would be no quarreling in my home. In my small mind I saw it was she who started them and none of them helped, only making it miserable for us children. And, quarreling fathers and mothers, these children listening to you are more hurt and miserable and ashamed than you realize.

Afterward, when we moved to Cripple Creek, things are running smoother. I say, 'We seem to be getting along better'; his answer was, 'Yes, you are getting some sense.' But I wasn't; I was only learning to manage him without his knowing it; also the use of 'hot air' and 'soft soap.'

Then Christmas is coming. I so want to send the children something, and go to Gunnison, walking up

and down the stores longing to buy so many things.
As I call to mind now, I had something like two
dollars to spend. I think I got the boys knives, and a
little white workbox for Jose, which I took home to
paint a rose on the lid, and this was the extent of my
purchases.

Then there is the child coming, a mingled pleasure
and sorrow. Now I will have something really my
own, something to love and cling to, but how to get
clothes ready, what to make them of, how to care for
it? This first wardrobe was made of the white outing-
flannel wedding dress, a pink cotton dress of mine,
and flour sacks. All the rags one could save, a piece of
real linen from a man's white shirt, a bar of castile
soap, a bottle of vaseline, and some safety pins were
the outfit. These and a twisted twine string were
packed in a box all ready. Rosie had helped me.

This winter word comes that Jamie has returned to
Bonanza and, while working in the Josephine Mine,
stepped out of a drift, missed his footing, fell into the
shaft across the bucket, and is killed. I feel conscience-stricken and very sad over this, but dare not
show it. Before this we have had a time over these
sweethearts of mine; of course more over Jim than
Jamie. In fact, I think in a burst of confidence I was
fool enough to tell him how I cared and always had.
At this all letters and anything burnable must be
burned, but I held out on him the plush workbox, the
butterfly booklet, and little white stone. He did not
seem to care because I kept things Jamie had given
me.

Now comes the third of July; there is to be a picnic in Iris, and I am determined to go. George never cares to go anywhere, but I coax for his permission to let me go, which was given, so I make two big blueberry cakes for my share of the lunch. We would go in freight wagons, but this is good enough, and I can probably sit with the driver on the spring seat. When I get up the morning of the Fourth, I feel strange, and soon start to have pains. They grow worse and worse; still I pack my lunch and dress, not intending to let a little stomach-ache stand in the way of my going to that picnic. But I am no better, so go and tell Rosie, 'Guess I won't go.' She knows at once, and says, 'Well — I guess you have knocked that picnic in the head for both of us. Go home and I will come over later.'

She comes, fixes the bed and lays out the contents of the little box, and sees that there is hot water. All this day I suffer, both Rosie and George helping me as much as they can, and at four in the evening Neita is born, the first child in Chance. 'Deacon' Hurley had gone by the house at noon, heard me screaming, and would not return that way; in fact, I think he went to the saloon and got drunk, but then the Deacon didn't need much of an excuse to get drunk.

George did the cooking and housework. Each day Rosie came and dressed Neita, also taking care of me — a born nurse. I have always felt I owed her a debt of gratitude.

On the third day I get very sick — such pain in my back and head. Rosie and George fill bags with hot

[184]

salt and put over me, but nothing helps. At last Rosie says that we must have the doctor; she has done all she can. (Oh, we hate to have the doctor — no money to pay him!) He is sent for, and, after hours of waiting, arrives with two girls in the buggy with him. He comes in, pushing the door wide open, walks over to the bed, and, throwing back the covers, grabs the neck of my nightgown with the other hand, tears it off, scattering hot plates and bags of salt in all directions. 'Don't you see this girl is burning up with fever? It is blood poison!' At once he gets his instruments out and goes to work. It was agony. And I don't think Dr. McIntosh was ever paid either.

Foolish as I was, I knew somehow it was better for the baby to sleep alone. (All babies I had known slept with their mothers.) So she had a bed made of a soap box. Many times I would look at it, longing for a real baby bed, consoling myself with the thought that one day when we are rich and great, it will be something to tell — 'My baby's first bed was a soap box.' We have become neither rich nor great, and this is the first time I have mentioned the soap box. It seems things of this sort are only a virtue when you rise above them; otherwise they are a disgrace.

Rosie insisted I stay in bed till the ninth day, which seemed foolish when I felt so well. When Neita is two weeks old, there is to be a dance, and I beg to go. We do go, taking her with us, but my pleasure is soon over. George doesn't waltz, and the first dance after we go in is a waltz. A man asks me and I can't resist and start to dance. George invites me off the floor. I sit struggling to keep the tears back through another dance, then we go home.

The inward struggle I had always had seemed to drop away now, I was so interested in Neita, and from the first she is unusually bright and good-looking.

One night before she was born a few are gathered in a cabin, among them a nice mild white-haired grandmother. Coming around the corner of the house, I see a building across the street is on fire. I run to the door and yell, 'Crail's house is burning!' Then this sweet old lady runs to the door and says, 'Damned if it ain't!' By this time I am at the house, have grabbed two full pails of water, jump down a step with them, but drop them to grasp my side, which is killing me with pain, and if I didn't have a doctor's word for it I would think Neita had been marked, because her side is covered with bright red marks like fire. I still think the doctors are right. Once I was passing a livery barn and saw two men fighting. One had just split the other's head open with a neck-yoke, and the blood was pouring in streams. I threw my hands over my face to shut out the sight and ran for home. Still, Neita's face is not marked.

After a time I have a partition in my cabin, also a pantry. These I papered with old newspapers. Once, while pasting on a strip, I found this ——

'Sometimes I stop with half-drawn thread,
Not often, though — each moment's time means bread.'

Then, when I expected riches from month to month, how little did I think that for many years I would sew for a living, and this little couplet would come to me ofttimes when I did 'stop with half-drawn thread.' 'Not often, though,' because 'each moment's time' did mean bread for me and my children.

They go on trying to make the mine pay, borrowing money to run it. Each night there is crushing of quartz in the mortar, then taking it to the pump and panning it. This is free gold, and by putting it in a shallow pan called a gold pan, covering with water, and rocking it from side to side, the particles of gold sink to the bottom, and the waste is washed over the edge of the pan. George panned enough in this way to make me a very heavy gold ring. (He is a generous man, with very good taste, and if we ever had money I had more than my share.) They even load two wagons with ore, hauling it sixty miles to a little stamp mill, and it doesn't pay expenses. Then a carload is taken to Black Hawk, Colorado, and it also is a failure. Each day proves to them that The Only Chance wasn't worth thirty thousand to them, even though the ground hadn't been scratched. Mr. C. starts to freight from the Lucky Strike and George also gets a job on this mine. Oh, the relief to have a payday!

Neita is growing fast, has curly golden hair, and I curl it in different places on her head, brushing it with an old toothbrush, then walk all around her to get the best effect, recurl, back off, and look again. Now, too, since we have had a payday, she has dear little gingham aprons and real shoes. And I have new clothes; a gray wool dress, trimmed with big revers of bright green; a black suit from The National Cloak and Suit Company, a long, heavy (very heavy) wide skirt, lined, interlined, and a wide velvet binding on the bottom, a tight waist buttoning up the side, with enormous sleeves at the top.

I remember The National Cloak and Suit Company from the time I was a little girl. At that time they made suits only to order. In the catalogue were pictures of the fashions — lettered from A to E; with this were sent samples of goods, also lettered. The A style and goods were the cheapest — around ten dollars, the workmanship and tailoring on this price suit being just as good as that on an E garment. These were the highest-priced goods and style, some of them silk-lined, lovely materials and finishing; these would be around twenty-five dollars. With my Si Dore money I had an astrakhan coat — fine material, made over for many years — little loops and fur heads for fasteners, well lined. The National made this to order for seven dollars. Every one but the Adamses wore shoes with thin turned soles, very sharp-pointed toes — from a dollar to two and a half was a big price to pay. The Adams girls wore shoes with a rather low heel, rounded toes, and an extension sole. These were called 'The Walkenfast,' and were made to order for three dollars. I coaxed many weeks before Mama would let me send for a pair of shoes costing that terrible price. The ultimate in shoes was the 'Sorosis.' Later, I had a pair of these, just enough to give me a reason for bragging on wearing 'Sorosis' shoes. 'You see, I have a foot that takes an expensive shoe to fit' — three-fifty, I think!

CHAPTER XIV

A man because of the fact that he had been drunk with another, felt that he could and should be favored by his companion. There seems to be a peculiar and particular tie between men who have been drunk together.

A. E.

A WOMAN may be very unhappy, not loved, and, she thinks, not understood, but a few paydays, a full cupboard, and some new clothes will grease the wheels of married life to a greater smoothness. This fall I want to go and visit the children, who live in Coal Creek now — Henry running a pump on an oil well. I want to show off my new baby and clothes, so I go, feeling very prosperous. Before this Neita has a second-hand carriage. Never before in our family, while there was always a baby, had there been a carriage.

It is Fruit Day in Cañon City, so I get rates. Some of the children will meet me here, and finally Jose comes, looking grown up. We go on to Coal Creek, where they have a house of three rooms built in the hillside. Everything is spick and span for my arrival, although when supper time comes there is a lack of dishes, which are discovered dirty, shut up in the oven.

I have a good visit, the children making much over Neita, fighting to see who will get to wheel the carriage. They are in bad with most of the neighbors, who are foreigners working in the coal mines. Gertie said, 'We are the only humans here.' They have fought and licked all these people's children. The town marshal has called and been bombarded with rocks — Gertie has held a kid on the railroad track (after pulling most of her hair out) till the train is almost on them; Moosie has punched holes in the top of each can in a case of fruit and sucked the juice out; but with the exception of a few little things like this a pleasant time is had by all. Ed is working away from home, and Frank has never been in Coal Creek, but comes while I am there, wanting so much to stay, but Henry sends him away. I thought it a very pitiful sight to see this boy's hand waving from the curtains of the stage, not wanting, but having, to leave home.

I go home feeling happier than since I left them, knowing they could fend for themselves. Soon after I am home, Neita (who has only walked around chairs) climbs to her feet and walks across the floor, and I stand with my heart in my mouth, thinking I am seeing a miracle.

That Christmas we decide to have a community tree, followed by a dance and supper. We all bake for the supper, and take it with us, putting it on tables and benches. The coffee is made in a wash boiler on the big box stove which heats the room. One man makes fine lemon pies and this is his donation, but this wasn't his lucky day, as he used pans with removable bottoms and started a kid with one in each hand, who had tin bracelets and no pie, before he learned how to carry them. Pete Peterson had a new girl and was spreading himself for her benefit. He brought her in, helped her off with her things, came back stepping high and handsome, and sat down, but felt at once that all was not well, and arose with all the frosting off Jenks's pie on the back of his pants.

The Iris people are invited over for the dance, and now we hear the sleigh coming. A sound of laughter, the door is thrown open, and people and snow drift in. They all stamp their feet and wish every one a Merry Christmas. By now some of our people who took more than their share of apples (Tom and Jerry, too, I expect), have begun to throw them at each other. As a big miner from Iris steps in, one takes him in the temple. I am not going to stand for any rough-house, as I had set out to have a ladylike, refined affair, so I jump up on a chair and yell — 'Here, you two stiffs, cut out the apple throwing!' At this, George drags me down and takes me home, but I guess it was just as well, as the dance ended up in a free-for-all.

We struggle along, things not improving any. This second winter the camp is at its best — many new log houses, a few store buildings, of course, saloons, and a schoolhouse. I am of school age, counted in to make it possible to have a school. In one cabin were several young men baching, some of them teamsters and some miners. They drank a good deal, calling these occasions 'birthdays,' and some one of them had a birthday at least every payday. Then they would play, sing, dance, and yell. One boy was a 'sorrow-ful' drinker and would fill the night with his mournful yells, 'Nobody loves me.' I often used to wonder how they could stand it to have so few hours' sleep, then up before daylight in the bitter cold (Gunnison County is the coldest place on the face of the earth), out with their teams hauling ore or timbers all day in drifts of snow, coming in wet and ready for a big time again. But they were young, and I suppose used no more energy than the young people of to-day.

There was one young couple very deeply in love with each other, but they could not marry because neither had enough to get a housekeeping outfit. It was a saying that all you needed was a bed and coffee-pot, but they did not have this much. One day the girl and I are at Rosie's, I, sitting holding Neita, rather rebellious at fate, Grace standing in the door working on a handkerchief for her lover's birthday, and crying because they cannot be married. I look up at her and think, 'Poor fool, you don't know how fortunate you are ——' When she left, I turned to Rosie and said, 'It would be a cold day before I'd shed any tears over a snub-nosed man like that.' Afterward I was to marry this man, shedding some of the most heart-breaking tears over him, and — our son wore this same handkerchief she was so lovingly making, for a bib.

But this is getting ahead. Along here the men decide to get a stamp mill and treat the ore themselves. They had to borrow money to do this, and it was the beginning of the end. It was a long haul from the mine to a stream large enough to run the mill, but at any rate, they built a five-stamp mill. With one of these, you dump the ore into a crusher, where it is broken into small pieces, from there going under the stamps, which are heavy pieces of iron, similar to a potato-masher. These rise and fall on this quartz or ore with a stamping, grinding motion, the fine ore running out over plates. There is a steady stream of water to keep it moving over the plates; these plates catch and hold the particles of gold while the water washes the waste away; the plates are coated with quicksilver; this is scraped off and strained through a piece of chamois skin and a lump of gold is the result. It is very heavy, a piece as large as an egg being difficult to lift, for me — but, oh, we had so few of these lumps.

Then there were expensive breakdowns and, I feel sure, poor management, although this had all been figured down to the smallest detail on paper, and, according to those figures, no chance of losing — George could and did make the most convincing figures on paper.

Seven of us, the Crails and our family, live in two small rooms. Neita has a small bed on the floor, in one corner. One night she wakens us screaming, we light a candle and find her covered with blood; a mountain rat had bitten her hand through and through. By now I am expecting another baby, and am very sorry, as things are coming so hard. One day the mill catches fire, and I am the hardest fire-fighter (not to save the mill, however). I grabbed huge tubs of water and carried them up a steep path from the creek, using every ounce of strength and straining every nerve and muscle in my body each trip. Time and time again I did this, was dripping wet, my hair hanging down, and working in a frenzy. Finally I dropped, exhausted, and thought, 'Well, if that don't do it, nothing will.' No one spoke to me. The next day I felt fine, and Rosie said, with a knowing look, 'Had all your work for nothing, didn't you?'

Yes, thank God, I had. In those days I would have been a fine believer in birth control, but the older I get the less sure I feel about this. After a time I am reconciled to this child and am more care-free and happy than ever before, having reached a don't-care state of mind.

Wherever I have been or with whom, the cooking always falls on me; perhaps because I do it well and enjoy doing it, so I cook for the bunch. But after a time, the Crails move back to town, and we give up the house to men who are working in the mill and move to a tiny cabin. The cattle have been taking shelter here, but it is cleaned out pretty well, and in I go. Just a few boards to hold the cook-stove on in one corner, and a bunk built in another corner. At some time there has been a floor, but now it is gone, only the sleepers which supported it are left, and I must step over these two-by-sixes constantly in doing my work. George works on night shift. It is very lonely, miles away from any people; the mill is the nearest, almost a mile.

Even under these conditions I try to fix up — flour sack curtains at the tiny window, pine boughs everywhere, and those pieces of board under the stove white as snow. In the daytime when George sleeps, I take Neita and sit on the hillside under the trees and dream. (No, none of them ever came true, but much better ones have taken their place.)

Soon we could see the mill was another failure, so we move back to Chance. I had lived, slept, and eaten in one room so long that I was frantic for a bedroom. Over at the mine there was an assay office with two bedrooms, and I insisted on going there. How I planned on fixing this place! It had the two bedrooms all right (the whole thing was built of one layer of boards). In addition to these bedrooms, it also had the kitchen stove about twenty feet away across a dirt floor and up a flight of steps. It took two nights of freezing weather to knock the bedroom idea in the head. We moved back to our log house.

Part of this winter I was the only woman in camp. At Christmas time, there was one other woman and myself, but lots of men, and they began early to fill up on Tom and Jerry. By night every man in town was either crying or singing drunk. The street was full of men; even those who had never been the worse for wear before were down and out to-day. They staggered and stumbled, fought and fell. One of the soberest, most reliable men in town fell by the town pump and was unable to get up. Mrs. W. and I watched them from the window. Sometime I am going to write up the different Christmases I have spent.

Along about here was the gold rush to Alaska. George wanted to go, but could get no one to grubstake him. He tried several plans, but one needed at least a thousand dollars, and he could not get it. The bank is going to foreclose on the mine and mill. Before this we have had a lawsuit and lost it. Sam D. Crump was our lawyer and a good one, although he did not win our case. A miner once told me that he was sitting in a poker game with Crump, and, 'By-doggies, I couldn't play my cards for looking at his hands, five fingers an' a thumb on each hand, an' he could sure handle the cards.' John often wished we could have had Frank Gowdy for our lawyer.

Ellen Jack tells this of Frank Gowdy and the early Gunnison boom days, in her 'Fate of a Fairy':

In Gunnison once I was very busy when one of the help came to me and said: 'There will be trouble in the bunkhouse, for Jim is full and has a gun, and is abusing one of the carpenters.'

I said, 'Well, go and throw him out.'

He said, 'Not me, by gosh, I don't want to be killed by that drunken whelp.'

I went in my room, got my gun, went to the bunkhouse, and said, 'What are you growling about? Get out of this.'

He said, 'Not till I have settled with this son of a b——' and pulled his gun to fire at the man. I pulled mine and shot the gun out of his hands and part of his hand with it.

I said, 'Now, go, or I will wing off the other hand.'

He began to yell, but got afraid that I would give him another shot, so he went; and as soon as he had gone the carpenter said, 'Words are empty, for you have saved my life and I have a wife and two children depending on me for a living.'

I said, 'What was the trouble?'

He said: 'Jim wanted to borrow five dollars of me and I told him I didn't have it. Then he began his abuse, and I am afraid that he will do something yet, for the very old Satan is in that lad.'

I said: 'No, he is a coward, for he knew that he had the drop on you, that you were unarmed, but he did not think of me being so quick and taking such a straight shot. He will never try to come at me.'

That night the officers told me that I was under arrest, so I went and got Frank Gowdy and gave a bond for $1000, and I would not let the justice try the case, but took it to the county court, before Judge Smith. When the trial came off, we all went to court and the jury was all sworn in. The man had Ike Stevens, and both the young attorneys began their case. All at once Stevens called Gowdy a liar, and Gowdy struck him a paster on the nose and the blood streamed down his face. When they both began to fight, all the jurors jumped from their seats and began scrapping too, and old Judge Smith jumped upon his desk and yelled out, 'I fine you both for contempt of court.' Then some one struck him with a chair and knocked him off the desk. The sheriff tried to grab some one and old Jack Seamon struck him and sent him head foremost over some chairs; the chairs were fastened together, and when I saw him go over, his coat-tails opened behind and his ears sticking up as he went on all fours over the backs of the chairs, I thought I would die laughing. But as soon as the men got out of the fight they made for the door and out. I never heard anyone say court adjourned nor anything more about fining for contempt, nor that any one was arrested. They all got out as fast as they could, and when I got out on the main street three old deadbeats that I had fired out of my place stood on the corner. Those men saw the bloody handkerchief and the black eyes of the two men, then saw me laughing. One of them said, 'There, I told you she had done it.'

Just then Frank McMaster, who had just got a little

newspaper, came up to the men and said, 'What's up?'

The man, who did not know anything only what he had surmised, said, 'Why, that yellow-haired girl has cleaned the court room up with a gun and licked both judge and jurors, and then turned loose on both lawyers and sheriff. They all have bloody faces and one a black eye, and the poor old judge is getting his wrist set, as she must have broken it with the butt end of her gun.'

The newsman went back to his office with all this, and as it was press time he put it all in the paper, with big headings how 'MRS. CAPTAIN JACK, THE DARE-DEVIL OF THE WEST,' had cleaned out the county court room, and a lot more that the man told him, when the truth was that I was the only one that was not in the fight. The only part I took was to laugh at George Hues, the sheriff, going over the chair backs.

Well, that paper went to Denver, then all the papers in the U.S.A. had me as one of the worst and most daring women that had ever lived. It seemed that every paper added a little more to it. They even sent agents from New York to get pictures of me to put in the Police Gazette and all this was through the vicious tongue of old man Kirkbe.

My trial did not come for several weeks after, and when it did I was fined $15 and costs for saving a man's life and at least $1000 expense to the county for prosecuting the murderer, but the game was to get what they could out of me, and they knew if they made the fine too large I would carry the case up. I was very angry at being fined, but paid it, and a few weeks after Judge Smith came to me to see about some land I had got, and after he got through with the land business he said, 'You see if you had not shot that man I would not have got my wrist sprained, and it gives me a great deal of pain and trouble.'

I said, 'Is that why you fined me for saving a good man's life and disarming a ruffian?'

He said, 'Well, no, not that.'

I said, 'Judge, you should have been in your grave ten years ago. You are not fit to judge between right and wrong. You remind me of an old piece of parchment that has done its work, and when election day comes I do mine. I cannot vote, but I let the boys vote for me.'

And when election day came there were stickers with names on them, and we cut off the name we wanted and stuck it over the name we didn't want. I was very busy fixing up my tickets and getting the boys to vote them, and the Judge was beaten. He started to sell out everything he had, and got his wife to help him, and when he had got all he could he took a seventeen year old girl and disappeared, leaving his poor old wife and daughter without home or money. That is a sample of the officers we had in those days.

We struggle on till the following July, when Joy is born, such a lovely brown-eyed baby, so healthy and happy, a real Joy. Rosie is my nurse again and I have no doctor.

When Joy is one month old, we see something must be done. George has a cousin in Denver who he thinks might get him something to do, so we, with barely enough money to get there on, go to Denver, and get one room, where I do light housekeeping (very light) and George goes to see his cousin, but does not get much encouragement.

George goes on to Cripple Creek, leaving me in Denver, broke, or with but a few dollars. How I count the nickels for kindling and a few pieces of coal! I wash the children's clothes in my room, much to my landlady's disgust. I lock the children in and go and buy a few provisions, always looking up at the window on my return, to see Neita's golden curls. She would be watching for me.

Then the room rent runs out, the landlady knows I am broke, and I see I must move. I have heard of pawnshops, so take the watch my father gave me, lock the children in (with the thought of fire tugging at me every minute), and go out to look for a building with three balls over it, walk boldly in, and get four dollars and a ticket. (I never return either of them.) He offers me twenty-five for my ring, but I hold on, then go to the room, pack and go to Coal Creek, where Henry and the children are.

CHAPTER XV

If one stands trouble bravely, there is more happiness in looking back to trouble than there is in looking back to joy.

A. E.

So I go to Coal Creek. When the expressman is taking my trunk downstairs (it was Mama's and has a swelled top), the landlady stands and swears at people who have all their belongings in one trunk. She wasn't insulting me any, because it was true. These two babies and the contents of that trunk, bedding, dishes, clothes — very few — cooking utensils, the mirror, and books, were all I owned in the world. I climb on the seat with the expressman and am off on my travels.

Henry is married again, to a lovely, cultured Southern woman. We never knew how it happened or where he met her, but I do know that Virginia loved him and made him a wonderful wife. She must have been brave; to go into that mess of children, trying to manage on seventy-five dollars a month for six of them, and doing it, when she had never cooked or washed in her life. Then think, too, how these wild ones must have suffered to have some one who had been used to the greatest system (she was a trained nurse) try to train them.

I remember very little of this time, except Virginia trying to manage, while I feel I am only adding to their burdens.

George sends for me after his first payday, and how

I watch for that letter! He was working on the Victor Mine. (Dave Moffatt once sold this mine to a French outfit for three million dollars. It worked a year or two, then Moffatt bought it back for two thousand and resold it to a Boston company for two millions.)

George has rented a little three-room house. It is luxury for me to have a bedroom; we have plenty to eat and pass a very peaceful, contented month. But soon George starts to complain that it was run by a bunch of 'red necks,' 'chaws,' 'flannel mouths,' 'Micks' — all names for Irishmen. At this time there was an agitation against Catholics by an organization of men called the American Protective Association, to which George belonged. (All my life I have had the utmost respect and toleration for any and all religions, and envied people who were brought up in any faith, whether Catholic or Jew.) All this fuss worried me and at last it reached such a state that George was either fired or quit.

He then got a job on the Vindicator at Independence. All these towns are in what is called the Cripple Creek district, the largest being Cripple Creek, then Victor (where we lived), four or five miles from Cripple Creek; Independence is halfway up the mountain-side, on top is Altman, at the foot Goldfield. Soon we move to another house and I help load, the expressman showing me how to take hold of a trunk so that it will load easy. Again the babies and I climb in with him and are off. This house was a two-room frame, built in the mountain-side. To get in the front room, one had to climb a flight of twelve or fifteen rickety steps, while the back door was even with the ground. It was newly papered, and I at once put newspapers back of the dry-goods box we washed on, and the table where we ate, thereby winning the friendship of the landlady, a German woman, supposed to be the hardest-boiled in the district. She owned the row where the fast girls had their cribs, and had the Indian sign on them, as she could and would fight any or all of them. Between-times she drove a burro cart to back doors collecting slop, but I found later that when I needed a friend she stood by. In the front room there was a bed, a stand, and always the same shelf in the corner to hang clothes under. On the floor was my first carpet, a bright red velvet one, over which I was much set up. I imagine she bought it for one of the cribs, then changed her mind. The house joined a livery stable, but I tried to think the smell coming through the wall was healthy, and got so the pawing and stamping of the horses was company to me.

If one would let one's self, one could be very lonesome, not knowing anybody, and with one's husband gone all day. Oh, it was a dull life! You see, there were no cheap amusements in those days, no picture shows; the kind of people I would have cared to meet I had no chance of meeting, and had I met them they would not have cared for me. I suppose I could have gone to church and met people, but I was too honorable to use the church as an excuse to 'get in,' when I felt no urge to go from a religious standpoint.

One cold night I was awakened by a strange dream,

a veil-like presence trying to give me a message. I was not at all frightened, and got up to put more cover on Neita, who was sleeping in her little home-made bed. I returned shivering to my own bed and cuddled Joy to keep her warm (she is six months old now); these little frame houses were so cold everything would freeze solid. Then I listened for a time to the horses pawing and stamping, then was asleep again, leaving a candle burning, and was again awakened by this strange dream. Now I lay there, neither asleep nor awake, wondering if there were anything in dreams, and, if so, what did mine mean?

Soon I hear voices in the front yard. At once I jump from bed, not stopping to dress, rush and open the front door, look down the flight of steps at the figures standing there, and ask, 'Why don't you bring him on in?'

Some of the men climb these rickety steps, take hold of me, and ask, 'Is this where George Fleming lives?'

'Yes, why don't you bring him in? Is he hurt bad?'

Now he calls down, 'This is the place, boys'—and to me, 'You must get some clothes on, it is very cold.'

I throw a quilt around me, and they come in, several of them, but they are bearing no burden. All carefully remove their hats as they enter the door. They fill this small room. One starts a fire. Neita is wakened by the noise and sits up in bed; Joy begins to cry and I go to her.

A man says, 'That's a fine boy you got there.'

GEORGE IS KILLED

Again I ask, 'Where is George?'

Only now do they answer, one for all, each looking helpless. 'Well, you see, he is hurt ——'

I break in, 'Yes, I know. Bad?'

'Well, Mam, you see he drilled into a missed hole, and here we didn't know he had a family. It is shore bad, and anything we can do only mention it, and — yes, Mam, he is bad.'

'Well, then, we will go to him.'

'But — well, Mam, you might as well know. He is dead, shot all to pieces.'

I just melt on the floor, the quilt covering me. One of the men says, 'Look, boys, and see if there is any whiskey or camfire,' and tries to raise me, but I, dry-eyed and voiced, ask them to leave me alone for a while.

They all troop through the kitchen and out the back door, except two, who sit there till morning with me, bolt upright in their chairs, only relaxing to hold the children. I still crouch there, gritting my teeth and clenching my hands. As it is coming daylight, Joy cries so hard that I know she is hungry and get up to let her nurse, but — there is no milk now, and never is again. After this night she has to be fed till I get a bottle for her. Strange, what a shock will do.

Now I dress and prepare breakfast for us all. These everyday duties are the saving of one in trouble. After eating, the men leave me; I am alone and glad of it. I go in the yard and a spirit of rebellion at fate comes over me. It is all centered around the fact that my children will be as I was, never a father to care for or look out for them. Most of my sorrow was for these fatherless children.

Then comes the landlady, very rough and swearing, still kind and gentle. Later in the day, some Knights of Pythias come, making all arrangements; then a lawyer from the mine with a paper for me to sign, but I know enough not to. In these times there was no Compensation Fund. I do sign this paper later, releasing the mine from any fault in the matter, and they give me six hundred dollars; in addition to this, each man working in the mine gives me a day's wages. This I take with a feeling of shame, because I know what a day's pay means to some of their families. Some of the miners' wives come, but how can they comfort this silent, dry-eyed creature who doesn't act like any other woman would, and it is as hard on them to make conversation as it is for me to answer. I am glad when they leave. That evening after dark comes a tap on the door, and a big Irishwoman comes in — under her arm a small bundle of dark outing flannel which she hands me. 'Here, dear, make a petticoat for the wee wan. Me man was kilt, too, about wan month gone. Oh, the throuble, the throuble' — and she begins to cry. I, too, at this, open up and we cry together, for ourselves, for each other, and for all sorrowing womankind. After this I feel better and go to sleep, making plans for the future. Henry comes for the funeral; also the cousin from Denver, the Crails from Gunnison, and George's mother from Saguache.

The cousin takes charge of everything; the rest are

helpless. I have a long veil, the miners send a big bunch of carnations — and I insist on carrying them! My only excuse is I never had any boughten flowers before, and that I love them so. I carry them much as one would a graduation bouquet, and have a feeling of importance as I step in the carriage.

George has been taken to the undertaker — the usual way now, but unheard of then. When we see him at the cemetery, he is only a form dressed in his clothes, with face and hands all wrapped in white bandages. Afterward in day-dreams, I imagined it was not he at all, and that he had left and gone to Alaska, from where he would return wealthy and shower gifts on the children and me.

After we are home again, this question comes up, What am I going to do? I don't know, except not give up the children. The cousin suggests I go and take a business course, but I will not hear of any one having the children, even for that long. I can see now how foolish this was, as in the long run it would have been better for all of us; but this was another move where I blindly changed our lives in a twinkling. Rosie and George's mother think I will manage somehow. I am glad and lonesome when they are gone. The first thing I do is to order a tombstone, no doubt foolish, but I feel he gave his life for these few hundred dollars I have, and that this is the least I can do.

The woman I am renting from has a little house nearer town and quite near the sporting district, which I decide to take and do baking — she says she will see that all the girls buy of me. She is even good enough to load me in her cart and move me. I went to one of the groceries and gave them an order, telling them I would pay as soon as the mine gave me the promised money. (They have paid all funeral expenses.) The clerk refused me credit, saying: 'I have to have the money in sight. I have seen too many of these new-made widows run bills, then, when they did get their money, blow it in for clothes to catch another man.' I walked out choking, and did wait till I got the money, but went to another grocery. Then I started baking bread, cakes, pies, also making candy, with the usual discouragements of a smoky stove and an oven which refused to bake on the bottom. I worked very hard and tried to manage, but made a poor out at it, and could see each day I was going behind. Jose now came to be with me, and it seemed very good to have some of my own people again. I tried this baking scheme for a month or two, but knew I was making a failure. There was the little red book where I kept track of what I sold and bought, and it did not come out even. One day the Superintendent of the Vindicator came to me. They wanted a boarding-house at the mine for just a few men, and he thought it a good plan for me to buy a house in Independence and start one. Just below my house was the depot which Harry Orchard blew up during the strikes, killing many men and injuring many others. It seems, as I remember it, that this first strike was justified, and the Union did win it, thereby raising miners' wages higher than they had ever been in Colorado. This went to their heads, and every time

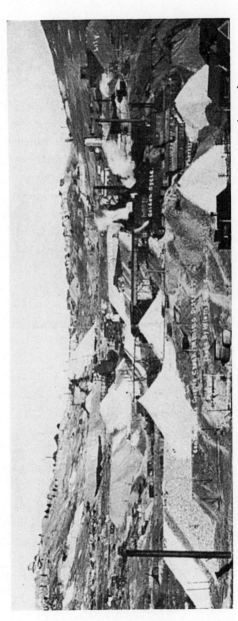

JUST BELOW MY BOARDING-HOUSE AT INDEPENDENCE WAS THE DEPOT (NO. **I**) WHICH HARRY ORCHARD BLEW UP

there was a difficulty they would go out on strike. Men were beaten and killed, property was destroyed, the Union blaming the mine owners and the mine owners blaming the Union. At last numerous agitating miners were loaded into freight cars, deported to the State line and dumped over and out, and ordered never to show their faces in the Cripple Creek District again.

After considering this boarding-house plan for a time, I consented to do it. How I hate to spend the money for a house, but I do buy a four-room one, and feel quite important over the fact that I am a landholder. No, not a landholder, merely a householder — all this ground belongs to some mine, and when they are ready for you to move your house, why, you move it. We move in and I start with five or six men, trying hard to have good meals and still keep the grocery bills down, and they were good meals, too good, as each week I go behind. Rosie and John are having more and harder trouble and she decides to come to me for a while. She helps with the children — Joy is sick most of the time, her food does not agree with her, and no wonder, as I was too busy to take proper care of her. I am getting sick, and tired, so when I get a chance to sell the place, I jump at it (Rosie has gone home before this) and sell at a loss, taking some silverware in part payment. (My first pieces of silver, pretty black and worn now.) The people move in, and are unable to pay for a time, so I stay in the attic till they do pay, a hot, smelly place, where I use an oil stove for the first time, and have hated them ever since. The girl of the house has lovely clothes, some silk-lined (an unheard-of thing to me), and a white powder which she uses on her face. She says it is harmless, as it is only rice powder. Now I think silk linings are bad enough, but when it comes to powder other than cornstarch, I don't know myself what the world is coming to.

Jose goes home and I am off to White Pine, a very foolish step, but then so many of mine seem to be that. I was homesick, not knowing where to turn, so turn to my old friends the Crails, who are now living in White Pine. She has written me that we might get a boarding-house there, so I go. The Crails haven't a bedstead for me, so I sleep on the floor. I find myself in a turmoil of family quarrels, drinking and fighting; they separate daily, make up and fight again. I manage to keep high and dry until one day John has a horse in the corner of the stable, and in a drunken rage is beating it dreadfully. I grit my teeth, trying to stand it, but it gets unbearable, and I sift in on him, when he lets up on the mare only to grab a hatchet and start for me. I don't know whether he would have chopped into me or not; I didn't wait to see. Finally he rolls his bed and leaves for good. All this time there is hanging over me, filling each day with worry, each night with fear, the thought, What am I going to do for a living? At this time I am doing a little sewing and all the washing we can get.

During this time there is a dance at White Pine. I have my doubts about going, George being dead such a short time, but I do so want to go that finally I compromise by going, but wearing a black dress. However, there was a rose-colored sateen lining showing through which I expect expressed my feelings. What a good time I had, and how I danced! And in spite of the black dress touching the floor all around, three men asked to take me to supper. This was served at twelve o'clock and was the main event of the evening, with boiled ham, turkey, cranberries, celery, salad, sandwiches, pickles, bread, pies, several kinds of cake and ice-cream, also huge cups of boiling hot coffee.

In this place lives a woman who has had more than her share of experience. She is stone deaf. One night she wakens and reaching out in the dark, her hand closes over another human hand. Never letting go of this strange hand, she jumps from bed, and there in the dark wrestles with this creature, over and over, around and around, she holding her own. Finally it or he breaks away and is gone, she never seeing a thing nor hearing a sound. The only way she knows it is not a dream is that morning finds her with a broken jaw and wrist. Another time she is in an old cabin and the dirt roof caves in on her, keeping her a prisoner for two days. Once again she is driving the stage between two camps, and meets a wounded bear on the road, also on the rampage, and is pretty well clawed, chewed, and slapped around before she can get away. And after all this, she is a meek, sweet-faced, pleasant little woman, trying hard to catch what you are saying by lip-reading.

Times do not improve any, and we decide to move

to Gunnison, so pack again, Rosie and her two children, I and my two babies, all loaded in an ore wagon driven by a half-witted teamster (also an admirer of mine), who sang every minute, 'Nobody knows how bad I feel, Nobody knows how bad I feel, Nobody knows but Jesus.' Again I am off for the unknown. It takes us two days to drive, so we stay all night in Ohio City, making all our beds down, pie fashion, on the floor — our teamster along with us, singing now, 'He et the meat, he gimme the bone. He kicked me out, he sent me home.' Oh, his songs were thrilling affairs!

As we drove along I would look at the prosperous ranch houses, wishing I lived in one of them; dreaming on, I would fancy there was a widower or a bachelor living there, and that for some reason he had to marry at once, before the day is over, and he would ride up to the wagon, halt us, and say, 'I am looking for a woman, I must be married before noon. Are either of you unmarried?' Rosie was to speak up and say, 'This one is'; and I, after he insists, tell him, just to save his life, land, or whatever it is, that I will. Then I go on, to the grinding of the wheels, and finish my house, buying silver, dishes, and linen, and many clothes, finally ending up by a big blow-out when I am expecting Neita home from college . . .

On arriving in Gunnison, we rented two small rooms upstairs in a building that had been condemned, therefore the rent was very cheap. Every time the wind blew, which was all the time, you wondered just how to save two babies from a falling building. Rosie got work at Parm Vadder's ranch, taking her children with her. This left me alone, and while I have a very hopeful, cheerful disposition, there were times then when I was afraid at night. Especially would I lie and count my money, wondering how long it would last, planning where and how to cut the cost of living, which was mainly rice and soup. I would lie and stare at the wall and pray that, if spirits ever do return, George's would come and show me a way out.

I had the coldest place in all Gunnison, and besides had to carry all my water up a flight of stairs and down a long hall to do my washing, then down a back flight to hang the clothes out. They would be frozen before I could get them on the line, and after leaving them a few days I would pry them off, again frozen stiff — both the clothes and me. (It's a wonder I haven't a darn sight worse than asthma!)

Now it grows colder each day. Sometime in December I get a letter from Ed, who is at White Horn, Colorado, working for Si Dore, in which he tells me that, if I care to come there, a mine is about to open and I can have the boarding-house. Again I pack and am off. Ed meets me in Salida, such a big boy, with such long hair and such looking clothes, and, much to my sorrow to-day, I wished then that he looked better. He was sensitive enough to know how I felt. Oh, if we could live some times over!

We go into a restaurant for dinner. I am given a menu (the first time in my life) and read it over. A porterhouse steak sounds good, so I will have that, and Ed, to be on the safe side, also orders porterhouse. When they come (the waiter smiling), never have I seen so much steak in my life, and we both burn with shame, and, instead of laughing it off, sit silently, eating very little. When we finish (many times since have I looked back and longed for the porterhouse left on that table), we go. Ed has a pair of broncs and a rickety wagon — the horses being so wild you had to leave the traces unfastened till ready to start. Finally he drives up with these mangy horses standing on their hind legs; gets out and holds their heads while the babies and I get in, I climbing in over the wheel, each move thinking the horses are going to run away. We are in and wrapped up. Ed makes a spring for the seat, and the horses lope away, my heart in my mouth — I have always been afraid of horses. Later, they simmer down somewhat or I am so cold that I have lost my fear of them. We suffer from the cold and the children begin to cry, I, too, have a lump in my throat and my arms are so stiff I can hardly hold the baby. After long hours, we come to camp, which I find consists of Dore's log cabin, another under construction, and a vacant tent about to fall down from the snow banked against one side. This tent looked as I felt, trying to hold up against the winds of Fate, ready to cave in with one last gust, and I am afraid, when I climbed down from the wagon, so stiff I couldn't stand, there were tears in both eyes and voice.

Dore, after kissing me, soon gave us a hot drink of whiskey, our cure-all for everything, which strangled and warmed me. Then I prepared supper. It seems I always get into the cooking, but I do not mind it, as these necessary everyday affairs take one's mind off things which trouble more, but are not nearly so worth while. Then our beds are made — mine in one room (all home-made bunks), Ed's on the floor in the same room, Dore's in the kitchen. There are two rooms in this cabin. By now I have time to ask about the boarding-house, when it will start, etc. Dore's answers are rather vague, and my heart falls. This is, I am afraid, another wrong lead.

For three days I cook the meals and wash in the bitter cold, Joy sick and crying, which annoys Dore. He tries to kiss me several times, saying it is so long since he has seen me, but I consider this no excuse, so object, while he, like many men, thinks I object only because I do not like him, but if the right one would come, I would fall for him, as 'every woman does.' The third day he tells Ed to go to town after feed. It would be necessary for him to be gone all night, and, as I have mentioned before, I have a Guardian Angel who is always on the job, so I tried to get Dore to wait awhile, but nothing would do — Ed must go. I talk Ed into refusing, and Dore fires him, thinking now he will have to leave, as, of course, he does, but I haul out the old trunk and pack again. The pitching horses are driven up, we pile in, and are away at a jump, on this same cold, cruel ride.

I feel guilty at making Ed lose his job. We stay all night in Salida, the next morning starting in different directions to fight the world, he driving toward Pueblo with these bucking horses, and five dollars I had given him from my rapidly diminishing pile. We do not see each other for many years, and when we do meet the first thing he does is to hand me that pitiful five dollars.

I start for Bonanza. I have been homesick for this place and it is the only place I know to turn to, although, after telling them how rich I expected to be a few years ago, this is quite a come-down to return broke and looking for work. Then, too, in the back of my mind was the hope that Jim would be home and that I might get to see him.

On the little narrow-gauge train running over into the valley I look at people and wonder if they know who I am or where I am going (our thoughts are so filled with ourselves). Joy cries very hard, and it becomes almost unbearable. I try everything to quiet her, getting so nervous the tears start and roll down my cheeks, and I wonder if I am turning into a weak sister. Then a red-nosed drummer — but with a kind heart — takes her and walks the floor with her till she whimpers herself to sleep. Arriving in Villa Grove, I go to the home of Mrs. B., the woman Mama had shaken so many years before because of me, and stay all night. They are very kind to me, and it seems so good to find people who know me and call me 'Annie.'

On New Year's Day I take the stage (a sled) for Bonanza. You may be sure I question the driver: 'Is there any work in Bonanza? What mines are working? Does any one give meals? Is any one baking bread? Who washes? Are there many coming in camp? Is Jim Chipman home?' When we arrive, I go to Mrs. Chipman's, where I feel I am an intruder, but stay nevertheless.

Now we find Joy has abscesses in her ears, but they are getting better. There is an epidemic of grippe in town; one whole family is down with it, and send for me to work. They give me a dollar each day and do not mind the children. Mr. Mahoney 'nusses' Joy, pillowing her little sore head in his shoulder and his white beard. Luck has turned, Joy gets better, they all get better, thanks, they say, to my good cooking.

CHAPTER XVI

'White wings, they never grow weary,
They carry me swiftly over the sea;
Night comes and I long for my dearie,
I'll spread out my white wings and sail home to thee.'
Old song, sung before aeroplanes were thought of

By the time the Mahoneys are well, I have rented a
house and furnished it with the few things I can borrow or buy; not much — a bed, stove, table, chairs,
and part of an old dresser. Every one is very good and
helps me in getting settled. I start in to bake and give
meals, and just manage to live. There is another
woman baking, she said, 'to pass the time away, I am
so lonesome.' I did so wish she would get over her
lonely feeling, and had a spirit of resentment when
seeing a man come from her door with a bundle under
his arm wrapped in newspaper. (These days only
unmarried men bought bread.) There are only a few
men in town, as the mines are closed till spring. One
of these men, Herbert, I had known slightly in
Chance. He, too, comes to buy bread — but remains
to visit, and I sympathize with him over his love
affairs, especially in not being able to marry Grace.
He seems to enjoy this, as he comes more often, and I
start to go out with him.

They are finding Jose rather hard to manage at
home and want her to come to me, which she does. I
now have two boarders, and try to have a good table,
losing money the first month; but, as I go on, find
keeping boarders is like any other business, one must

[218]

learn it. One-Eye Thompson is a sometime boarder and a constant visitor, and so glad to see me each time that he must either kiss me or put his arm around me. After the first time, which I stand for old time's sake, I object, and, whenever he comes after this, am behind a table sewing on what I called my 'Thompson dress,' as I kept it for just this occasion.

Our first dance supper we cook days before, borrowing dishes and tables. That night after the evening meal the work is rushed in order to reset the tables, then, when everything is ready, we rush and dress for the dance, running in and out to see how the supper is coming. (We live right by the hall.)

Once I go in alone and get the stove boiler of coffee on, when the door opens and a young fellow comes in, his face covered with pimples, the price tag still on his clothes, and with well-blacked, smelly boots. He begins to talk at once, 'Say — er — er don't you want to get married with me?'

I am thunderstruck (and, of course, pleased). 'Why, you must be joking.'

'I ain't. Only I want to be married, and you seem to be a rustler. But if you don't want to, all right, no hard feelings, just wanted to ask in time, that's all.' And while I laughed (silently) at him, still I was thrilled.

Time passes. I work hard each day, but I am now making a living and able to buy some new clothes. (Nothing like clothes to give a woman morale.) I am going to all the dances with Herbert, the children left in bed (no excuse, except I was young). Jose is going with a cousin of Herbert's, so that every Saturday night there is a 'settin' bee' in both the front room and the kitchen. All this time I visit with Mrs. Chipman as much as possible, trying to get some word from Jim, or news of when he might return, but I suspected then, and now know, his mother didn't want him to come to camp while I was there. One Christmas (I want Mrs. Chipman to think me popular) I sent to Montgomery Ward and bought a photograph album, and pretended an admirer had given it to me. And I surely got my money's worth in the effect it had on her, as well as in the album, which had a bright green clouded plush back, the front a brown mottled celluloid affair, over which a spray of apple blossoms rested. On top in large gilt letters was the word 'Album,' so one would not mistake it for anything else.

One spring I take the boarding-house at the Hanover Mine, up on the hill near timber line. It is a two-room cabin, and as soon as I get it cleaned, I tear up a white nightdress to make window curtains for the dining-room.

We put the meat in an old tunnel to keep it cool, and the first meal Neita walks in and tells the boarders 'she is just scraping the snow off the meat.' (The flies had got to it.) I hush her, but before dinner is over, she comes running again; this time Joy has fallen through the toilet hole and is just hanging on by her hands. Luckily it is a new one.

This day we have visitors, a girl I had gone to school with, who now lives in Denver, and a woman we have always known. When they come in care-free and well dressed to where I, so tired, rushed, and worried, am trying to get a meal ready for fifteen or eighteen men, I will own up a feeling comes over me, 'Why is it always thus? Why can other people have a good time while I must ever work?' (You see, I was almost having a dose of self-pity.) I laughed and talked with them, gritting my teeth to keep the tears back. When they are leaving, Mrs. Sharpe turns from the door and quickly steps to my side, patting me on the back. This is too much, and now the tears come, and I am afraid drop in the dinner.

When we return to town, the first telephone is being run in and the switchboard is to be at my house. It was very funny to see and hear some of these miners use it. (Just as funny the first time I tried it, but not to me.)

There was the old Indian scout, Mark Biedell, who once, when the Indians were on the war-path, located 'the bloody butchers,' as he called them. He bravely climbed on his horse and rode from the Canero to Fort Garland, a matter of one hundred miles, without stopping. He wanted the soldiers. When he rode up to the fort, his horse fell, and Mark Biedell was pulled from under a dead horse. He was not this brave the time he saw his first telephone. How he did tremble, backing off, and rolling his eyes. After I had almost forced the receiver on him, he handled it as though it might be a rattlesnake, finally getting within three feet of the transmitter, with the wrong end of the receiver in his ear. I said, 'Say hello.' He fairly bellowed, 'Hello!' then sweatily turned it over to me and I talked for him.

Here it was that Helen, our resident fast woman, came very often to talk to headquarters in Salida, bossed and supervised by the 'Madam,' who, when times and occasion demanded, would send over extra girls. She explains to me, 'You know we own the girls' clothes and, when they do not do to suit, why, we just hold out their clothes on them.' She also said, 'I have worked' (only she didn't say 'worked') 'from coast to coast, and never yet have seen such illiterate women as there are in Bonanza.' (And my copies of Dickens and George Eliot right in sight, too!)

Finally she married a saloon-keeper, and lived among us, respectable and respected for a time. Only Mrs. Smeltzer never could stand her. One time we were having a Christmas tree, and Helen was asked for a donation, also to come to the tree. Mrs. Smeltzer heard of this and objected, saying, 'If old Helen comes, I will climb her frame,' so we sent a bag of candy to her. As time went on, Helen grew tired of this quiet life (they usually do) and started drinking and fighting. At last she left her husband and went back to her old life.

I was running the telephone board when Helen came in one day, wishing to telephone Laura White, the 'Madam,' who lived in Salida. She sent her girls out from Salida to the different mining camps on or near payday.

When I got the call through, Helen said, among other things, 'No, don't send Queenie, they don't like her. Send Grace and Lillie — no, I think they will be enough; there are only about twenty-five men.'

When she was through telephoning, she watched me make out a slip for her call, and said: 'Is this the way you keep track? Now, I keep tab of all my girls and all business transactions on the door facing.' The 'Madam' is still alive and 'doing business,' but she is not as prosperous as formerly — for she was seen recently in a store buying a paper pattern and some gingham, and she remarked by way of explanation, 'Business in my line is so damned bad, I have to go to sewing.'

In these early days we took the sporting women as we did the saloons, as a matter of course. They, like the saloons, never bothered us, so we had no feeling for or against them, and even now, when I hear talk of raiding or running them out of town, I never pay any attention, considering it none of my business. At one time in my married life their house was just back of mine on the mountain-side, a flight of steps running up to it. Nights when they and their friends would be drunk and fighting, I have heard curses, screams, the break of falling glass, wild laughter — some of them have the shrillest, emptiest, most cutting and unfeeling laugh — then the sound of people falling down this long flight of steps, bumping and cursing each step, till, in the morning, when I opened my door, I expected to see the ground strewn with maimed people. But — much to my disappointment — there is nothing in sight. Once my creeping baby disappears, and I finally spy him, his yellow curls shining in the sunlight, crawling step by step up this flight, and I watch him to see he doesn't fall backward, letting him go, much to the disgust of my neighbors, but I know these girls can't hurt him, and he may help them.

In some ways I am not a popular telephone operator. The general manager has been in town for a week in a big poker game, where he even has his meals carried to him. Each morning and evening his wife calls, wishing to talk to him, and each time the saloon-keeper says he knows nothing of him. I, in turn, lie to her, telling her I can't find him. Finally she gets desperate (expecting and thinking all sorts of things about him) and begs me, 'Do please try and get some news of him, I am so worried.'

I thought, 'Ethics or no ethics, I'm going to put you out of your misery,' so I call the saloon, asking for Mr. S. and telling the barkeeper the telephone is out of order. Soon S. comes to the telephone talking sleepy and mad (I expect he was losing), 'Well, now, what's eating you?' I never answer, only ring and connect him with his wife in Salida, listening in long enough to hear her ask in a strangled voice, 'What in the name of God do you mean?'

Another time I meddle. A married man and wo-man — not married to each other, however, are carrying on quite an affair, every one knowing about it except those most interested. One day this man's child is very sick, and they have me call every place he might be. Then his brother calls again, rather blaming me for not finding him, so I tell the brother, 'I can't get him on the telephone, but if you go to the

cabin in the head of Raleigh Gulch, you will find him.'
He does find him, but not alone. This was one love
affair blighted, but not soon enough.

By now Jose and Will are engaged, also Herbert
and I. I don't know just how this came about, as, although we go together, I never had any idea of marrying him, and he always said he never asked me. I
don't think he did, more than to say once, 'You would
never marry a man like me, would you?' But I must
have been willing to consider it, since we are engaged.
I don't think he was crazy about me at this time, but
I was getting so tired, and wanting and wishing for
some one to share the burdens with me. (I could see
waiting for Jim was a hopeless matter, as I never got
any word from or of him.)

In this camp the event of the day is when the stage
comes in, and a few men are always sitting or standing on the corner, waiting for it. Some one might
come in, or now we will get to see the paper. (I, too,
watch each day, hoping some one will come.) This
day I am watching out the window (he may come yet),
and see a small figure climb down. I know at once he
is not one of our kind, with his tight-fitting suit, and
his little round straw hat. He moves as fast as a chip-
munk, putting off a telescope, a bundle, a violin, and
a camera. The first thing is to discover who he is and
where he comes from, what for and why? But much
to our distress, we learn only just as much as he wishes
to tell, which is that he is Dr. Right, lately of Alaska,
formerly of New York, and, in thirty years we have
been unable to learn what for or why. As you know

him, you find him a wonder — a jack of all trades and master of each, but still a failure, as men count it, always busy with these same quick movements, ever smiling, a cheerful word or story for all listeners, never doing an unkind deed or saying an unkind word of any person or thing. Often when you would pass an unfavorable opinion on some one and ask, 'Don't you think so too, Doctor?' — you knew he felt as you did — his only answer was 'Um—mm.' You could take this any way you wished.

He gets a job assaying on one of the mines and is accurate and reliable; when there is need he practices his profession and is very successful; he gives music lessons on several instruments, and is a fine teacher; he plays for the dances, is a carpenter, a cook, and can sew. Then, too, he is an inventor, having built several mills in which he had a new process for the treatment of ore. He was a very artistic photographer, finishing and mounting, and sometimes tinting, his pictures. But the thing he did best was bringing beauty and music into our lives by plays or light opera. For these he wrote the words and composed the music — he may have used parts from other operas he had heard — planned the dances, designed and helped make all costumes, did all the coaching, keeping every one in a good humor, although having them go over a dance or song many times. He would stop playing long enough — his chin drawn down on the violin, his eyes rolled up taking in everything — to say, 'Now' (giving the violin a sharp tap) 'we will try once a—gain, once a—gain.'

THEATRICALS

There is very little talent to draw from (I say 'is' because he is doing this very thing to-day, under the same conditions), but he would work them all in — old and young, and make them sing or dance. Jose, Herbert, and Will all sang well, so had prominent parts, while I was used as a filler-in. One Christmas I am queen (I think this play was Cinderella) and a tool sharpener on one of the mines is King. Doctor has a time with us, trying to make me sing, and teaching Kaufman to be a little less the tool-sharpener and more of the King.

The night comes, we all are dressed in our kingly and queenly robes (cheesecloth, tinfoil, and cotton ermine, made with splotches of ink), Doctor out in front playing the quivery, thrilling beginning; time for the curtain (a boy on either side to pull it back, their lives threatened if they made a miscue), when the King starts to hunt frantically for something.

I whisper, 'What is it?'

'Oh, my specter is gone.'

I don't know what he means, and pass the word out to Doctor, 'Kaufman has lost his specter.'

Doctor, tucking his violin under his arm, trips behind. 'What is it, what is it — your specter?'

'You know — the thing I carry in my hand.'

'Oh' (not even a tone of disgust), 'you mean your scepter.'

We go on. Once Doctor looks up startled to see Kaufman chewing gum during the whole performance, even while singing.

Another play called for four people singing and

playing. I, used as a filler, am supposed to pretend to sing and play a guitar, and I think, since I can neither sing nor play, that I will make up on my dress. And I do, making a much-beruffled white affair (I am being daring now, as married women, especially widows, didn't wear white), with beading heading each ruffle. In this beading (I must have some color) are run endless yards of bright red ribbon. When this confection is done, I spread it on the bed, where I can admire it. Besides this dress I have made one for Jose also, never being absent from rehearsals, the boarders to be cooked for, a dance supper besides, and helping the Doctor with costumes. The day before I do not feel as well as usual, and before evening am broken out in huge red blotches, which turn out to be from chicken pox, but nevertheless I go on moving my lips in the song and dragging my fingers across the guitar, the red ribbon in my dress matching the polka dots on my face.

This time the Doctor has a ballet of small girls. I have made the tarlatan dresses which stand out above their knees (we have only accomplished this by coaxing, it wasn't considered decent), and for tights they have long white stockings (heavy cotton). When we come to dress them, all have on long-sleeved and long-legged red, gray, and écru underwear, with the instructions from the mothers not to roll it up or down, so it hangs below as to sleeves, and is concealed the best it can be in the white stockings. Now I know what is meant by a 'nobby effect.'

Doctor is living in an old store building that is high,

bare, and cold, but he builds a house within a house, by throwing up a light framework, then covering this with canvas. By now his wife has come from New York, and is just as much of a character in her way as he is in his. He gives a dinner in his house to which I rush in at the last minute (it seems I am always in a hurry), sitting at the table at once, reach for a huge cup half filled with what I supposed was water, taking a large swallow before tasting, and thereby almost wrecking the party. It was clear gin, and by the time I was through gasping, spluttering, and wiping tears, I had learned that if you don't taste, it pays to sniff before taking.

As we work, either sewing or cooking, Jose and I have happy times. We both read a good deal, only she remembers while I forget. You see, I was always so tired that when I stole the time to read it was for amusement, never for instruction. We could carry on a conversation, using sayings and characters from Dickens, and others would not understand what we were talking about. One day we are baking cakes, and the little try cake has just been put in the oven to bake. We are discussing marriage and trial marriages which we had read of, and I ask, 'Well, Jose, what do you think of these trial marriages, anyway?'

She opens the oven door, pulling the little try cake toward her. 'Well, I think they would be fine, only' — here she hesitates a minute — 'what would you do with the little try cakes?' — meaning the children.

Another time Neita is reading, looks up and asks, 'What is a virgin, Aunt Jose?'

'A woman who hasn't been married.'

'Oh, and what is a man virgin?'

'A eunuch.'

One day I have a miner fixing my stovepipe for me, and wished to compliment him, and keep him in a good humor — this putting up stoves is such a hard matter — so I hold the pipe for him and rush around and hand him tools, look up at him where he is wiring it together, and say, 'You would surely make a good second-hand man' (meaning because he could mend things so well), but he is Dutch and doesn't get it. He looks frowningly down on me and informs me that he 'don't intend to be a second-hand husband for any widder.' So that was that.

The day comes when Herbert goes and breaks to his mother that he is considering getting married, and she, a lady and ever brave, never objects, nor lets him see the misgivings in her heart over him marrying a woman with two children and no money in sight anywhere. (Come to think of it, I guess we were all brave.) At this time he has a small butcher shop, so small that he gets only a quarter of beef at one time. He has had a partner, but they dissolved partnership over the question of whether or not you should sell sausage after the flies had been to it. No business is small enough to escape problems.

I am getting our dresses ready, dark blue near (not very near) silk, trimmed in rows upon rows of tiny white lace. I shudder when I think of them, but thought them pretty then. Jose and Will are married first and move into a little cabin.

HERBERT AS A HUSBAND

Then one morning I leave the children with a friend, we climb into a buggy, drive seventeen miles to Saguache over Ute Pass, and are married at his mother's. A few are invited in, we have a lovely dinner, and get several presents. In the afternoon we load into the buggy and make the homeward journey, I, though I try to fight it off, with a feeling of disappointment. Had I made another false move? My friends said I had, and that 'Herbert was all right, an honest enough sort of a person, still — he would never set the river afire.' He never did, but who wants it afire? He proved to be the best man I have ever known. Too honest, and believing every one just as honest as he; absolutely clean in every way; never an unkind thought or action toward man or beast; a very hard worker and a most cheerful disposition. We never had but one disagreement in the years we were married, and when I hear some one say, 'Of course, we had our quarrels as all married folks do,' I think, 'I know one couple who did not.' Of course, part of this was due to me, as a wife married the second time (if she has any brains at all) makes a much better wife, having learned how to manage both herself and husband. To-day I am a better woman for having known that there are men like him.

CHAPTER XVII

A plea for the beggar on horseback. It seems to me the fault-finding, if any, should be with the one who puts him there. Instead, it has been the beggar who has been sneered at, it being expected of him to sing his booster's praises rather than enjoy the view from his exalted position. Then, too often, the beggar finds it is an ass he has been set upon.

A. E.

AFTER a time we buy a house, using the last of my money — some two hundred dollars; and while it wasn't much of a house (in the boom days it had been a saloon — when I was a child Lil had lived here), it had four rooms, two of them very small, and bulging in the back where they were built in the hillside. On the front room was dreadful wall-paper. (Sherwood Anderson isn't the only one who is bothered by wall-paper and water-lily pictures!) We start to tear out and build up, Herbert working every spare moment, before and after shift. I have a new rocking-chair or two, a new dresser, and an ingrain carpet; this was rather large as to figures, but then — you can't have everything. I filled the large windows with plants, and, oh, the endless wrapping up of these plants winter nights, then lying awake worrying about them, only to get up in the morning to find them frozen stiff. Then, without dressing, I would sift around in the cold, throwing cold water on them and shedding a few tears. We are very nicely settled here, better than I have ever been before, Herbert working hard each day in the Juretta, which was owned by Colonel S. T. Everett, of Cleveland, Ohio.

HERBERT WAS GETTING THREE DOLLARS A DAY IN THE EMPRESS JOSEPHINE MINE

FOOD AND DRINK

For many years Colonel Everett was a provider for Bonanza, spending his money just out of kindness, I used to think. The dream of his life was to strike a paying mine. He owned and operated the Empress Josephine. Many times men had found pockets of very rich ore there, some of it running one hundred and forty dollars per pound. There was a tradition that at one time miners had broken into a glory hole of this rich ore, and being 'on the outs' with the management had timbered over it. To this day men search for the lost ore in the Josephine.

Herbert was getting three dollars per day, and on this we saved. I am so anxious to get ahead. We live very well, I am a good cook and manager, and take pride in having his lunches better than other men's. It has always been an opinion of mine that if men were fed better they would drink less, as part of the craving they have for booze is hunger. Many times I have seen men coming off shift stop at the saloon for a drink, and I knew they had done a hard day's work on a half-cooked breakfast, and a lunch at noon which was not satisfying. So in my home there was a hearty breakfast, fruit, a cooked breakfast food, meat, potatoes, and usually hot biscuit, coffee-cake or cookies, and coffee. The lunch was good home-made bread, meat, fruit, cake, and pie, always a change each day. Then a big supper at night consisting of a salad, two vegetables, meat, bread, and two kinds of dessert always. Each day I baked pie and cake. Miners did and do live well, when they are working.

Neita is six now and ready to start to school, and

I am glad, as she is a strange child — doesn't know how to play, and cries a good deal. I call her Niobe. I have known children to come to the house to play with her and she would stand and cry, not a mean, hateful cry, just the tears running down her cheeks. When I would tell her to go on and play, she would answer, 'I can't, I don't know how.' It seems to me she was reading before she ever went to school; at any rate, she soon did read; then the question was solved. From that day to this she has never lacked for entertainment and has to be pulled and driven from books. She was always unusually bright in school, and I hoped great things for her — that she might do and be what I had always longed to do and be. I encouraged her every minute, never anything she wrote but was praised if it was worth praise, and always criticized and helped, in so far as I was able. She had, and has, the words and the gift, and I had some sort of feeling. Like most writers, she wished to write of something else than what she knew, and of some other place; then I would tell her: 'Oh, Neita, there is so much to write of here. Can't you see it? Why, there is a story in every house. If I could only write!' — never thinking I would try it after over twenty years!

When we had lived in Chance, Herbert was one of those hard-working teamsters who occasionally had 'birthdays,' and he had had several in Bonanza. At these times, he had a high plug hat he wore. I don't know whether he was more daring then, or was trying to live up to the silk hat. He never brought this hat home, but was keeping it in reserve somewhere. One day I hear the singing and yells that mean a birthday, but even then, when I look from my window and see Herbert in the midst of the bunch, the silk hat on one side of his head, I can hardly believe it. A weakness comes in my knees and stomach, but I go quietly about my work. Neighbors come to see how I am taking it, but I talk on every subject except drunk men and high hats. When evening comes, so does Herbert. I have a good supper waiting; he comes in daringly, still hatted, and looks at me as much as to say, 'Yes, I am drunk, and what are you going to do about it?' Just what I had been wondering myself. I say and do none of the things I had intended to say and do, only, 'Come on to your supper before it is cold.' When he is eating, I walk to the bed where the high hat is resting, pick it up in my hands, carry it to the kitchen table, ram the butcher knife into it, then hack it up, lift a stove lid and cram it into the stove. He opens his eyes rather wide, but never says one word and neither do I. Neither of us ever speaks of this again, but it must have been the right thing to do, because there were no more birthdays, at least not that he took part in.

We have been married almost a year when Earl is born. Just a short time before this, Doctor gives a play. It was Pocahontas, and Herbert was John Rolfe — Doctor doesn't ask me to fill in this trip. After they have it in Bonanza, they decide to go to Saguache with it. Of course I am asked to go along — they know I can't — and I make Herbert promise to return the same night, making myself and him think I might be sick while he was gone. (I knew I wouldn't be, but couldn't stand for him to dance all night and I home alone. Aren't women selfish?) So he promises to return, and just as soon as the play is over, he gets a saddle horse and rides over the pass, getting in just before the break of day, and I am startled to see him standing in front of the dresser, taking off his large plumed hat, his face still with all the make-up on, in the entire John Rolfe costume. I laugh, thinking how funny he must have looked riding along this silent road, dressed as he was, a bottle of whiskey in each saddle-bag, that Johnny O'Neil had given him just before leaving, because, 'You took your part so well.' I wished that some sheep-herder or prospector had seen him — I fancy they would have thought him a spirit.

Again I am sick without a doctor. No excuse in the world except that I don't want to spend the money — wishing so much to get ahead, and twenty-five dollars took a long time to save. Rosie comes again and helps me, but informs me this is the last time she will ever do it. Herbert stays home from the mine for two days and does all the washing, then after that we manage till the ninth day when I get up and start to work again. I shall never forget the first time I go to the window. When I had gone to bed it was winter, and when I looked up on the hillside nine days later, I saw a faint tinge of green showing on the aspen, and it seemed good to be alive. Summer comes late here. It was the fourth of June.

I can see we will never get ahead by day's pay, so talk Herbert into going to Saguache and buying the stage line, which we do, going in debt for it. This worried him, as he was never a plunger, so we only remain here about one year, when he returns to Bonanza (you can never wean a man away who has worked in the mines) and I soon follow.

We have sold our first house, but now buy a much newer and better one, and all the furniture goes with it. Now I have a Home Comfort range and a lovely bookcase, or at least I think so. I liked it because it was very plain in this time of Grand Rapids, pressed gingerbread, golden oak furniture. I had to scrub bear grease off the kitchen floor. Some man had more bear oil than brains and had used it to oil the floor, but it refused to oil and caked around cracks and corners.

Herbert has steady work and we are getting on fine. I have plenty to read, having books sent me from a traveling library in Denver. After a lot of consideration, I branch out by sending for some books myself. They are advertised and sold by the 'Woman's Home Companion' — are called 'My Lady's Library.' With them comes a shelf to hang on the wall and you could hang cups under this and place other dishes or small art objects on top if you wished; at least the advertisements said so. They also said if one read the contents of these books one would know all that was necessary or expected of a lady in art, poetry, history, and fiction. This was just what I wanted, so sent for them, one dollar per month till paid for. They were all as advertised, and much more, but I could never make myself read so many of them, that is why

THE LIFE OF AN ORDINARY WOMAN

I fall short of knowing what a lady should know. 'Makers of Venice' was never opened, 'Emerson's Essays' but very little, 'Elizabeth and Her German Garden' was well worn, as also was Charles and Mary Lamb's 'Shakespeare.' The most read and worn of all was a copy of Dickens's 'Chimes' and 'A Christmas Carol.' But they have all lent an air to the cabins I have lived in.

Here, too, I go in for art by the yard — a yard of violets, a yard of roses — but I drew the line at a yard of puppies or kittens. I also send and get several Copley prints.

I remember a Fourth of July in Bonanza when Herbert is to be Marshal of the day. Now the duties of a Marshal were, I supposed, to ride around, with a bright sash over one shoulder — and look full of business, but, Herbert, much to my disappointment, thought differently. He does ride, but there is no sash nor any trimmings. But he sees that all the events start on time, that every one is looked after, that all the races are as fair as they ever can be, and that there is not too much drinking. This is a copy of one of the programmes:

OFFICIAL PROGRAMME

July 4th, 1905

BONANZA, COLORADO

FORENOON

9:00 A.M. Double Hand Rock Drilling Contest
First prize, $50.00, Second, $25.00
11:00 A.M. Baseball Game

[238]

THE FOURTH OF JULY IN BONANZA

AFTERNOON

1:00 P.M. Horse Races
1/2 Mile dash, first prize, $25.00; second, $10.00
1/4 Mile dash, first prize, 20.00; second, 10.00
Novelty Race, first prize, 15.00; second, 5.00
Tug of War, $3.50 to winning team
Men's 100-yard dash, first, $10.00; second, $5.00
Boys' 50-yard dash, 7 to 15 years, $2.00 and $1.00
Little girls, $1.00 and $.50
Little boys, $1.00 and $.50
Boys' sack race, $1.00
Burro race, $1.00 and $.50

It doesn't sound very thrilling, but you should have been there to see the drilling contest. The men stripped to the waist, a handkerchief bound around their foreheads, some of them hairy, some smooth, all white. There is money bet on the different teams, and much excitement. Each team has its drills all sharpened and in a pile. The contest is to see which can drill the deepest into a rock, in a given length of time. This huge rock is up on a platform where all can see. One man crouches, turning the drill when his partner strikes it with a large hammer, putting all his strength behind each stroke. It would be a lasting disgrace should he miss the head of the drill and hit his partner's hand. The sweat pours; each time a man strikes he expels his breath in a rasping puff; mud and water fly from the hole. They change drills — 'Pretty work! Pretty work!' — the turner letting loose with one hand and reaching for a sharp drill, all with one movement, it seems, pulling one drill out and slipping the other in, the striker never missing a stroke. (These drills fly into the crowd, and it is part of the entertainment to miss them.) Then the men change places. They are dripping wet with sweat, mud-bespattered, and maybe have bleeding hands, when time is called. The hole is measured and another team takes their place.

Herbert came down from his horse and his distinguished place, long enough to win the men's footrace — and loaned the horse for a race, meanwhile sitting on the fence. The races were run up and down the street.

Along here I see my first picture show. The people are driving through and stop one night in Bonanza. It is of Jesse James and his gang, and it doesn't seem so remarkable to me that they move as it is that they could get these intimate pictures of Jesse James. Afterward, when I talked it over with Eli, he thought perhaps they might have faked some of it, and I thought, 'Now, isn't that just like Eli? Always picking things to pieces.'

Again Herbert had an honor conferred on him, or at least I thought so, but he had his doubts from the first, and it turned out that he was right. He was elected Mayor. Now this may sound like a small job when it is such a small town, but not so; there is more depending on him and he seems far more essential than the Mayor of Denver. In the first place, everything that goes wrong, from a drunken husband to a leak in the town pump, is laid at his door, and he is supposed to do something about it. When a cow breaks a fence, destroying a garden, or the stage gets in late, he is to look into and correct it. There is no money in this job, but a man is supposed to be at all the town meetings, or be called from his work at any and all times.

There had been a good deal of complaint about the girls on the hill disturbing the peace. (No matter how small the place, there are always uplifters.) Herbert is supposed to see about it. Any one else would have sent the Marshal, who would either not have gone at all or gone and made a profitable visit; but Herbert, when he had a thing to do, did it; so he marches bravely up these steps, in the daytime, too. I never knew what was said, but this is as it would be.

When Mabel opened the door, dressed in a distracting kimono, mostly open, Herbert would lift his hat (he was always very polite, never asking me to dance in his life without saying, 'Would you please dance with me this time?' and thanking me when he seated me); then he would say, 'Miss Mabel' (if these girls have last names I never heard them), 'can't you carry on your business a little quieter?' I know Mabel would laugh at him, but would respect and like him for his earnestness and would, the next time, if she wasn't too drunk, try to be a little less loud.

Sometime along here Alice Roosevelt is to be married. We felt very near to her. You see, this was Romance, and having none of our own we took part of hers. I was especially interested because I am but very little older than Alice Longworth. All the country was sending her gifts, so we, not to be outdone, decided to send one also. It seems to me now that we held a meeting to decide what, and how. We thought of a quilt, each woman doing a certain amount of work on it. This was voted against as not being dainty enough. The final decision was a centerpiece of Battenberg lace. One woman did beautiful work and we had her make it — each of the rest of us, except one, chipping in fifty cents. She said, 'My cousin's wife, what lives in Californie, saw these Roosevelts coming in to a show once, and when the band played "Hail to the Chief," this Alice danced all the way down the row between the seats. I don't call it reefined nor dignified. Our family don't hold with any such doings.'

When the centerpiece is finished, I have the honor of wrapping it — 'You're so artistic.' I spread myself. The finished product was tacked on pink tissue paper, 'to make the different stitches show up better.' We inserted a paper — we had no cards — with all our names on, and sent it, then waited, reading the papers to see what other people had sent. Each day we watched the stage come in and then would gather to see what Alice had said. Long, long weeks we waited — the papers never mentioned any 'lovely gift from the West.' We never heard a word. Alice, how could you?

There was almost the interest in this wedding that there had been in that of Frances Folsom and Grover Cleveland. I was a little girl then, and she a fairy princess. Later, when her first baby came, a girl, we were disappointed and understood that Grover was, too. Then, when other girls came to them and the papers were making light of Grover, I was mad at all newspapers, especially 'Puck.'

CHAPTER XVIII

A swarming of human bees and no one to beat on a pan in order to hive them.

A. E.

I AM getting tired of this little mining camp (had I only known it, I was eating my white bread then), wanting to get a start in life and seeing no chance here. I am afraid I harped on this one string a good deal, as one day Herbert said, 'There is no satisfying you. You no more than get one thing than you want another.'

'Sure I do. This is what makes progress, men trying to satisfy women.'

About this time work slackens up and we have a few hundred dollars saved. There is an opening or drawing of Indian land near Lander, Wyoming, and Herbert and a few others decide to go to this. After he leaves, I, to burn the bridges, sell the furniture and house, and pack, ready to go any time.

Herbert writes that he did not have any luck at the land drawing, doesn't like Wyoming, anyway, and for me to sit tight till he finds a place. But I am ready to move, and do move to Cañon City, thinking I will rent a cheap room for a while. The outstanding event of this trip is that, since we are seeing the world, we don't want to miss anything, so ride outside on the observation car going through the Royal Gorge and are blown to pieces — our eyes are full of cinders and clothes full of smoke. Neita loses her hat. (I have just made it, an old Leghorn, steamed and pressed into shape, and trimmed with washed blue ribbon and a pink rose dropping gracefully over one eye, or at least I, when I hung it on the back of a chair and backed off, squinting at it, thought so.) I scolded, she cried, and rubbed the collected dust and tears all over her face.

In those times I am afraid to spend, so we drop in on a woman who has lived in Bonanza. She is very kind and shares all she has with me, but, in her excitement, forgets to tell me one of her boys has whooping cough. He is generous, too, and gives it to my children.

I get one little back room, hot as hot. It has two beds in it and we have the privilege of eating in the kitchen. There we hole up, myself and three children all whooping it up, Joy quite sick; I herding them, to keep them off the lawn, out of the street, and making all of us generally miserable. No good news from Herbert and no nearer settled. He thinks he will go to Bingham Cañon, Utah.

After several weeks, Herbert sends for me, and I go to Utah. Going uptown in Salt Lake is the first street-car any of us have been on, and when the conductor holds out his hand for the fare, Joy, thinking she has found one friendly person, grabs it and shakes hands with him. At the hotel we have finger bowls — also something new — and Neita, as many have done before and since, drinks from hers. Herbert meets us here and we go to the opera, my first and last. He'd rather go to something else, but I have read of operas and want to see one. It is 'Parsifal.' I am really thrilled, and now, when in a group of women who are discussing opera, I can hold my end up by breaking in, 'The first time I saw "Parsifal" I did not think much of Kundry.' (They have more respect for you if your criticism is unfavorable.) Or, 'So-and-So is in Denver. They often have good operas in Denver.' (So they do, but we failed to be there at the same time.)

We go on up to Bingham, a copper mining camp, where steam shovels are cutting down huge mountains. There is an overhead tramway, carrying ore, running the length of this town, which they said was seven miles long and seven feet wide. The gulch is so narrow, there can be a sidewalk only on one side, and it is only three feet wide. The houses are built on, and in, these steep hillsides. We had a two-room house built on a mining dump. Many other houses, filled with Italians, crowded us close, and never did I know so many people could hive in one room. They seem numberless, and I am quite sure the beds never had a chance to cool from different miners coming off different shifts and using them.

Herbert has quite a long walk to the mine where he works, and I think he does not care for the foreigners he has to work with. Here he joins the Union. When leaving the hall, a man takes his hand and, pressing it in a peculiar manner, whispers a word in his ear (I expect it was 'Bill Haywood'). 'Now,' he said, 'you have the *gripe* and the *pess* word.'

We remain here only a short time. I have been getting letters from a family in Goldfield, Nevada — a new booming gold camp, and it all sounds so interesting and prosperous that I urge Herbert to go. He is

[246]

slow to make a change, but does consent to give up his job, sell the furniture (at a loss), and again we are on the road. This move was entirely my fault, and all that followed I had to swallow without a word of complaint. Herbert was big enough never once to say, 'It is because of you we are here.'

The Goldfield train was just pulling out as we came into Hazen, so we had to spend the night there, in a green-lumber, just-put-up hotel, crowded with people going to this gold boom town. Outside along the railroad track was the largest pile of goods that I had ever seen — tools of all kinds, tents, bedding, provision, merchandise, lumber, barrels of whiskey, and everything, the owners frantic to get it into Goldfield. In the big bare office where we crowded around an enormous heating stove, we all talked of gold and Goldfield. Miners, mining men, prospectors, business men, promoters, and men of every sort were there; not so many women, but what there were, were more excited than the men. Mine were the only children in this adventuring crowd.

That day as I sat there I thought, 'I wish I could write about these people and describe their actions, faces, and clothes'; and I considered getting a pencil and doing it, but writing seemed impossible to me then. Here we saw our first big automobiles owned by very rich men. We, too, expected to have one soon; I had even bought a big automobile veil so as to be ready. In all the pictures they had their heads wrapped in a veil, the long ends blowing straight out behind them.

THE LIFE OF AN ORDINARY WOMAN

The doctor at home had one of the first automobiles. It had to be pulled up the hill every time he came to Bonanza. It was 1910 before I ever rode in one, and then and always my seat has been a back one, the guest's seat.

We arrived in Goldfield soon after the Gans-Nelson prize fight. People were wild over it and made a hero of Joe Gans. I wish I had tried to write then and tell of the stirring times; but there was no time for writing in this mad but thrilling search for gold. (I have heard that Peter B. Kyne first started to write in Goldfield.) The cost of everything was soaring; wages were also high. Whiskey was cheaper than water, and used more. We had a time getting into a hotel (a thrown-together frame building), and I remember it was alongside the 'Velvet Bar' Saloon. After standing in line for a long time, we find there are no more rooms. A man who had a room reserved said he 'could sleep on a billiard table,' and gave the room to me, to be shared with two women who were in line back of me. They turned out to be a nurse and a fast woman, and these two and myself took this tiny room. Necessity does make strange bedfellows! I use coats and things and make a bed for the girls on the floor; Herbert takes Earl and goes to the 'bull-pen,' a large tent full of cots, running over with all sorts and conditions of men. The next day I look for some kind of shelter, and while the sound of hammers fills the air, and houses and shacks are going up day and night, still there is no place for us. I walk, coax, and beg for a place till both my feet and heart ache. It is three days

before I find one. During this search, I am passing the
Mohawk Saloon, where there is a greater crowd than
usual, although the streets are all so crowded you
could hardly walk. Two men are fighting; some one in
the crowd calls, 'Look out for the knife, kid.' I don't
know whether this was a plan to stop the fight or not;
at any rate, it did, both men letting go at once and
backing off in opposite directions.

When almost desperate, I find two tiny rooms for
forty dollars per month, and we move into this,
promising to give it up in case of a sale, which happens
on the third day, so again we are out in a cold, cruel
world. After searching, we find a small one-room tent
which had been boarded up, then covered with tar
paper. For this we give three hundred and seventy-
five dollars and move in. Our beds are made of bed
springs which during the day can be closed against the
wall; in one corner is a tiny inkstand stove; between
the foot of the bed and table is one trunk, which two
children can sit on while they eat. (On wash days this
trunk is used for a bench.) The big box is unpacked
and used for a dresser, lending quite an air when it is
draped with a piece of Battenberg on top, with the old
mirror hanging above. I hemstitch curtains for the
one window and door, and after the books are unpacked and put on a shelf, and the few pictures tacked
up, we are quite cosy.

Now I am seeing life in big gobs; fortunes made or
lost each day on the stock exchange, in the saloons,
at the mines, or at stealing, buying, and selling high-
grade. I knew men who made, in addition to their

wages, from twenty to fifty dollars per day, depending on how rich the ore was where they were working. The ore was a dark porous formation, no gold showing till it was roasted. In almost every family, either in the oven or on the back of the stove, there were pieces of this ore roasting; then, when you poured water over the hot ore, blisters of gold came out. Gold does not glitter, only the baser metals do. Mark Twain knew this, and said, 'However, like the rest of the world, I still go on underrating men of gold and glorifying men of mica.' After selling the house, we put all the money we had left, not much, into mining stock — United Mines. Each day after we buy it, it drops, till it is taken off the board. This was our luck. Other people around us, with seemingly no more judgment, were buying stock and making money. We are forced to be honest, as there is no high-grade on the Kewanas Mine where Herbert works (nor low, either, for that matter). Wages are very high, prices accordingly. We find that we must all work and I get a place in a laundry, five dollars per day.

The woman who owned it was a Swede who had been a servant in the old country to a wealthy family. One of the sons comes over here, goes broke, but has the luck to run across this former servant (much older than he) and she helps him. Finally they are married, and she heaps favors on him, providing fine clothes, a house, and the best of everything, all the time thinking he is conferring a favor on her. She is coining money in the laundry, has several to help and is very good to each. The work was terrible. It did not take

WE LIVED ON HIGH-GRADER'S HILL IN GOLDFIELD

her long to find out I wasn't much force as an ironer, and I was glad when she let me out. The afternoon (I expect this was to soften the blow) when I went home for keeps, she passed little Swedish cakes, and anchovies on toast.

Afterward, when times got hard and the husband discontented, I heard that she sent him to Sweden on a visit. There he fell in love with a young girl of his own class (I wouldn't call it high), and refused to return. Then the provider, after consulting many fortune-tellers, and finding no hope, takes an overdose of headache powder and is at rest, beyond the reach of husbands, love, or laundry.

Goldfield was discovered, so I heard, by some cowboy prospectors (I believe George Winfield was one of them) riding into Tonopah. Their horses kicked rich gold-bearing quartz from the side of the trail. This is all desert country, covered with tufts of yucca, Joshua palms, and, in the spring, beautiful flowers. Low hills rise to the east, and on the northwest is the Malapai — this is in the form of a plateau, desert on top, with a rocky, steep rim.

In the lower part of town some one was fortunate enough to find and stake a small spring, and from this they made more money than if they had found the Mohawk or the Little Florence. Water was hauled around on wagons in big tin tanks, a short hose which could be unhooked giving you a pailful for fifteen cents. Never was water so precious. One never used more than one could help, the family all bathing in the same tubful, then using it to mop with, then pouring it, very sparingly, on a small patch of wheat planted beside the door. Many tired and dusty men would stop and look at this little bunch of green, but it did not last long, as the sun soon burned it up. I know of one woman who kept a boarding-house, who would boil the dishwater, then skim it, and strain it, in this way using it time and time again.

We lived on High-Grader's Hill, looking down Hall Street, across Sundog Avenue. On the upper end of this avenue the prominent people lived. There were many lovely homes, some of stone, a great many on the bungalow order. Later they built stone school-houses, banks, churches, hotels, and business blocks, that, one would think, might last for ages.

At that time there was a population of thirty thousand. To-day, eighteen years later, I understand only two buildings are left standing, one, the Gold-field Hotel, a seven-story brick structure covering one block. When it was built it was considered the finest building between Denver and the Coast.

Floods and fires! Yes, in this desert country once in a while they do have floods which would take these tents and lightly built frame houses down with them like eggshells. We also had dreadful wind storms. Once a booster was telling a newcomer (the wind taking them off their feet, also lifting and transferring roofs), 'One thing — it blows this way only three days at a time.' The newcomer, meeting him a few days later (with the wind still blowing), said, 'I was under the impression you said the wind blew this way only three days at a stretch.'

'So I did. It then turns and blows the other way.'

Looking down toward town one saw tents like mushrooms, all in orderly rows, the largest the Rotunda Hotel, which looked like a circus tent. All lots were on mining ground, so, first come, first served. This led to jumping lots, and this to many fights and shooting scrapes.

One day I heard a big racket, and in these times a commotion meant there was something doing, so I ran to the door, and just below me saw a woman throwing the foundation off a lot. The moment the last stick was off, a mule team was driven in on the run, drawing a tent house on skids — smoke coming out of the stovepipe. So Mrs. Enright jumped and held her lot, a gun in her hand in case of trouble. Later her gentleman friend (to-day we call them 'Sweet Papas') moved in with her, both of them fine-looking, well-dressed people. Comes a day when they fight; he fires her out, she pounds on the door, screaming and swearing. Finally he opens it a crack, sticks a gun out, and shoots a few times, just to show her he means business. We are glad, as she is a tough citizen, having killed her man before this.

Fuel is very scarce and expensive; at one time there is a real famine and people suffer. Coal and timbers are stolen from the mines; a car of coal is taken right off the tracks, and guards are put out to take care of it. During this time Herbert is sick, and we try in every way to get fuel, but there is none, only promises from day to day, then talk of the coal being shipped elsewhere, or of other towns taking over whole trainloads. Finally, through the influence of some one in power, a car does come to Goldfield — I just have to have some of this, so go early in the morning to the Tonopah freight yards, over a mile through slush and mud, to find a huge crowd — all of the same mind — before me, all talking and arguing. We form in some kind of line, trying to slip and squirm nearer. After standing for hours, I come to where the man is doling it out, only to find that there is none left. I tell him, 'There is no use in talking, I just have to have coal; a sick husband at home,' etc., and make it pretty strong. He gives me a gunnysack full — supposed to be one hundred pounds, for which I pay three dollars and a half. Then begins the search for an expressman to take it home.

During this lack of fuel, Herbert 'lifted' the foundation from a vacant tent, bringing it home in the night. He sawed it into blocks and hid it under the bed, but we were punished at once, as the blocks were so green they were hard to saw, and brought forth much puffing and sweating. They never did dry out enough to burn. So was justice meted out.

This time that Herbert was sick, we were so frightened of dread pneumonia, people dying like flies with it — nurses being rushed in on every train. But I kept him well plastered in onions and one morning was delighted to have him turn in bed and say, 'The bacon smells good; I think I can eat some.'

Neita, then eleven, had a job taking care of two little children. The father was a stock-broker, and the mother, a sparkling, pushing, dark-eyed woman, who never let any grass grow under her feet. She entertained a lot. Several times when Neita would go in the morning, she would find five- and ten-dollar gold pieces on the table left from the game the night before. All money was gold then and these pieces were used as counters. I would go and help with the cooking. Mrs. L. was very good to me, and appreciated everything I did; in fact, she gave me a confidence I had lacked before. She said, 'If I could cook and manage as you do, I would make a place for myself.'

Before this, when Herbert is sick, I manage to land a job in the San Francisco Bakery, waiting on people. While I was a quick worker and could stand a lot, this was dreadful. First, to learn the cash register was hard, as an egg-beater is as far as my mechanical mind reaches; then the standing every minute of the day, reaching, wrapping, and breaking string till your fingers bled, and handing across the counter in an endless motion. Two of us kept this up, as people were formed in two lines which sometimes reached out to the sidewalk. What a business that was, and the money they coined only to lose it in stock gambling! One day they tell me they will not need me any longer, the woman whose place I had was able to return to work. Going up the hill that night, I am heartsick and so dreaded telling them at home. I wonder, when a man gets the bounce, if he has the same feeling?

The first Christmas I remember only by having huge bunches of California peppers hung in the window, and by the Elks giving every child a gift within reason. This within reason was five or six dollars. The children wrote a letter to Santa Claus, telling him just what they wanted. I don't remember what the girls ordered, but Earl got a football. These were delivered along with big boxes of candy. You can see by this how free money was. This must have cost thousands of dollars. Every one, man or woman, was bucking the stock exchange.

I knew one woman, a clairvoyant, who had made some money at her trade. She had now retired, in a way, but each day consulted her dead husband (through an Indian guide) just what stocks to buy. Then other women would watch and buy the same, but they must have got the wires crossed, as she spent all her money and was flat broke the last I heard of her. No trade now, because if she couldn't see for herself, how could she see for others?

One would see coming out of small shacks or tents the most beautifully dressed women. This was the time of the Merry Widow hat, a large wide-brimmed sailor covered with flowers. Maude Adams was playing in 'Chanticleer,' and there were little red roosters on hatpins, embroidered in ties, in fact, everywhere.

Each store had its counter for wines besides all the hotel bars and saloons. One day a grocery store advertised a sale, unheard of, and the first sale in Goldfield. By daylight — I know, because I was there — the crowd reached several blocks, their money tightly held for fear of pickpockets. The congestion near the door is so bad that finally it crashes in, policemen are called, and a good time is enjoyed by all. In the mean

time, all who can crowd in, rush madly and buy everything in sight, only to find when they got it home that
it was spoiled. 'They said' (not the grocers) that
these were goods shipped to the sufferers from the
San Francisco earthquake, and held up, intentionally,
in Nevada.

I now go to sewing for a dressmaker who, it seems,
is asking and getting wonderful prices. She gives me
five dollars each day and my dinner. She was lovely
to work with, and for years afterward we were close
friends. She married a mill man, who I heard grew
rich from the gold he carried home each night under
his finger nails. If so, it did not help him any, as he
went broke with the rest when the bottom fell out of
real estate.

Every saloon had its side entrance to the wine-
rooms, where women went. There were also several
places for both men and women. The Rendezvous is
the only one I remember now. Here one could drink
and gamble. Most of the women did lay bets on the
roulette wheel, but I never did, as there was no money
to lay. Once I did go in one of the back rooms with
Billie and his wife, and have beer and club sandwiches, but considered it a very tame affair, as I
didn't like beer, and you got only a rumble from the
front, where things were really doing.

A big theater was built, The Hippodrome. I don't
think it was quite finished before it was condemned,
but they had good shows in it. (My first and last
shows, and how I revelled in them, taking the last
cent to go!) There I saw Nance O'Neil, Nat Goodwin,

THE LIFE OF AN ORDINARY WOMAN

Grace George, Weber and Fields, Kolb and Dill. The latter sang, 'I don't like your familie-e, I don't think your Uncle John ever had a collar on,' etc.; also, 'Thursday always was my Jonah day. If I bet my money on a Thursday's race, you could see the smile on the horse's face.' Some of the chorus girls remained in Goldfield, and married miners, and some stayed without marrying. Here I saw 'The Wolf' played, and from somewhere they had brought small pine trees to decorate the stage, which was a show in itself. I enjoyed this play because it was so human and real.

'The Mikado' and 'Pinafore' were put on by local talent, with no expense spared — hand-painted Chinese lanterns for programmes, lovely embroidered Chinese costumes, and startling decorations.

The day Lew Dockstader was there, I was unable to dig up enough cash to attend, so went to town to see the parade. Here they come up the street, all dressed so wonderfully, the music thrilling you through and through. A teamster has stopped his big ore wagon, four fine horses hitched to it; the music frightens them (or maybe they wanted to run and dance, as I did) and they ran away in that crowd. Such excitement! As they run they are stopped by a telegraph pole, one of the lead horses going on one side of it, and the other on the opposite side, the tongue of the wagon just sliding up that pole and staying, so both horses are suspended there. The parade stops to see the strange sight, and I rub up against Lew Dockstader, looking to see if his white satin coat is of a good grade. It was. Then I go home feeling that I had seen enough for one day. I also attended one prize fight. Herbert had insisted on my going, I think because he felt guilty at paying so much for the tickets, and wished me to share his guilt. I refused, but my saving disposition could not see this ticket wasted, so I said I would go down and see the crowd go in. I did, and was one of that crowd, feeling out of place, although seeing many women there among this crowd of men. Boys were carrying bottles of beer around to different groups. There were a few tame boxing bouts to start with, and still I didn't see anything in prize fights, and considered my money wasted. Finally the main event was called, a white man and a negro. There was much fun made of the negro, and so many insulting things called to him that from the start I was for him. As it went on, I got more interested, and when the knock-out blow came, I found myself standing on my chair pulling at the coat tails of a man in front, so that I could see over him.

He was Jake, the proprietor of Jake's Dance Hall. I, myself, never got to go to his place, only walked slowly by, twisting my head and eyes, trying to get a glimpse of the 'goings-on.' But the windows I enjoyed most were in the Palm Restaurant, because in them were tiny pine trees, which made one think of home. (Although I was fed up on pine trees while at home.) I knew of an Italian who longed so much for something green that he set a post in the ground, cutting leaves from tin cans and nailing them on the post, then painting the whole thing green.

So passed the first year, Herbert working all the

time and I occasionally. Each day we studied the stock reports and each day we were disappointed. I was frantic to make money, and rebellious at so many around us getting rich, and returned to that age-old wonder, 'Why do they prosper and get along when they do not lead half the good life that we do?' Yes, I had reached this pitiful stage, and was due for a good hard slap, which came later, the worst I have ever had in my life.

CHAPTER XIX

Many people believe in turning the other cheek, especially when it is your cheek.

A. E.

Now comes the strike. I never did understand what it was all about. The following are some of the reasons given: that the Miners' Union had — very foolishly — taken into their union the I.W.W.'s — Industrial Workers of the World. We afterwards called them 'The I Won't Work's,' and much worse than that. They were made up of the barbers, barkeepers, butchers, waiters, and dishwashers. Something, it seems, peeves the dishwashers and they walk out. This doesn't look as if it would amount to much, but strikes, like many other things, start from small beginnings. The miners go out in sympathy, thinking, I imagine, that they would have to extend that sympathy for but a short time. The mines are not paying so well, and 'They say' the employers are glad of a strike, and, underneath, urge it on. 'They' also say that during a strike the agitators and strike leaders are paid much more than when everything is quiet. I know they, being good talkers (this is about all), do influence the hard-working, peaceable miner, who asks only for a day's work and the pay for it. Some strikes may be all right, but it seemed to me this one was uncalled for, and, oh, how it dragged out!

Day after day, week after week, and the money almost gone. During a strike all suffer, but I think it must be harder on the wife. The husband, tramping and looking for work, sees other men and can talk matters over with them, thereby forgetting himself and gaining a sort of courage, but she, at home, is planning what and how to feed her children in the cheapest and most nourishing way possible — counting and recounting each penny, so much for fuel, so much for water, so much for a soup bone. They told of a woman who asked a neighbor if she could borrow her yesterday's soup bone. The answer was, 'No. Mrs. So-and-So has it to-day.' The wife worries every hour of the day, not knowing which way to turn, and in the evening, when the man returns from his hopeless wanderings, she, looking up at his gray face, can tell at a glance that there is no good news.

I try to get any kind of work as do so many others. One day I have sewed and got two dollars, which goes into the family exchequer, we having only one pocketbook in our family, kept in a common place, so that there was no asking or giving of money. When I go to pay the water man, the two dollars is gone. I ask, 'Herbert, did you take any money?'

He answers, red-faced, 'Why, yes, I didn't think the two dollars would help much, so bet it on a horse race, four to one.'

'And did you win?'

'No; it was a muddy track. Luck seems to be against us. Others were winning all around.'

I turn away, but do not say anything, as I see he is about desperate, and besides keeping myself in order I must not let him lose hope. There is talk of trouble,

[262]

and a call for help is sent to the Governor. He sends in the United States regulars, who make a camp over on the hill near us. They help the stores, saloons, and amusement places, and, as there is no trouble to quiet, have an easy time of it, skating at the rink, and getting drunk. But they were never arrogant with the miners, and I think they realized that having been ordered here was a mistake. Some of them did do a good turn by stealing provisions from the Government and selling them cheaply to the miners. At this time we had with us a Socialist element, which talked a great deal. One day, after a strong demonstration, they marched, carrying a red flag, which some man was brave enough to take from them.

Always the more trouble there was stirring, the more I would dream, and in this way forget, and, in spite of this good husband, there is never a day that I do not think of Jim and dress for him. Never a time, walking along the crowded streets, that I don't think I might meet him; never a shadow passes the window but I think that it might be he. I have kept this in my own heart till now. I wonder if other women are as foolish as this? I mean, do they have their dreams? And had Jim come, would I have gone with him? I think not; the kind of woman he would have liked to go with him was the kind that wouldn't.

During this time Joy gets a sore throat. I have always been my own doctor, so now do all the things I have formerly done. While she does not seem bad, playing each day, she gets no better, and still I do not pay much attention to her. She and Neita are sleeping in an old tent beside the house, and on the third day, when she comes in covered with blood, I see there is more the matter than I can reach with my Listerine, tincture of iron, and Wizard Oil. (How I hated to spend the money even for these!) I send for the doctor, who pronounces it diphtheria (that dread word!) and gives both her and Neita antitoxin. I hate it — although it may save lives, it leaves many cripples, or did then. I doctor Joy every half-hour day and night, and she seems to be improving and I am so glad to see her strong. The doctor did not caution me in regard to her heart being weak. Diphtheria is such a loathsome disease, with such an odor, and, you see, we were cooking, eating, and sleeping all in this one room. It was summer and very hot. Each day, I would wash and mop, and I kept a wet blanket hanging from the ceiling in a draft, trying to keep things cool. (When you reach a certain stage, you do not think of expense.)

Comes a day when she is very much better. We are invited to a Masonic dance, and I am very anxious to go, as this will be the first time I have gone to a social gathering in Goldfield. I know I cannot go, yet put my hair up in curlers. I have made Joy some paper dolls to play with while lying there. Everything is very quiet. I am sitting on the trunk reading 'The Count of Monte Cristo,' and when she asks me for a drink I never look up (oh, the bitterness of it!) but say, 'Neita, give Joy a drink.' Neita is reading also, and doesn't move. There comes a gurgle from the bed, 'I want a drink.' How I throw the book behind the

trunk (and shudder at the name even now) and jump
for the bed, but it is too late — Joy turns on her side,
and, with a sigh, is gone. I scream at Neita to run for
the doctor, which she does, down the half-mile of hot,
dusty road, while I am doing all in my power for Joy,
tearing at the curlers with one hand, feeling them
burn into my head, to think of being so foolish when
she was so bad.

The doctor comes and pulls the sheet up over her
face, and now I know this is the end. Some one goes
in search of Herbert, who is out looking for work. I do
not remember what followed, only that I would not
let her be taken to the undertaker's, but did all things
for her myself, combing her beautiful hair for the last
time, dressing her in her many-times-washed-and-let-
down white dress. Each thing I do, each move I make,
I am choked with bitterness and sorrow, thinking of
the many times I have punished her, of the time she
must learn 'Old Glory' to speak at an entertainment.
She was always so full of play that she put it off to the
last minute, then I whipped her, making her climb on
the old swelled-top trunk, not letting her come down
till she knew it. Even now I can hear her,

'Old Glory, say — who, by the ships and the crew, or the long
　　spangled ranks of the gray and the blue —
Who gave you that name, that name that you bear with such
　　pride everywhere?'

Of the day the Governor was coming to town and she
rushed home to change her dress, and I, after making
her wash her neck several times, put on and take off
her dress while I shorten a petticoat, scolding with

each stitch, and send her down the hill nervous and crying. (If we might turn back!) Of the Fourth of July — when I dress her in the Indian blanket and she wins a prize, but escapes in the crowd, and I, frightened, nervous, and scolding, find her in the judges' stand, her brown eyes dancing. And the day she drapes the veil around her and dances on the rock up by the Malapai, I stopping her for fear some one might see her. And what if they had, she was so graceful and pretty!

And thus my thoughts go on and on, filled with sorrow and regret. Night comes and Mrs. S., the woman whom I had sewed with, sends a bunch of flowers, carnations and baby's breath. I have her fixed in the cabin, we go in the tent to sleep, and at once I drop into the deepest sleep I have ever known. Neighbors come to see, and to sympathize with us, and, instead of finding me prostrate and grieving, find me in this deep, peaceful sleep. I think both they and Herbert wondered at me. I, myself, wondered and felt ashamed until I read Corra Harris's 'My Book and Heart,' in which she describes this same deep sleep coming to her after her husband dies.

The next day, just our family and a minister in one carriage — she in an express wagon — go out the long road to the cemetery, where she is laid between a murdered fast woman and a famous gambler, and, I thought, if she can, she will put in a word for both of them at the big gate. I crouch beside the grave, and when I arise am a better woman than ever before, more human, more lenient toward faults in others,

with more feeling and understanding for people, seeing now that money isn't everything, and, from that
day to this, while I may have fallen short in some of
these things, I never have been as frantic for money
as I was before. (It was never the money, only the
things I wanted to get with it.)

When I was putting her school books away, her
reader fell open at this —

'There is a Reaper whose name is Death, and with his sickle
keen,
He reaps the bearded grain at a breath and the flowers that
grow between.'

The first birthday (hers, the tenth, came in a few
weeks after she was buried) is the time mothers suffer
most. Then, during the holidays, there is more of that
aching loss. And it is many, many years before you do
not look up, startled — no, not startled, because you
expect it, feeling they are with you. Hundreds of
times you start to put on their place at the table, or
plan for clothes — she will have this; but the keenest
of all is when it is stormy, and you think this one is
safe here or there, for a moment it flashes in your
mind — that she isn't in yet. And now, when I sit
resting and thinking of my children's well-being, running over in my mind just where they are and what
they will be doing, always at these times I count one
boy and two girls. Barrie writes so wonderfully of
this in 'Dead These Twenty Years.' (Queer — how
he could read the writing on a woman's heart and
describe it better than she who had it chiseled there.)

Before the quarantine is over, Neita comes down

with it, but I am on the job this time, and do not let her move head or hands. As I work, I am having a struggle with Fate and myself, although it is a silent one, as I never told Herbert any of my thoughts. First, you see, I had no religion or faith to fall back on. Would I ever see her again? I could not bear the thought that I might not, and I think the thought of this, and the feeling that I must have some one to lean on, brought me to find God — I wonder if we would have much religion without trouble and sorrow? Then there was the fight — what is it all about, anyway? There is no use in trying, we are only born for work and worry, and I wished I was dead and out of it all. I am taking care of a miner's room near by, and when I make the bed, find a gun under the pillow. I often think to-day I will end it, and go so far as to lift the gun (very carefully, as I am afraid of guns, and the darned thing might go off) and stand in front of the mirror seeing just how to place it.

One day, in my ceaseless round of work, just after putting a large washing on the line and scrubbing, I have a miscarriage. If I think at all, I am pleased over this, and never stop working day or night. On the third day I am lifting something and have a dreadful hemorrhage, and I, who so lately wished to die (I have often smiled to myself over this), call some passer-by to get the doctor quick, then go to bed (with Neita), piling pillows under my hips, and lying there scarcely breathing, waiting and praying for help. I have never thought of killing myself since. Fate was slapping me hard, trying to knock some sort of a woman into shape.

Neita is now so she can be up a little, dragging herself by a chair — is partly paralyzed from so much antitoxin, and is unable to talk. Herbert has a few days' work and is away. I am lying there trying to console myself with the thought that Joy missed a lot of suffering, going when she did. Herbert before leaving had put on some dried apples and a chicken to cook (I wonder where we got that chicken? Joy's pet, I expect), and I had told Neita to put some sugar in the apples. She, holding herself by the wall, gets the sugar, goes to the stove, takes the lid from one of the kettles, and, before I can stop her, pours the sugar into the chicken. Now, this is a calamity, and I scream at her. She drops the cup, and such a change comes over her face as she grabs something to hold to. I almost faint — thinking, now I have killed her, too. I get out of bed — that chicken must be saved if we both die, so pour all the broth off (almost crying to do this), and start it again in new water, then both climb back into bed. Brother all this time is kept outdoors, except nights. Of course, all mothers and children run from him, so he has things his own way, and puts in hours running around and around four blocks. As soon as Neita is able, she, too, is put out in the sun.

I can hardly wait to visit the cemetery, and go when I am very weak. Then I find a miracle has happened — especially does it seem so in this desert country — the flowers we had left on her grave (the baby's-breath) had been full of seed pods; since then there had been a heavy rain, and it seems unbelievable, but her grave is covered with a quilt of green.

CHAPTER XX

I sometimes wonder after all,
Amid this tangled web of fate,
If what is great may not be small,
And what is small may not be great.

ROBERT SERVICE

WE could see no end to the strike, and, talking it over, decide Herbert must go back to Colorado and find work, but have no money for his fare. Now I take the bit in my teeth and make a bold move. I have never done housework before, only for myself, but know that I can, so I watch the paper and ask for the first job offered, cooking, washing, ironing (how hard this was!), and cleaning for a family of five. Their name was Grain. I feed them fine for two days, then ask for my month's wages in advance, telling them what I want it for. They look me over for a few minutes, ending by giving me four ten-dollar gold pieces. Herbert gets ready and leaves, taking Brother with him — such a little fellow in a home-made Buster Brown suit. In his suitcase he has his Teddy-bear, which he had found — a burro was eating it — and the first night after he arrives he makes my sister get out of bed, and get this Teddy-bear for him to sleep with. When they are gone, I go to work at daylight each day, not getting home until after dark, leaving this sick Neita alone all day. Here is where the doctor comes in. She has moved beside us while we have been quarantined, and discovers that Neita is left each day, so commences to take her things to eat. She

sees the condition of her palate, and sprays and treats
her throat for her. (She was one of the best women I
have ever known.) As soon as Neita can walk, she
insists on going to school, and tries it, but is sent home
because she cannot talk plainly. I drag to work each
day.

I give this family a good month's work in spite of
being sick, both mentally and bodily. Christmas time
is drawing near, and I make all kinds of candy, cakes,
and a big plum pudding. The day before I work extra
hard, even have the turkey stuffed ready to go in the
oven, but this night my month is up, and I feel that I
cannot go on much longer. Christmas morning I go at
my usual time and start the fire, but see I can't hold
out. I am just able to get home and fall into bed, lying there all day in a quiet, peaceful daze. Mrs. S.
sends our dinner.

I never go back to work, and decide to ask help of
the Union, which I do. Along about here Father
Dermody, the Catholic priest, comes to see me, saying
he had heard we were in trouble and needed help. At
this I cry, and answer through my tears, 'No, we don't
need help, and besides' (now I can hardly talk for
crying), 'we don't belong to your church, anyway.'

'That makes no difference if I can do anything, and'
(I shall never forget him for this) 'if you do not need
anything, take this and buy a present for the little
girl.' And with this he laid a ten-dollar gold piece on
the table and left.

The Union, after a lot of red tape, gave me five
dollars each week. (You know, a certain amount is

paid into the Union each month by every miner who belongs to it, so it wasn't charity.) Neita went to the office for it each time, I sending her to do something I cannot bear to do myself. In a short time the S.'s have their trouble, and she has no money, so I give her part of mine. Both families, I am afraid, eat beans as a steady diet and more than is good for them. Comes a day when we have a snow, and Mrs. M. and I are sweeping our steps at the same time, and whisk snow upon each other. She was one of the kind who enjoy the joke best when it is on the other fellow, so when I let her have a face full, she goes into the house mad, and, being impulsive, before she has a chance to cool down, she went to the Union and told them I didn't love them; also (and I did say it) that we 'never would have joined if not compelled to.' In a few days I have a committee call on me who rake me right and left, fore and aft, bringing me to time for daring to criticize them, and, 'Besoides, yer mon wint away, whin he moight have stud phat and helped us fight.' Good Lord, what did they mean 'fight'? He was no talker. He was only like so many an honest miner wearing out his heart and shoe leather looking for work. And so they kept their five dollars.

We manage until Herbert gets a job in Bonanza and has a payday. He has left Brother with his mother. In the spring the strike comes to an end, no one having gained anything — all losing. It just dies a natural death, and is a forerunner of the end of this prosperous camp.

On Herbert's return from Colorado, again they

stay with my sister, and this time she has to get up, not for Brother's Teddy-bear, but to hear him say his prayers, his grandmother having taught him. It seems good to have them home again, and Herbert goes to work soon. His trunk fails to arrive and we are worried about it. One day they are holding a séance in the doctor's. Mrs. Frazer is there and has brought with her a wonderful clairvoyant, and when it is over they call and ask if I would not like to meet this woman. Of course I would. What if there were something in spiritualism and I could communicate with Joy? We visit a while, but nothing is said of my trouble or anything pertaining to spirits. Neita runs to the door, calling me; then this woman looks at her vacantly and says, 'There is another with her, a dark-eyed, laughing one, who points to the ring and says, "It is mine."' (It was an Indian ring of Joy's that Neita was wearing.) 'Now she comes in and stands by you; she doesn't want you to grieve so much because she wants to run and play with the others' (Joy would have wanted just this), 'and your sorrow is holding her back.'

Did she see? I don't know. Mrs. Frazer vowed she had told her nothing of me. Only I do know that what she told me that day I have passed on to many bereaved mothers, thereby helping them. Then, too, I had this to strengthen my belief. I am so thrilled that I run home and insist on Herbert coming and seeing her. He comes reluctantly and stops midway of the door, feeling embarrassed and out of place. Some one says, 'Tell his fortune.' He, man fashion, half believing, still making light of it, says, 'I have no fortune; the only thing I want to know is, where is my trunk?' She hesitates a moment, then answers: 'It was missent and went to Hazen. You will get it Friday morning at nine o'clock.' And — I am not trying to explain it — only telling you, at nine Friday morning we see an express wagon coming up the hill with the trunk.

It was while working for the Grains that the following happened: I have written it in the third person. It was easier to do it in this way — but I was the thief.

Going to work that cold gray morning, she passed them lying there. When she saw them, she, so tired and hopeless a moment before — no, heavy-hearted, she was never hopeless — thought, 'Oh, wouldn't they be fine for that? I do wish I had one. I wonder if they got them in Goldfield here? I wonder what they cost? But — I could never afford one.'

Now it was getting lighter, the sun would soon be shining over the Malapai, and there was so much to be done this day that she must hurry on. As she lifted the ashes, built the fires, put the oatmeal and coffee on the stove, and cut the bacon, she thought of it. As she set the table and made the biscuit, she still thought of it.

She was glad when breakfast was over and she was alone. Thinking and longing for it more and more, she did her work in a daze. There was extra work to-day, company coming from California, so she dreamed and cooked, every move, every thought, somewhere else. 'I want it — I cannot buy it — I cannot bear to ask for it; they would not understand. Dare I take it? —

But I couldn't without help. I couldn't move it — well, maybe I could — and maybe it wouldn't be so bad to steal it. But I know I will be caught — only I could be very careful — but I couldn't get it home. No, I couldn't get it home, much less move it, and will stop thinking about it. It isn't right, anyway.'

Before supper the guest arrived. Mrs. Grain said, 'This is our new maid.' As the guest did not care to say, 'Glad to meet you, Maid,' she merely lifted one eyebrow. (This working woman thought she was a hired girl, and that maids only opened doors and wore caps and dinkey aprons.) Mrs. Grain went on, 'She is a very good cook, and we think we will like her.' (Must not praise too much, as one's cook should be kept in her place.) Now the guest lifted both eyebrows, as though she had her doubts of all this, and the cook brought her teeth together, saying to herself, 'Bet I make you sit up and take notice before you leave.'

As she cooked, she went on with her planning. 'I will make some of those little piecrust dodads — bet she never ate any of those. There is that kid's little express wagon, it looks strong — might as well make some tarts, too; I have the crust and I make pretty ones. I'll slip in and get a thimble to cut the holes — what if it should break the wagon? — and, besides, I don't think I can get it on. To-night I intend to decorate that table. I'll show her to lift her brows at me! Let's see, I will take some sprays of wandering-jew and geranium blossoms, they will look lovely, and the salad I will fix on the plates like a flower, the mashed potatoes I'll pile like a small mountain, the

[275]

butter running down the sides will look like sunshine. Then the parsnips in small golden strips, and the pork roast I will brown till it tastes — well — like a good pork roast. I'll boil those apples so carefully not to break them. Well — I don't care — I want it so much, and I'm going to try and do it.' Her mind made up to this crime, she planned just how to go about it, the best, quickest, and safest way. When she found time, she slipped out and greased the wheels of the wagon with lard.

Mr. Grain came and leaned over the table where she was working. Before this he had intimated to her that his wife did not understand nor appreciate him. She dared not make him angry, because she had borrowed her month's wages in advance in order to send her husband to Colorado to find work, as the Goldfield workingmen had been on a strike for months. She had never understood why this strike was; only knew there had been long months without work, grinding poverty, and all the worry and troubles that come to miners and their families through a strike.

While the family were eating dinner, she slipped to the door and listened; maybe they would say something of the strike, or, better yet, how stocks were going. Mr. Grain was a stock-broker. She and her husband had put all their spare money in United Mines mining stock and each day since it had gone lower. (How little people know what their cooks are thinking!)

After dinner she did her work quickly. While she worked, she wondered what the child at home was doing, too sick to go to school and left alone all day in their tiny cabin.

At last the work was finished. She left at once, in the darkness, carrying the wagon so that they might not hear. Some Joshua palms along the way seemed to point accusing fingers at her, up toward the Malapai a huge cloud frowned on her. Still she staggered on with her burden until she reached the place. The first trial lift, and, oh, thank God, she could move it. Then the pulling and pushing, the dragging, the lifting of one corner and twisting it a little, first one way, then the other, the sitting on the ground and shoving and pushing with feet. Listen! Some one is coming. She drew her feet up sharply and squatted, picking up pieces of board and chips and throwing them into the wagon. The footsteps pass on, as after these months of poverty it is nothing new to see people steal fuel. Then she pulled the wagon in below the load, bracing it with huge rocks. One last shove, and — yes, it is going on. Now, if only the wagon does not spread, but there is no quitting now — breathless and trembling she grabbed the wagon tongue and was off down Sundog Avenue.

She must hurry now before some one sees her. It was downhill at first; along Sundog and Ramsey she had to hold the wagon back. Soon she came to High-Grader's Hill, where it was hard pulling, and she must strain every muscle to move the wagon a bit at a time. Then, so tired that she must rest, she held it from the side, moved behind, and sat down flat on the ground, feet down the hill and back against the wagon. Once more she got her breath. A man was coming. She hunched up pretending to fix a wheel, and he went on with a short 'Hello.' Now she pushed from behind, digging her toes in the road and almost flattening out at each shove. She saw a man coming off shift, down the trail, swinging a dinner pail; he must have a lease or they would not let him work. Now she hovered over her load, praying he would pass, but, no; 'Looks like a heavy load you have there. Ain't been high-gradin', hev you?' He knows she hasn't, as high-grade never came up the hill, but always went downtown where it was sold.

'No, it is some boards I have been picking up for wood.'

'Don't you know only a few days ago they shot a man at the Mohawk for swiping wood? Better be careful.'

Would he never go? After an age, it seemed, he passed on. She couldn't have held out much longer. Up again now, pulling with all her might. She was a slender woman with small hands, and just a few weeks before this had had a miscarriage and was not yet strong. With her back breaking and a hurting in her throat, she becomes frightened. If she should injure herself, what would become of the child at home? But she cannot let loose now. One last superhuman pull and she reached the top of the hill. Oh, thank the Lord, she had done it!

She went on quickly to a small tar-covered house. Leaving the wagon at one side, she grabbed an old gunnysack and threw over it, then stopped at the olla jar, left out at night with a wet cloth around it to keep it cool, and took a big drink, thinking, 'I must tell her to-morrow to have it filled with water. No, I can only get one pail now; that will be fifteen cents.'

'Is that you, Mama?'

'Yes. How have you been to-day? What did you have for dinner? I'll fix you something now. See, I've brought you some of those little nut dodads,' drawing a bundle from the front of her dress.

'Didn't I hear a noise when you came?'

'Yes, Fay's little wagon. I brought some pieces of wood on it.' She did not say how much, as she never lied to her children. 'Wouldn't you like to go over to the McCarthys'? I think she has a new magazine, and you can stay a little while.'

The child went slowly out; she was just getting over diphtheria and could hardly walk. Her mother knew if once she started to read, she would not return until she was called for or sent home. She waited for the McCarthy door to slam, then went to her stolen goods and threw off the covering, eased the wagon up over the doorstep and hauled it in. There was a tiny closet off this one-room cabin with a blanket for a door. She took the wagon through this opening, lifted it up on the hind wheels and dumped the load against the wall. It slipped out on edge, and now she had only to tip it over. She moved quickly, took the wagon outside, returned, found a hammer and an old file, then got a pencil and drew three designs on her booty, and, kneeling down, tried these rude tools. They will not do, so she hunts a big steel nail, and Glory! she can do it.

THE LIFE OF AN ORDINARY WOMAN

After she finished her task, she covered the whole thing with old clothes, and went to the door and called the child home, asking her if the McCarthys had any news of the strike? Oh, if it would only end!

When the child finished eating, they went at once to bed, the mother so very tired, but with a glow inside. In the morning she wakened more happy than she had been in months. She made the fire, dressed herself, then called the child and told her what to have for breakfast and not to forget the waterman and to be good. She always told her children to be good as a sort of blessing. When she left, she looked down at the child, longing to kiss her. She so wanted to show her love for her children, but something held her from any demonstration. So in the darkness she started to work, taking the wagon, and as it grew lighter she saw such a spraddled-out little vehicle. She must hurry to be there, build the fires, and have breakfast by seven. She went a different way to miss the place of her crime, and never in her life did she see that place again.

Mr. Grain going in the yard during the day said, 'I'd like to know what's happened to that express wagon?'

She (liar as well as thief) answered, 'I saw several kids on it at once yesterday.'

He slammed the door. 'Oh, well, they ruin more around here every day than a man can bring in. I'm getting about fed up.'

She would work hard each day, returning to her labor of love at night, then she would chip away, often missing the nail and hurting her hands. She wondered if a new miner had this trouble using his first single-jack. Three nights and it is done. At the foot of the hill an expressman lived; she stopped and asked him to do a job for her.

'Where to?'

'Out beyond the railroad tracks. How much will it be?'

'Dollar and a half.'

Her heart fell — 'Well — I've got only seventy-five cents,' and went on before he had a chance to speak, 'To-morrow being Sunday and, you taking your load from this end — and — it is not as if you had to come all the way from town.' There must have been a great longing in her eyes.

'All right, then, at daylight.'

At daylight it was ready when he came. She never explained to the child why he came or what for.

'It is here, and is heavy. I will help you load it.' (All covered now with an old blanket.) Both lifted with all their might.

'Hope you are not having me haul high-grade.'

'No, it is not,' and she threw in an old pick, then talked very fast in order to keep him quiet. 'What a good-looking horse you have, and how fast he goes; you must be a good provider. What do you think of the strike? Do you suppose it will end soon? And do you think there will be any trouble? Did you hear when Jack London was here — you know he spoke at a Union meeting — when the miners talked of blowing things up, he said, "I am a Socialist, but no Anarchist." Are you an old-timer?' And so on and on, never giving him a chance to answer.

They rattle on downhill, on down Ramsey, a turn here past the skating rink. So many of the soldiers here, sent in to keep things quiet. She hated this place. Days when the burning sun had beaten down and into her cabin, where she was nursing her sick children, had come the ceaseless roar of the skaters and the never-ending throb of 'Come awa-a-y with — me-e, Lu-cile — in my mer-rie Olds-mobi-le.' Here they turned and went down one of the main streets. On the corner was Tex Rickard's saloon, the Great Northern. The miners' wives liked Tex better than the usual run of saloon-keepers, because it was said of him that, after a man commenced to be the worse for wear, Tex fired him on home.

On across town, on through scattered tents and shacks, on over the railroad tracks, on across the desert toward the west. Now, the expressman knew where they were bound for, and what was in the blanket behind, but he remained silent. He had had some queer jobs in his day and never asked questions.

Arriving finally, he offered to help her, and she — knowing he felt embarrassed — talked very fast and even joked a little. Neither mentioned the job in hand, only worked, he digging where she showed him, she dragging away at the cactus. Soon the place was ready, and they both lifted out the burden, uncovered it, and placed it on end in the hole, bracing it with rocks and dirt.

He turned quickly, 'Must be on my way, it is late.'

JOY'S GRAVE

She undid her handkerchief, giving him the three quarters tied in the corner, and started to thank him, but fearing she would spill over, he muttered hastily, 'That's all right, that's all right. So-long,' and drove off.

Then she found more rocks and built around it, and, as the sun came up, it saw her kneeling there beside her child's grave. At the head was a white headstone with the name 'JOY' carved on it. She was smiling.

Now she must hurry back to work, and, as she walked the mile and a half, she wondered what the builders of the Sundog schoolhouse thought — when they missed their white stone step?

CHAPTER XXI

She smoothed her work and folded it tight
And said, 'Dear work, good night, good night.'

From an old reader of mine

HERBERT worked steadily, and after a few paydays we built on a lean-to kitchen. One could stand by the stove and reach the cupboard, which was a box nailed on the wall; by turning slightly, reach the cook table — another box on end; still it seems as if we had much more room. But now we have another worry. Herbert, even before we left Bonanza, had some kind of spells; he would be in dreadful pain, then better, and able to work again. (And as long as people can work, they think they are all right.) Now these spells were coming closer and harder. Each day, when leaving for work, swinging his dinner pail — never since a night in Cripple Creek have I looked at a miner with his lunch pail without a shudder — I glance at him to see how he is feeling. Never a time as he opens the door, returning from work, but my first thought and look is, 'Is his face drawn and gray?'

We had the doctor, who did not know just what it was, but would give him a shot of morphine and leave. Yet, with this hanging over him, he still works on. In a little hole under our floor, in a cocoa can, is a fast-climbing pile of twenty-dollar gold pieces, being hoarded to get out on when the mines shut down. He got five dollars per day; out of this, fifty were saved each month.

[284]

NEITA AND EARL AT SCHOOL

Neita gets strong and well, and in the spring graduates from the eighth grade. At the same time they have their first class graduate from high school. There is a big time, many speeches and flowers. I had made Neita a much-tucked and lace-inset dress, and when she delivers the farewell to her class — carrying a big bunch of carnations over one arm (we practiced this at home; even then she forgets and sits on them), I am very proud and think she is the best-dressed, the best-looking, and far the smartest there.

Earl is in school and has a wonderful teacher. In fact, all the teachers here were fine, most of them being from Ypsilanti, Michigan. One day in his room they are having some sort of entertainment (he isn't in anything), and I go. After many small girls get up, either speaking or doing whatever is expected of them, the teacher said: 'Now there is one little boy who can sing. I don't know whether he will or not. Will he come up here and stand by my side and sing, "I'm a little soldier boy"?' And — my heart jumps when Earl wiggles out of his seat, straightening the belt on his little gingham Buster Brown suit, and marches up front. I know he has made a mistake. But she starts playing, and his clear and sweet voice rises without a quaver,

'I'm a little soldier boy, brave and true.
Follow me, my Captain said, and see, I do.'

And on for several verses. On returning to his seat, cocking his head and peeking at me like a robin, he sees me weak and crying.

[285]

THE LIFE OF AN ORDINARY WOMAN

So the months pass, bringing their daily round of work, looking forward to payday, thinking I will try and manage better next month. We had given up being rich, and when the fortune teller said we would have a blacksmith shop and a little home near by, we were pleased, and this was all we asked for. But we do not get this (she failed to see right). I wonder what was the trouble with us? Was Herbert too timid and I too much of a dreamer to snatch anything from the hand of Fate? Surely I was not asking too much.

I could write on and on of the strange, interesting people in Goldfield, but will only tell of a few, although all people are interesting to me. Earl stalks in one day and tells me very calmly that he has 'just found a dead man in an old tent,' and wants something to feed him. 'Maybe I can bring him alive.' He fixes up something and carries it out. When he returns, wanting some whiskey, I think I had better look into it. It was true. He had found in an old tent, partly down from the snow drifted against it, an old bearded man, a 'desert rat' who had been on a big drunk, gone to bed, and, when Earl found him, had been three days without eating or drinking. He claimed Earl saved his life and, being very grateful, he came to the house and wanted to deed him an interest in some claims he owned. Now if this weren't a true story, we would be rich from those claims.

Then there was the famous Scotty of Death Valley. He would take a team and go into Death Valley to some mysterious place known only to him, from which he would return with a load of gold. His money was spent very lavishly, on one trip to New York paying for everything with gold, and having whoever he bought from keep all the change. When he did happen to have a bill, he lighted his cigar with it. I have forgotten how many thousands this trip cost. Men would watch his movements, intending to follow him into Death Valley, but he was too slick. After a time his notoriety waned, either the mine played out or was — as some said — a big advertising scheme of Goldfield's boom times. He had a fine big car, and he thinks he is so famous he can do anything. One Labor Day, with the streets so jammed with people one could hardly move, Scotty is drinking and drives his car full tilt into this crowd, expecting them to make way; but he is not the idol he was, and the running boards are quickly covered with men piling over each other like flies, trying to pull him from the seat. I, who have been milling around in this crowd, trying to make myself think I am having a fine time, and failing, see all this, and, jumping up on some boxes where I can get a better view, find myself shrieking, 'That's right, drag him out, drag him out, show him — start him for Death Valley!' Now I had never seen Scotty before, and had always admired him. It only goes to show what a mob spirit will do. Herbert was ashamed and pulled me down.

There was a girl who loved a man very dearly, but did not seem to make much headway with him. She ran a bakery in a tent — and made such good things to eat. The hot desert sun beating down on the tent, the hot stove within, going from early morning till late at night, made her have headaches which drew her face, and she, to keep young-looking for this lover who came so seldom, wore little squares and half moons of sticking plaster on her face to keep the wrinkles from coming. Some laughed at her when she would look up from her work all plastered as though she might have been in a wreck, but I thought it pathetic.

Another woman I met one day at the Frazers' was dressed in a green velvet dress that, ten years before, had been very expensive, made by an experienced dressmaker, and, at some time, I fancy, had a French name sewed in it. Now it was pitiful in its old age; many bald spots where the velvet was gone, many open places where the buttons, of which there were many, had given up the ghost and dropped off. Her hat was of the same vintage as the dress, velvet (this was in August on the desert), with little ostrich tips hanging sorrowfully in every direction except the right one. When I get through looking at her clothes, I look at her (a bad habit of mine) and see such a hopeless, wistful little woman. Her cheeks and hair, like her clothes, had been beautiful once; and, like well-made clothes, would always bear the trade-mark of better times.

She told me that day (while I read much more between the lines) that her husband was a college professor, with all the things that go with it, and in the course of human events a friend tells them of the easy fortunes to be made in Nevada, so they take their savings and come here, and love the strangeness and romance of it. Then they are roped (she never used any expression of this sort) into buying a claim out by Ryolite in the desert, where they hopefully go, taking two miners with them, and start to work.

For a time they are very happy; the interest each day of thinking they might strike it; the added interest and love for the desert, which gets any one who lives on it; but to run any mine even on a small scale takes money, and they soon have to let the men go. Now the husband, who has caught on to how to work, works in the hole, and this woman, who has never done anything of the kind before, helps him, sometimes in the hole and sometimes on the windlass. Thus they go on for a long time, until the money is gone. They have a mule team which they drive out after provisions and water, and when the man and wife are just about on their last legs, these mules desert them, as rats do a sinking ship.

A day comes when there is only a little water, very few groceries, no money at all, and they decide to abandon this place where they had put in so much hope, work, and money. The things they wish to take are divided equally between them, their clothes, a few books, and, of course, he would have a bunch of samples taken from the last bucket they had hauled up. (They always hope on, when bitten by the mining bug.) She wants him to carry one of their two cats, and she will take the other. He will not hear of any such foolishness. 'Do you think I will carry a cat twelve miles across the desert? Not much.' When they start she is a little behind him, her pack strapped on her back, but besides her share there is a gunnysack with two cats in it, carried so that he cannot see. For many miles they go this way, then the cats get into a fight, clawing, spitting, and scratching, and the cat is out of the bag, as it were. They run up and down her back, are frightened and tear the sack open, she trying to hold them with her bare hands and getting scratched from elbow to finger-tip. But she cannot hold them; they break away and tear out across the desert. She follows, calling and calling, until they are lost to sight, and she has to go on without them. Now, as she sits telling it, her words and worries are not of the squandered time, hope, or money, or of the lost faith in man in general, or of the tinhorn gambler who sold them this prospect, but of those lost, hungry cats on the desert.

Then there was the Piute woman with a string tied across her forehead holding a patch over her nose. When I asked the cause of this, I was told that this is as all Piute women are served who have been unfaithful to their marriage vows, or, if they do not make vows to their husbands. I saw no men wearing patches, so I expect none broke vows.

The time comes when the mines close every day; the bottom has fallen out of the stock market, and we do not know from one day to the next how long the Kewanas will work; but now the cocoa can is full, holding just five hundred dollars, and we prepare to leave. We manage to sell the house and contents for forty dollars; thus in four years do values drop in a mining camp. Herbert went over to Manhattan, a later boom than Goldfield, but finds it overrun with miners looking for work. When he returned, he brought me a newly minted ten-dollar gold piece which was withdrawn after the first issue, because the stomach of the eagle was so large that the coins wouldn't stack. I have managed through thick and thin to hold on to this.

So we leave, my greatest regret the little grave toward the west. I keep my eyes on it till the train rounds a point and it can be seen no more. I promise myself that some day I will return, but never have, except in dreams, when I search for the little tar-covered house, never finding it. But not even in dreams do I see the white stone marked 'JOY.' Once I was awakened from a deep sleep by hearing her clear, ringing laughter — this is much better than cold stone.

We don't know where we are going or what we will do, but are on our way toward Colorado, three full fares making a hole in our little store. I am thrilled at the first tree I see, and when we arrive at running water, it seems like something precious being lost and found again. Jose is living in Salida, so we go there. Gertie, a sister, and her husband Mots, also live here. Now, while I am not especially fond of Mots, still he was different and interesting, a rather small man with a sharp-featured face, wearing his hat on one ear and walking as though he had a chip on one shoulder, absolutely ignorant as far as education went, but sharp, sly, and daring, ever into something shady, never reaping the benefit himself. I think he did these things for the adventure. He was very good-hearted and would steal with one hand and give it away with the other. This is a sample of one of his stunts: When he was in Goldfield for a time, a man named Hutchinson wanted to buy a gallows frame. Mots and a partner, who could read, saw the ad, and decided to be prominent mining men and sell him one. Their overalls and jumpers are not suitable for this act, so (this shows Mots's hand and cunning) he goes to the hotel and steals Hutchinson's clothes, dresses in them, and swaggers into the office. He has Hutchinson paged, and tells him he has just the gallows frame he needs, but it will have to be a quick sale as he has a big sale on in Tonopah. He has such a prosperous, go-getting look as he stands there (in his listener's clothes), that he does sell it, some money is paid down, and Hutchinson doesn't recognize his clothes and never knows it is a stolen gallows frame till it is torn down and at the depot ready to ship. By this time Mots has made his get-away, only making twenty-five dollars out of this deal, but enjoying every minute of it.

On arriving in Salida, we find Mots is there in full bloom, putting over a big mining deal. He has all the prominent business men in town putting up money for him. In an old abandoned mine he has discovered wonderful gold-bearing quartz; assays and enthusiasm are both running high, large specimens being displayed in every store window. Mots is stepping high in his expert's boots, his hat on one ear, a fine cigar in his mouth, balancing the hat; Gertie having fine clothes and living on the fat of the land. He, in a condescending manner, offers Herbert a job. We know him of old, but a job is a job, and, 'You know it might be straight goods this time.' We rent a house and Jose and our family live together for this winter.

The mine keeps on working, but they find no more ore. Mots goes East to sell stock, bringing Gertie a wonderful fur, which, in his next drunken rage, he cuts to ribbons. Toward spring, faith and money give out at about the same time, and the mine closes, 'They say' expecting to start in a few days, but it never has. We realize that Mots has salted it by shooting a lot of high-grade into it. He had brought this high-grade from Nevada for just this purpose, and I bet that, if he should return now and try to put over another deal, he would do it. You know there are two 'born every minute.'

Here at Salida I see Ed for the first time since our parting long ago. He has grown into a large, handsome man, the head of a big cattle concern, having taught himself to do the bookkeeping after getting the job. And although he has associated only with cowboys and miners, he has never tasted whiskey nor played a card. No, not religion; it just didn't amuse him. He paid me the five dollars I gave him so long ago.

We go to Saguache for a visit, intending to go on to Bonanza, which we had left years before, expecting to make our fortune. We stay at Herbert's mother's. A lilac bush in full bloom peeps in at the window; her currants were ripe, too, and one morning, while sitting in the grass picking them I think — 'Herbert's spells are coming faster, and we should be where there is a doctor. Neita is ready for high school, and must go — I like it here and want to stay — I am sick and tired of mining.' (The currants are falling into the bucket.) 'I am going to stay and will talk him into it.'

Soon I start my campaign; not dwelling so much on his sickness as I do on the fact that Neita must be in school, and he consents to try it for a time. A brother-in-law has a contract to build a telephone line over one of the high mountain ranges, and Herbert and I go along, taking Earl, leaving Neita with a sister-in-law, Herbert to work on the line, I to cook. There are from fourteen to twenty men, and I have a boy to help. There is a big tent to cook and eat in, with smaller ones where the men sleep. In spite of the flies and hard work, I am never so happy as when I have plenty to cook, and enjoy this being outdoors by the side of the streams, among the trees, and living in the tents. The men usually took their dinners with them, huge boxes of it, and I am glad when they do, as then I have the day to myself to work and think. Almost always they would break down or something, coming in; then it was cook an extra dinner.

One day after breakfast all leave, even the boy who helps. Brother and I are alone and things go swimmingly. I have baked and piled on the table four large cakes for their to-morrow's lunch, a fleet of deep, rich brown, fragrant pumpkin pies, and a huge pile of bread, with the oven still crammed full. It begins to rain. I see that I have plenty of wood in to finish

supper, then have Earl come in from his playing and
help me tighten up the guy ropes, then tie the tent
flaps, and think — 'Let it rain. We are cosy and warm
here.' Soon it rains harder and harder, and the tent
poles begin to sway. There are three of them inside,
besides those at either end. Now the wind comes in
big blasts, bringing sheets of rain with it, the middle
pole starts to bend, and I run and grab it, holding it
against me and trying to brace it. Earl is looking on,
crying and frightened. The thunder and lightning are
terrible, and soon the wind tears the pole from me and
it is snapped in two; then the tent begins to sway, and
I yell to Earl to crawl under one of the tables, at the
same time jumping to miss the tent poles which have
all given away at once. The wet heavy tent is on us,
knocking me flat on the ground. I am up on my
hands and knees at once, creeping in the mud and
water toward the stove, which is sending off clouds of
steam from the wet tent lying on it. My first thought
is fire. I get sticks of wood or anything I can reach to
brace the tent off the stove. All this time Earl is
screaming at the top of his voice. I call to him to
hush, and finally threaten to whip him if he doesn't let
up, but he only screams harder, and I have to creep
over to comfort him. (Afterward he said he had 'as-
tericks.') When it stops (of course, none of the men
return this day) I have Earl go to the nearest ranch
and bring help; and when the men do get in, we manage to have supper, but such flat squashed pies and
such soggy bread. I always kept the day's menu.
This day's report is: 'Aug. 18 — 69 meals, steak,

string beans, potatoes, fried rice, cookies, pumpkin pie. *Fatal pie.*' The fatal pie was underscored; that was all the time one had.

This contract was a loss from the start. There were three crews on the payroll, one working, one coming, and one going. The unrest grows worse and worse, until one day they call a strike, or I guess it was a walk-out. I am fixing their lunch for the day when some of them walk up to me with a 'We are quitting and so must you.' I have a long sharp bread knife in my hand, and reach for the steel, making it still sharper, then glance up, saying, 'Piffle; I like my job and am not leaving it,' and go on spreading bread and butter. (As Charlotte did.) Finally they gave me up as a bad job, and all of them walked down the hill. We soon go home, as it is time for school to start, and Herbert gets a job clerking in a store. He felt sure we could never manage on the small wages, but I knew if any one could make ends meet, I could. We rent a four-room house, with big cottonwood trees in the yard which I am never tired of looking at. I build in a few shelves, and stencil curtains, so we are settled and very comfortable. And the joy of having one's man home for all three meals, and not having to change shifts every two weeks, but the biggest relief was losing the fear of accidents which ever hangs over a miner's wife.

Miners should have good wages, as, aside from risking their lives every time they go underground, there is the feeling of being buried; at least this is my first feeling whenever I have gone down a mine; then the dampness, the sound of dripping water, the smell of burned powder and bad air, the feel of darkness, the dirt sifting and slithering around rotten timbers, rats slipping around corners, the fear of a companion's carelessness, or of an open trap-door not noticed in the darkness. Well, the sump catches everything that falls. A drunken engineer might miss their signal and hoist a cage or bucket full of men into the shive wheel — I have known them to. If a mine is working three shifts, it is hard to get used to the different hours for sleeping and eating. From 7 A.M. to 3 P.M. is day shift, from 3 P.M. to 11 P.M. is night shift, and from 11 P.M. to 7 A.M. is graveyard shift, hated by all miners and their wives.

The children are in school and doing well, and, with the exception of watching Herbert to see how he is feeling (he never complained), things run along smoothly. One day a woman is kind enough to invite me to a party, and I go to my first big affair, being careful to watch every move so as not to get in wrong; as, no matter how faithfully one reads 'The Ladies' Home Journal,' one may make some bad breaks. This winter we join the Eastern Star, I intend (since I am going into society) to do it proud, so make a dress for the occasion. The crowning feature (I am determined to do this up brown) is *a train!* (I had always wanted one; also a parasol and feather fan.) So at this time I get my train — I am still waiting for the fan and parasol — and practice with this thing so as not to trip over it; and any one who is a Star can imagine me dragging it around the five points and corners. Somehow (like many other things we think we want) it was a disappointment.

Neita has won first place in the county declamatory contest, and now is to compete with the valley. While she is practicing in closets, the barn, and in the kitchen while washing dishes, I am making her a simple little dress. It is pale blue (men, I have found, are partial to light blue, and two of the judges, anyway, would be men), and it is very becoming. As I take each stitch I am wishing and praying that she might win. They leave early in the morning, her throat well wrapped so as not to be hoarse. All day I wonder, and when night comes, think, 'It is about time now and she will be dressing. Hope her hair looks all right and she doesn't take this time to daub on some paint. Now it is time to begin. She will be among the first of this curved line of boys and girls sitting on the stage, all looking solemn. I hope she doesn't get frightened, and that the judges are good, and really just.' We have no telephone, so I am left wondering till toward morning when I hear her come in so quiet and easy that I know she has lost, and feel sorry for us all. I never make a sound, knowing the more I might say, the worse she would feel. In the morning I get breakfast over, letting her sleep. Finally she gets up. 'Did you have a good time? Was there a big crowd? And' (I cannot stand it any longer) 'who did win first place?'

'Why, I did, of course. The gold medal is there pinned on my dress.' (So the judges were just!)

As the days pass, Herbert feels well very little of the time. The doctor comes, but seems not to arrive at any definite conclusion. We plan as soon as we have the money to go to the hospital and find out just what the trouble is.

One night there is a very large Japanese party, every one to wear a kimono. Some have lovely silk ones, but as always, I fix the cheapest thing. I get a finely woven white cheesecloth, and make bands on it of pink; also a big sash; then paint delicate flowers trailing over it, and as a last touch add scrolls of gold paint. It was very good-looking. After the party (I am very happy having so many compliments on my dress) we dance, and how I do dance, letting myself go, doing all the fancy steps I know and some I don't, finally calling a quadrille, and ending by doing a cake-walk! (How it does go to one's head to be noticed a little!) I treasure this night as the last care-free one I was ever to have. When I returned home, all in a glow to tell Herbert about it, I find him very sick, and as I drag off this kimono, it seems, in the face of suffering, to be such a flimsy, no-account sort of thing. I change into my house dress and apron and rush after the doctor. It seems to take an endless time for him to tie his shoes. When I return, I roll up my sleeves and all night long work with Herbert. Now I see something has to be done whether we have the money or not.

He went over to Salida and they decide on an operation. Then I follow. He is waiting on the station platform to meet me, standing there so gray and thin. At once they operate, finding it is a bad case of appendicitis. He was very sick from the ether, but still seemed to be doing well. In a day or two we have a visit, the

Masons from home having made up a purse of money for him, but this we decide not to accept, he refusing more strongly than I. We plan how we will manage, and I tell him I am going to take all the sewing I can get. 'But,' he answered, 'you know you cannot sew because of your bad side.' (I find that, if you have to do a thing, bad sides must, and can, be put in the background.)

One day he is so hungry he begs for something to eat. They will give him only a glass of hot water. As soon as he drinks this, large drops of sweat break out all over him, running and dripping off his face, and at once he is different. I am making a pallet on the floor of large bath rugs and towels the nurse had let me have. (I had a room at the hotel, but this night he coaxes me to stay with him.)

He is watching me, and says: 'I am going to sleep there. It looks so cool.' 'Why, no, you are not, you know you mustn't move.' 'Oh, please let me, I'm burning up.' (Now he starts to throw off the covers, putting one foot out of bed). 'I am going to.' I run to him. 'Of course you can have it. Wait till I call a nurse to help you move.' I run for help. Nurses and doctors come, and when I look in their faces, I know there is no help. After a time I ask them to leave us. He calls for me, not knowing I am there, also for his mother and sisters. (I find when death comes, it is usually a woman that is called for.) I fall on my knees beside the bed, holding his hand and trying to make a pact with God, promising him if he would spare him — 'I will serve you all the days of my life,' until it is a mere jumble of 'all the days of my life — all the days of my life.' But — God had other plans.

Again, alone and penniless, I am left to fight the world for my children and myself. Did I make a success? I don't know — that would fill another book — besides, we can never tell — can we — till the game is played out?

THE END